Get on the Rollercoaster

Get on the Rollercoaster

Oasis in New Zealand, March 1998

Karamdeep Sahota

Balmansa Books

A catalogue reference for this book is available at the National Library of New Zealand.

Cover design: Caitlin W at G'Day Design

Front cover image: Liam Gallagher, Queens Wharf Events Centre, Wellington, March 10 1998. Image by Lee Pritchard
Back cover image: Queens Wharf Events Centre, Wellington. Image by Wellington City Council

Published by Balmansa Books, Wellington, New Zealand

ISBN 978-1-7385817-0-2 – Paperback
ISBN 978-1-7385817-1-9 – Ebook
ISBN 978-1-7385817-3-3 – Hardback

Typesetting services by BOOKOW.COM

Foreword

In 1998, I saw Oasis live in Wellington. I went because I was enough of a fan to go. I had been a huge fan of the first two albums, less so the third. But I had a mate who was very keen to go – so why not right? Back then, it was about seeing as many shows as I could anyway. Banking experience, trying to translate that into knowledge. Fast-forward 25 years, and just as I thought I was a bit jaded from seeing thousands of shows I'm suddenly hungry for them all over again.

I never saw Oasis more than that one time. To date, I haven't seen Noel or Liam solo, with their respective bands – both of them paying more than lip service to the band that made them, with roughly half a set of Oasis material on any given night. Maybe, one day I'll go to another Gallagher gig. But the one I saw seemed to sum them up so perfectly at the time, for the time.

First of all they were fantastic. A real rock'n'roll band. They sounded – instantly – huge. And direct. And there was an animalistic urge to the music. Liam had swagger. And Noel knew all the right chords. They were sultans. And they were naughty little schoolkids too. Which we loved. But we also hated it a bit, since it left more than a few of us slightly perplexed and definitely underwhelmed at times when the brothers argued on stage and walked off; was it all staged? Was any of it staged?

Oasis was – briefly – the biggest band in the world. Because any band that becomes the actual biggest only ever manages it briefly. It is, after all, a herculean feat. Those people that lift boulders up over their heads to win strength competitions…we never ask them to hold it up there for a bit longer. We're just impressed they managed it at all.

That was Oasis selling out Earls Court for nights on the trot. Or, somehow, miraculously, playing to just a few thousand in little old New Zealand right around that same bloody time.

Shit we were lucky.

I think that now. Reading back these memories from so many lucky, and grateful fans. I was one of them. And though my fandom detached itself with time, I've always talked up the fact that I got to see Oasis when they mattered most. They mattered most to me then too. I was in a covers band that played over half of *(What's the Story) Morning Glory?* and a fair sway of *Definitely Maybe* too.

It was music that spoke to us. Our Beatles. Or whatever.

It was a moment in time.

And to see that moment frozen here. Held up not really for scrutiny but held up entirely by and for love, well, that's what music's about init? That's the very best thing about music. It brings us together, builds communities, even sitting in a bedroom or walking down the road now with our headphones on, or in…the music of the moment makes us feel less alone in this world.

The accounts in these pages reminded me of what it was to be hyped to see bonafide rock 'n' roll stars.

We live our lives for such stars to shine.

Simon Sweetman
2023

Simon Sweetman is a writer from Wellington, New Zealand. He has concentrated on music and pop culture in much of his works.
www.offthetracks.co.nz

Preface

Why? is probably the first thing anyone would ask. Why write a book about such a fleeting moment in New Zealand's music history, long forgotten from public memory? The answer is, why not?

Twenty-five years ago New Zealand welcomed one of the most talked about, headline-grabbing rock 'n' roll bands of the 1990s. For a brief moment in time, this self-proclaimed biggest and best band in the world actually might have been.

While critics and fans will remember how their first two albums cemented them a place in rock and roll history and spearheaded British guitar music across the globe, their only visit to these shores came after the release of their divisive third album, *Be Here Now*.

At the time, New Zealand was a country with its musical ear more in tune with Grunge, Metal and American Alternative Rock throughout the 1990s, but this cultural and commercial phenomenon penetrated through all the noise to reach the masses. Used to playing stadiums and headlining festivals in Europe and Asia, the New Zealand crowds were smaller, the venues makeshift and the attention less.

As an Oasis fan following the band since the *Be Here Now* era, I wanted to understand the impact of their visit. What did the press think? More importantly, what did the fans think? I had met some of them in person over the years, and they had little positive to say. I began to ask myself - was that the legacy of their only visit here, or did some people actually enjoy the experience? So, I started digging. I found reviews for the gig in Auckland which were relatively positive. I wanted to know more, so I launched a search for concertgoers near and far, anywhere I could find them - Facebook groups,

Twitter, Instagram, classified ads in the paper and even broadcasting my idea on community radio. Slowly, but surely, things started to come together. The first attendee reviews were in, mostly negative. But then the floodgates opened and more people were happy to share their stories, many with more favourable recollections. Alongside these stories are brilliant pieces of New Zealand journalism and magazine media from the 1990s. Many publications are now defunct, thankfully archived by the National Library of New Zealand where many hours were spent researching.

Ultimately, I wanted to create a record that documented this tour and the history of the band in New Zealand for the fans - for those who lived through the era, and fans of the future. Those who will likely never experience the thrill of seeing the band live, but who can live vicariously through the personal recollections of those who did.

Compiling these recollections and the history that goes alongside them has been no mean feat. This tiny piece of music history is pre-internet, pre-smartphone, pre-digital camera and pre-social and online media. Newspapers, magazines, radio, and television were the outlets of choice, and where I found all the information I needed to supplement the ever-growing pile of recollections I was receiving. From the early ripples of excitement in magazines profiling an up-and-coming band from Manchester storming the charts in Europe, to the full-scale media onslaught that sometimes focused more on two bickering brothers than their three multi-platinum award-winning albums. The rise and fall of the Gallagher brothers, and their first and last visit together to New Zealand right in the middle of it all, in an era where music consumers showed dedication to the cause, queuing for concert tickets and lining up outside music stores to buy the latest record – a far cry from the industry we see today.

What you'll see in this book is Oasis' journey in a New Zealand context, from their early success with *Definitely Maybe*, right through to *Be Here Now*, a suitably bombastic album and tour that somehow swaggered its way all around the world, with the wheels just starting to come off as it headed down under. In everything from magazine coverage, reviews, insights from those who were in the band's camp and most importantly, the experiences of the fans, Oasis' brief stint in New Zealand tells a story of triumph, joy and disappointment, a story that finishes abruptly after the band departs on March 11, 1998, never to return.

This is the unofficial story of Oasis in New Zealand.
Karamdeep Sahota
August 2023

Acknowledgments

There are far too many people to thank for making this a reality. To all the fans, crew and Kiwi artists who contributed, this would not have been possible without your support and insights. Thank you for your time and patience with my numerous requests for help.

A few individuals I have to mention:

Lee Pritchard – Great photographer and top bloke. An inspiration! Go check his books out.

Michael O'Connor – Brilliant memories and a privilege to talk to him. We could have spoken for hours.

National Library of New Zealand – To the many librarians who assisted me. Thankyou.

Sarah Moffat – For putting up with endless Oasis chat even though she has no interest in the topic. And for giving my work a reality check. I promise not to mention Oasis ever again.

Trish McCormack – For all the tips on how to publish and going through the book with a fine toothcomb.

Simon Grigg – For helping me find numerous copyright holders and allowing use of *Rip It Up*.

Simon Sweetman – For the brilliant foreword, finding Luke Peacocke and support in making this happen.

Richard Bowes – For his expertise in Oasis, writing and publishing, and the kick up the backside he provided to get me to the finish line.

Steve Passiouras at Bookow.com – For making this a reality and piecing it all together.

Barney McDonald – Thanks for great recollection and reuse of *Pavement* magazine material.

Amee Munro - Waikato University Library – For enabling easy access to *Nexus* which was proving hard to find.

Imroze Sahota, John Porter & Derek Clear for their continued support in pushing me to the finish line.

Contents

Chapter 1 – Definitely Maybe

'We haven't got any master plan. I don't think we have much control over it. I'll only sit back and reflect on all this when the band is no longer in existence anymore, and I'll sit down one day in the old rocking chair and I'll write me book and get the comeback tour going. At the moment the fantasy's still to be lived out.'
Noel Gallagher, September 1994 [1]

To understand the impact of the 1998 tour, it is important to look at the history of Oasis going all the way back to the beginning, albeit briefly. The band formed in Manchester in 1991 as The Rain, with members Paul Arthurs, Tony McCarroll, Paul McGuigan and singer Chris Hutton. Hutton was replaced by Liam Gallagher on vocals and the band name changed to Oasis after the band saw the name on an Inspiral Carpets tour poster. Noel Gallagher was present at their very first gig at the Boardwalk in Manchester in August 1991.[2] Initially offered the role of band manager he declined, instead taking on songwriting duties and de facto leadership of the band. Fast forward to May 1993 and the band trekked up to Glasgow for their 13th show, at King Tut's Wah Wah Hut, where Creation Records supremo Alan McGee saw them perform. As the story goes, he was so impressed he offered them a record deal that night.

By the time their debut single 'Supersonic' was released in the UK in April 1994, there was a huge buzz surrounding the band. From their first appearances on BBC Radio to adorning the covers of various UK music magazines, and three successful singles under their belt, the Oasis juggernaut was in full swing. In August 1994, their debut album *Definitely Maybe* was released, reaching #1 in the UK and becoming the fastest-selling debut album in UK chart history.[3] Oasis signed a worldwide deal with Sony, but relicensed to Creation Records in the UK.[4] Sony Music Entertainment New Zealand distributed their records, working off a close relationship with Sony Music Entertainment Australia. A CD processing plant opened in 1993, in Western Sydney, serving Australian and New Zealand audiences.[5]

Throughout the 1990s the New Zealand music press also started to hone in on the band. Cue contrast of opinion and pages of detail spread across fashion, music and entertainment publications. From *Rip it Up*, *Real Groove*, *Pavement* and others, interest in Oasis was evident. Overseas publications such as *Melody Maker* and *NME* were available, but on sale weeks after release in the UK. Even before their first single was released in New Zealand, they were on the cover of the local street press magazine *Swerve,* in July 1994. The edition also included a great interview with Noel Gallagher.

Swerve, July 1994[6]

Oasis are being hailed as the next big thing out of England - and we're talking REALLY big. Guitarist and songwriter Noel Gallagher is on the phone from the UK, it's a Monday morning there so I thought he'd be mellow. I was wrong.

So Noel, who do you reckon are the best band to come out of England in the last 10 years?
Easily us. (I laugh - he doesn't - whoops) I'm not sayin' that tongue in cheek at all. Aside from us I'd have to say The Smiths. I'd like to say the Stone Roses but they haven't done enough.

Does a Marshall stack and a Gibson Les Paul signify rock'n'roll to you?
No. John Lennon never used either did he? I don't think rock is a fashion thing - or is about sayin' the right things in interviews about 'the sixties' or 'The Rolling Stones'. It's a spiritual thing, it's about communicating that spirit to your audience. I hope that when kids think about rock'n'roll these days that they think about Oasis.

Some English bands have attributed their not being able to crack the American market on too much advance hype in the English press - leaving audiences at American gigs standing there going 'well go on - impress me' - instead of getting into it. Is that a fair comment?
You know what that is, that's an excuse! Those bands fail for this reason right. It is to do with the hype of the NME and the Melody Maker sure, but when these bands go over there, they automatically assume they're the next big thing, because they've been on the cover of the NME, and so they get there and they do six gigs and it doesn't take off, so they come home and start slagging America off saying "Aww they don't understand us bla, bla" What they've got to do is go to America and spend six months touring as you can't expect to crack a country of that size with six gigs, it just doesn't happen, so they've got to stick it out and really deserve the hype.

I suppose the reverse is true though, as the grunge thing doesn't appear to have gone over as big in the UK as it has in the rest of world.
Well the Melody Maker tried to make it take off, but they couldn't. You get all these middleclass fairly wealthy American bands, who cut a hole in the knee of their jeans and buy themselves a heroin addiction and then go around singin' about how fucked up they are and how they were abused as children. People in England aren't into that. People in England want you to tell them how shit their life is, not how shit your life is. People here want you to 'express the things they can't express, and I would never write about how shit my life was.

What's your impression of the English music press?
It's so full of its own importance it's unbelievable. We have two national weekly papers (NME & Melody Maker) that basically can either make you or break you. One's as bad as the other and they play the bands off against each other - so you get your Melody Maker bands and your NME bands, so if one likes you the other will hate you. It's shit, It's nonsense. They believe they are the worlds music papers, but honestly, you go to New York and no-one gives a crap if you've been on the cover of the NME. So they don't mean jack-shit outside of England.

What's the live scene like in Britain at the moment?
Well it's the best it's been for 4-5 years and the venues are starting to open up again, but unfortunately most of the bands aren't any good. The scene needs a band that can inspire the imagination and for the last five years or so if you asked what rock'n'roll was, you'd have been told Guns & Roses. Now they're hardly likely to inspire the imagination of a 16 year, unemployed kid in Manchester are they?

Could you tell us a little about being signed by Creation?
Yeah well it's quite an infamous story actually. We'd been practising around Manchester for about two years and we'd never actually played outside of our home town until some friends of ours who were in a band, had to go and do a gig at King Tut's Wah Wah Hut up in Glasgow and they asked us to support them, so we said OK. We get to the gig and the promoter said we couldn't play 'cause there was too many bands. We stood our ground and insisted we play or else and eventually he gave us a shot but there was only about 5 people in the club at the time and we only got to play 4 songs. One of those people was Alan McGee who's the head of Creation Records and he comes back stage and asks us if we had a record deal - 'no' we says - 'would you like one' he says, and we said 'yeah, suppose so.' So that's how we got signed.

How come you were a roadie for Inspiral Carpets?
Cause I needed the money. Someone offered me quite a lot of money to go and set up a drum kit and travel the world so I went for it. Took me a few years to get out of it though. But I was by no means a fan of their music.

You've got a reputation for being pretty rowdy on the road. Trashed hotels and the like. Is there any truth in that?
Well it's not me personally. Chairs are for sitting in, not for throwing out windows. But the other guys have never seen this sort of thing before so they do tend to get a bit carried away. I mean a year and a half ago they were all unemployed going nowhere and now they're on Top Of The Pops. It's got to affect you one way or another. But I'll tell you this, I'd rather they smash up rooms than get into heroin or something. I mean you can always fix a chair up but once your'e gone, your'e gone.

So is there still a lot of heroin in the UK?
I wouldn't know the first thing about it to tell you the truth. I'm not really interested in that drug as it's just fucked up too many people. Heroin has taken Kurt Cobain from me so that drug is the Devil. He was as big as John Lennon in my eyes and he always will be. It's such a shame - you get twats like Eddie Vedder who live and Kurt Cobain dies - it's just sad.

> "You get twats like Eddie Vedder who live and Kurt Cobain dies - it's just sad."

The worldwide muscle of Sony music seems to be poised to drop right in behind Oasis' debut album. How does it feel to be on the verge of such massive success?
I haven't really had time to sit down and think about it yet. I mean it would be presumptuous to say that we're going to be huge because it might never happen. So we're just getting on with it one day at a time. When the accountant comes in and says that we're gonna have to buy a Lear jet to avoid a big tax bill - then I'll believe it. It's just the big adventure at the moment and we want to see how far we can take it before we lose it.
. D McNickel

Swerve, Noel Gallagher interview – David McNickel[7]

3

Rip It Up, New Zealand's premier music magazine at the time first mentioned Oasis in June 1994, with a brief but positive review of 'Supersonic'. An early flag bearer for the band was *Rip It Up* journalist John Taite. He understood Oasis was a little bit different, a breath of fresh air to the UK indie scene. He interviewed Noel in September 1994.

singles

For the third consecutive month there's a bundle of non-dance singles worth crawling from the wreckage for. Tops are Manchester's new saviours, **Oasis,** who've stepped into the vacuum left by the Happy Mondays if their debut single 'Supersonic' (Creation) is anything to go by. In Liam Gallagher they've got a front man with the same swagger and dulcet tones as **Shaun Ryder** and in 'Supersonic' they've got a great British rock single in the same street as 'I Wanna Be Adored' or 'Step On'. Of the other three tracks 'Take Me Away' is an OK ballad but guitars and urgency are back on track on 'I Will Believe' and 'Columbia'. Compulsory.

Rip It Up – 'Supersonic' review - George Kay/Simon Grigg[8]

Forget for a minute that the English music press cry wolf every damn month. One word. Oasis. This time you can forgive the press for salivating. This time it seems a genuine hope has arrived, and Oasis are hope, not hopefuls. They are (whisper it) THE NEXT BIG THING. After their first couple of singles they were compared to the likes of the Stone Roses. Upon hearing their debut album, *Definitely Maybe*, they've made peers out of the Beatles, Stones, Pistols, Smiths and the rest of the history makers. The Stone Roses opened their album with 'I Wanna Be Adored'. Oasis open with '(I'm a) Rock n Roll Star'. That's the difference.

At the core of Oasis are brothers Noel and Liam Gallagher. Liam sings and acts like he was born into the roll as front man, older brother Noel writes all the songs, lyrics and plays guitar. Oh, and Noel does all the interviews as well ("We don't let Liam do interviews, 'cos he tells a pack of lies").

The band rose from a city devastated by the media hype blitzkrieg. They're the Steve Austin of Manchester, better, stronger and cooler because of the crash. At the time Noel was a roadie for the Inspiral Carpets ("I learnt a lot of don't"), and even though the record companies were waving around the chequebooks, he hadn't even thought of starting up a band.

"We were just having too much of a good time really. Just going to clubs and following the Stone Roses around. We were too busy just going out, taking drugs and having a good time to think about forming a band. It was only after things died down in Manchester and there was nothing else to do, we thought about getting a band together, by accident, we stumbled into a rehearsal room one day cos we had nothing better to do, and after six or seven weeks we had a couple of songs, and after a couple of gigs we thought 'we may as well call ourselves a band'."

There's something familiar and inviting about Oasis's style, something that makes their music easy to get fanatical about. Noel's timeless chords (played on a guitar that Johnny Marr gave him), the melodies the occasional lyrical spaz outs ("I know a girl called Elsa, she's into Alka Seltzer/she done it with a doctor in a helicopter" —'Shakermaker') delivered perfectly by Liam's casual sneer. It would seem the perfect partnership, that is if you didn't know about all their sibling rivalry. Most of the interviews with the band have resulted in punch-ups between the two. Like Ray and Dave Davis in the Kinks or Reed and Cale in the Velvet Underground, their flaring personalities certainly play a big part in of the band dynamics.

"He's always at my throat. Sadly it's not just a media concoction. I wish it was to tell you the truth because its becoming a bit of a chore. We get on with each other when we're recording, it's just when we get bored we seem to pick on each other. But he is my little brother so it is allowed."

It seems that everyone focuses on the punch-ups and the drugs when it comes to their interviews.

"Drugs have always been part and parcel of what we do, not for any particular reason. It's just that's the way it is in Manchester, especially when you're unemployed and you've got nothing better to do, you just do drugs. I don't need it to be creative, it's just when I'm bored. It's come out a lot in the media just because we're honest. We won't deny anything for the sake of it, if people ask us do we take drugs then we'll say 'yeah we do', because we do. If you say you don't you get found out in the end."

The album title, *Definitely Maybe*, sounds rather hesitant for you guys. Who came up with that?

"Well I did, you know. I am the creative force in the band. If anyone else was to come up with a musical idea I'd probably die of shock. They're all quite happy about it because they don't have to do any work, they're probably still in bed right now.

"To the people outside the band, from what they read in the press, we're this ultra self-confident bunch of chaps. But *Definitely Maybe* is just a phrase we'd use in the studio, like I use it all the time. 'Shall we use such and such a sound on this record?' and I'll go 'definitely, well maybe'. I think the average man in the street, no matter where they live, can understand that indecisive thing. I wrote a song called 'Definitely Maybe' about a year ago, but it was a shit song, and I just thought the title would fit the album, and then after about a week I thought I shouldn't have done it because I'd have to answer questions like this."

Since signing with Alan McGee's Creation records last June and already it's easy to say that *Definitely Maybe* has surpassed the heights of Ride, Swervedriver, Primal Scream and the rest of the Creation roster (even when you are a huge fan of said bands). They've only released three singles in the UK: 'Supersonic', 'Shakermaker' and 'Live Forever', all of which have been indie number ones, and the last two cracked their national top 10.

But it's live that they've had everyone reaching for the thesaurus. It was during one of their first shows that an astonished McGee ran on stage and signed them.

"We were doing a gig and there weren't very many people there at all. There were five or six bands and we were bottom of the bill, and McGee just happened to miss his train back to London, and he had half an hour to kill so he went into this club to have a drink while we were playing. And we only played like four songs, and afterwards he came up and said 'what's yer band called', and we said Oasis and he goes 'do you boys have a record deal', we said no, he said 'do ya want one', we said 'who with?' and he said 'Creation', and we kinda went, 'oh suppose so.' At first we just thought he was some Scottish bloke taking the piss, so we weren't going to get excited.

"He invited us down to Creation's offices the next day, and I'm saying 'well I'm not paying to go to some bizarre address in London' — Hackney of all places — you know, to find out it's all been a wind up, and he says he'll pay for the tickets, and we're like 'where's the money?' and he's going 'well I'm not going to give you any money 'cos you'll just take it and spend it all on drugs, but I'll leave the tickets at the station'. And they were there."

It was another Oasis gig that caught the eye of Crazy Horse, Neil Young's backing band, recently. They were so impressed with Noel that they invited the 27 year old to play on stage with them at their gig.

"Yeah, after the gig someone came into the dressing room and said 'there's two old fellahs outside to see you lot', and we were like 'oh dear, well let them in then' and when they walked in the door I was going, 'fuck me, that's Crazy Horse'. Anyway they said they really liked 'Supersonic' and asked me to show them the chords, and they're going [puts on an American accent about as good as Americans put on English accents] 'Yeah man, yeah man, Neil'd love this'. And then they said 'we're going to do a show, would you fancy getting up on stage and playing with us.' And it was fuckin' great. I'm thinking of changing my name by deed poll to Noel Young and Crazy Horse is my new nickname in the band.

"Neil Young's like a big influence, 'Slide Away' could have been a Neil Young song, I hope someday he'll cover it. That and 'Live Forever'. There's only two people that have played with Crazy Horse, one's him and one's me, you know. So if I ever see him in the street now I've got a reason to tap him on the shoulder and say 'Your backing band's shit aren't they', and he'll probably turn around and go 'Yeah man ... so's yours!'."

One of the album's highlights is the quiet closing track, 'Married With Children', an anti-'Creep' lament. There's a softly strummed, bare acoustic guitar with all these great, acerbic lines like 'I hate the way that you are so sarcastic and you're not very bright/You think that everything you've done's fantastic/You're music's shite it keeps me up all night'.

"Well that's a song about my ex-girlfriend actually. She didn't like that fact that I used to get up at four in the morning. Like I'd been having a musical dream or whatever and I'd be writing songs in my sleep, and I'd sit up in the bed and grab me guitar and start writing songs. Which is where the line 'You're music's shite it keeps me up all night' comes from. It's a universal type song, you know when you're living with your girlfriend and you have this love/hate relationship. The first verse is me addressing her, the second verse is her addressing me. She hated the way I was so sarcastic and she didn't think I was very bright. It's probably one of the best songs I've ever written, actually."

There are eleven tracks on *Definitely Maybe*. All are fuckin' deadly. And after my interest in 'Married With Children' Noel eagerly grabs a track-listing and gives me a run down on the inspiration behind the rest of the album.

"'Digsy's Dinner' is just about this mate of mine called Digsy who invited me over for dinner and said 'do you like lasagne?'. Seriously. 'Slide Away' is just a love song really. 'Cigarettes and Alcohol' is about being young and down on your luck and it's saying all you need is a ghetto blaster with your favourite albums on and a bag of booze and a packet of fags and everything will be all right. 'Bring it on Down' is one of those tracks that should have been on *Never Mind The Bollocks*. 'Supersonic' is like ... well I don't know where that come from. 'Colombia' was an instrumental that we decided to put lyrics to, and that doesn't mean anything. 'Up In The Sky' is about people who claim to be the voice of their generation and then when you actually see the emperor without any clothes on you go 'ha ha you've got no clothes on you bastard'."

Aimed at who exactly?

"No-one really, just like school teachers, the police, governments, you know. The only person that can tell you where you're going is you, and everyone else are just empty uniforms. 'Live Forever' is a love song, and 'Shakermaker' is in the same vein as 'Supersonic' — that's just too many drugs, too much booze and a lot of rhyming couplets. 'Rock and Roll Star' is about wanting to be Mick Jagger."

Do you or does Liam?

"Liam doesn't just want to be Mick Jagger. He thinks he *is* Mick Jagger. I wouldn't mind being Mick Jagger now, he's got quite a nice wife really hasn't he. Lovely kids, nice car, beautiful house, loads of money."

I read somewhere that you didn't like talking to the media about anything other than the music.

"Well I don't want to talk about my life in the media. And I certainly don't want to talk about my life in the songs. I never wanted that out of a band, somebody telling me how shit their life is. I wanted someone to tell me how shit or how great *my* life was. I'm not interested in Kurt Cobain's heroine addiction, or Morrissey's celibacy, or Brett Anderson's, fucking homosexual experiences, it don't mean anything to me. It might mean something to them, but for people to put that in the context of a song is very, very, very, very arrogant, as if to say 'you need to know I was abused as a child'. Like who gives a fuck, you know, not me. I don't think the record buying public does, they just want to hear music. If it's got a good tune its got a good tune."

Definitely Maybe doesn't sound like a debut, it's full of great, assured tunes. Nine out of the eleven tracks could be fantastic singles.

"My debut album was written when I was about 14. Sadly I never got to record it cos I was still in school. This is like my seventh album. I've been a songwriter since I was 11, seriously. So here we have the supposed debut album when I've been writing stuff for 16 years."

How long have you had the songs for the album.

"Around March this year we recorded them, but the songs were written a year and a half ago. With the exception of 'Slide Away', they were all written before we had a record deal. They're quite old songs, but they're timeless if you know what I mean. We're already getting songs together for the next album, so we're already two steps ahead of everyone else."

Two steps ahead indeed. It seems that in the retro state of 90s English indies, Oasis are the only guitar band really forging ahead. Not that they're completely original in everything they do. Their second single 'Shakermaker' is like some (strangely fantastic) cross between 'Strawberry Fields' and 'I'd Like To Teach The World To Sing'. 'Cigarettes and Alcohol' pinches the riff from T-Rex's 'Get It On'.

"Well we've never denied the fact that we had. But you see when we wrote that song we didn't have a record deal, so it was like who the fuck cares anyway, but now it's become this big statement, that we're harking back to the seventies or something. But it's a great riff so why not pinch it. It's better than pinching a riff from fucking Inspiral Carpets, for instance."

Sure they plunder the odd moment from pop's past. But then, if everything *has* been done before, Oasis are the sparkling hope that it can be done a whole lot better.

"I believe in fate totally, I think that everything is mapped out for ya, and now's the time to do it. Everything has seemed so natural from the way we formed the band to the way we got the record deal. We haven't got any master plan. I don't think we have much control over it. I'll only sit back and reflect on all this when the band is no longer in existence anymore and I'll sit down one day in the old rocking chair and I'll write me book and get the comeback tour going. At the moment the fantasy's still to be lived out."

JOHN TAITE

20 ripitup

Rip It Up – Noel Gallagher interview - John Taite/Simon Grigg[9]

Newsnight, a TVNZ production presented by Simon Dallow, Alison Mau and Marcus Lush featured Oasis on September 27, 1994. This would be one of their earliest references on New Zealand television. 'Supersonic' first charted in New Zealand on August 14, 1994, landing at #36. The song peaked two weeks later at #28 but remained in the top 50 for 10 weeks.[10] The band's debut album *Definitely Maybe* was released two months later in October 1994, landing in at #8 in the chart, an impressive first appearance for a band still relatively unknown.[11] The album remained in the top 50 for six weeks. As was the case in the UK, the album received (mostly) widespread critical acclaim from the New Zealand reviews.

Oasis

Definitely Maybe Sony

Not since the emergence of The Stone Roses has the collective hopes and aspirations of so many English music critics been placed in the hands of one band. But where so much of the hype surrounding The Stone Roses came from the 'Madchester' musical scene which they helped to create, Oasis have attracted as much attention for their own hype as for their music.

On the strength of *Definitely Maybe*, however, their PR machine can safely discard the already tiresome stories of the Gallagher brothers' feuds and hotel room trashings, and instead concentrate on the virtues of the best British pop album in years. From the opening Sex Pistols-inspired riff on *Rock 'N Roll Star* through to recent singles *Shaker Maker*, *Live Forever* and the John Peel favourite *Cigarettes and Alcohol*, Oasis synthesise some of British pop's finest moments into a gloriously crafted whole that leaves the opposition in the shade.

Some critics have already questioned whether Oasis will last long enough to pull off this feat twice. But really, who cares? *Supersonic* and *Digsy's Dinner* would make better epitaphs than most bands manage to produce over five albums, let alone one. Forget the preaching of Public Enemy, with *Definitely Maybe* you *can* believe the hype. Buy this album. ***Jock Laurie***

Pavement - Definitely Maybe review - Jock Laurie/Barney McDonald[12]

albums

Oasis

SUGAR - File Under Easy Listening
(White)

Copper Blue was a fizzing pop hit, spawning all sorts of singles with Bob Mould's melodic guitar and (did somebody really call him the alternative Cat Stevens?!) distinctive voice. The follow up mini-album, *Beaster* (recorded in studio time left over from the *Copper Blue* sessions), was a belligerent, religious bile fest'. After the two, Mould had a breakdown, convinced he could never better them.

Well, *F.U.E.L.* doesn't so much better the previous albums but it does define more clearly what this Sugar thing is all about. You need to know that Mould, ever the perfectionist, made the band completely re-record this album after being initially unhappy. Perhaps as a result, we've got a band that's come to terms with the contradictory demons that dominated their two previous incarnations, blasting electric tumult and melodic pop shade.

The album opens where *Beaster* left off and throws 'Gift' in your face, which rages with a guitar line that found a home for a My Bloody Valentine experiment. We dive into a bit of a Ringo track with bass player David Barbe's 'Company Book'. Then in soars the single, 'Your Favourite Thing', with a tale about relationship objectification and some blazing guitar to put things back on track.

It's halfway through *F.U.E.L.* when things really start hotting up. There's the compulsory head nodding pop of 'Gee Angel', about buying a pair of wings that don't work. Now we're in the midst of modern Mould's genius. 'Panama City Hotel' puts on some strummed time out and glides you onto the "do do dos" of 'Can't Help You Anymore'. Then 'Granny Cool' grunts against the attitude of the "hate everything" idols. The lament 'Believe What You're Saying' gives us bunch of sad lyrics and tearful guitar. We finish off with the cyclical 'Explode And Make Up', which is exactly what Sugar's fantastic career has been all about, really.

As for filing under easy listening, I don't think so.

JOHN TAITE

PUBLIC ENEMY - Muse Sick N'Hour Mess Age
(Def Jam)

Public Enemy have always had a message in their music. But now, as one of their sound bytes puts it, "the red, black and green machine is back to clean up the scene". The rap scene that is. It seems Public Enemy are less than impressed with the spliff head gangster, direction the black CNN is taking, and they love something to roar about.

Muse Sick is PE's fifth album and, in a genre that eats it's old, it was always going to be a tricky one. Regardless of rap's recent period of hyper innovation, PE have remained true to themselves. Despite the accidents (Terminator X) and drug scandals (Flavour Flav) this album is full of what they do best: going BOOM, that is, with the assistance of The Bomb Squad.

The sounds more than make up for the flawed concepts, which almost advocate some kind of clean up censorship in order to protect the black community. The single 'Give It Up' sets the tone for the rest of the album. The lyrics are a big preach about the ill effects of weed and malt liquor, but it's saved by liquid funk and addictive hooks providing something that's, over all, spectacular. Moments like the uncredited 'Stop in the Name' and the super smooth 'So Watcha Gonna Do Now' take aim at "dat gangsta shit", and once again they're aided by slammin' backing. Over and over they prove they've still got the musical cred' and creativity to kick it in '94. Want more proof? Check out 'Live And Undrugged', or Flavour's bounce around 'God Complex', or the highly controversial 'Hitler Day', with its loud, dense live sound of layered madness (which seems a bit over the top for a song about American Thanksgiving, but who cares).

It's a brave move to dis the major innovators and to try and top them; but if you've ever liked PE in the past, well, here's the next episode.

JOHN TAITE

OASIS - Definitely Maybe
(Epic)

Oasis are what you've been waiting for. *Definitely Maybe* has just become the fastest selling album of all time in the UK, some 150 000 copies in the first two days. There are hundreds of reasons why.

If you're just tuning in, Oasis are from Manchester. Brothers Liam and Noel Gallagher are the core of the band. Liam sings and does the sneering front man bit, Noel plays guitar and writes all the music and lyrics. Phew, that was restrained. It's also got to be said that they're gonna put your faith back in English pop, give you a new set of guitar idols and completely change your life. Noel's talent for hooks and melodies puts Oasis right up there with the history makers. They're so much more than the empty hype we've become used to.

First there were the infectious singles; their White label 'Columbia', 'Supersonic' with it's cocaine addled babble: "I know a girl called Elsa she's into Alka Seltzer . . . she done it with a doctor in a helicopter." 'Shakermaker' their catchy cross between 'Strawberry Fields' and 'I'd Like To Teach The World To Sing', burns a hole in your memory. Then there was the love song 'Live Forever', with its swooping, caressing guitar.

Stepping inside *Definitely Maybe* is like walking into another dimension, where every rock/pop guitar legend has provided some Obi-wan Kenobi advice. There's deadly rock 'n' roll in the form of 'Cigarette's and Alcohol' (complete with T-Rex riff and all), 'Bring It On Down' and, of course, 'Rock n Roll Star'. There's the speedy 'Up In The Sky' and the pogo fest' 'Digsy's Dinner'. Then at the other end of the spectrum there are the wry, tender moments like 'Married With Children', with a beautifully bare acoustic guitar and the quietly sung lines: "I hate the way you're so sarcastic and you're not very bright/You think that everything you've done's fantastic/You're music's shite, it keeps me up all night."

With the exception of 'Slide Away' (a heart aching love song that'll have your speakers weeping), all of the songs here were written nearly two years ago, before the band got their deal with Creation. This just adds to their familiar timelessness, really. They would've sounded as great in '92 as they do in '94, and as they will in '96.

There are 11 songs and it's hard to find fault with any of them. The worst thing I can say is they've filled the Stone Roses' figurehead shoes, or they've provided a Beatles for the '90s. A couple of listens and you're hooked. A couple more and you're a fan. A couple more after that and you spouting off about them to everyone you know.

Definitely Maybe is the perfect debut, a showcase of strength and diversity; pop flavour, rock 'n' roll vigour, guitar mastery and, most of all, personality. It's given my stereo a daily blasting for the last two months, and it still sounds as fantastic as the day I got it. Easily the best album to come out of England in the last seven years. Definitely definitely THE BIG THING.

JOHN TAITE

DINOSAUR JR Without A Sound
(Warners)

Singer/guitarist/drummer J Mascis would have been asleep on his lazy boy and realised that he should probably, maybe, sort of do a new album. So he did. He wrote a brilliant opening song 'Feel the Pain', which is full of all the things that are brilliant about Dinosaur Jr; the simplicity, the pretty melodies entwined in fuzzy basic guitar chords, and J's simple 'generation X' (ha ha) lyrics. After 'Feel the Pain' J's sugar rush peters out. He slips into mellow mode and the rest of the album consists of low key, relaxed ditties.

Dinosaur Jr started off blisteringly in the late '80s, released their mega rockers, 'You're Living All Over Me' and the brilliant 'Bug', and

GET A SLI

SEMI LEN

BEFORE

chronic

DEBUT 3

OUT

CD FEATURES
ON TOUR
THROUGH

Rip It Up – Definitely Maybe review - John Taite/Simon Grigg[13]

OASIS
Definitely Maybe
(Epic)

From the moment I picked up this album, I knew I was going to like it, and I wasn't disappointed. This music is great!

It can be compared to nothing else, it is in a class of its own.

They are very Beatles. In one song he mentions the Yellow Submarine.

They also have a bit of T-Rex in them (especially on 'Cigarettes and Alcohol'), but they have their own unique sound. Wailing guitars, great harmonies, feedback and heavily echoed vocals.

There are no gooey love songs or 'Let's-All-Change-The-World' dribble. Instead we have lyrics like "I want to build myself a house out of Plasticine", and a song about lasagne!

If you want to listen to something that breaks free of the worn-out musical mould, get this album! – PAUL, Designer

Tearaway – Definitely Maybe review[14]

In complete contrast to what was going on in the UK music scene, Grunge reigned supreme in New Zealand throughout the early 1990s, with Nirvana, Soundgarden and Pearl Jam all delivering #1 albums in 1994. Nirvana topped the singles chart in 1992 with 'Smells Like Teen Spirit' and Pearl Jam and Soundgarden both managed top 10 singles. The Stone Temple Pilots were another American band successful down under, notably with their sophomore album *Purple*. British bands, especially indie bands, never quite reached the same dizzying heights. The Stone Roses failed to have a top 20 single or top 10 album. *Pills 'N' Thrills and Bellyaches* by Happy Mondays peaked at #27, lasting four weeks in the chart. Even the breakthrough album by Primal Scream, *Screamadelica* failed to chart in the New Zealand top 50. Despite the success of their hit single 'Creep', Radiohead's debut album *Pablo Honey* peaked at #44 lasting just one week on the chart. Britpop contemporaries Suede had minor success with single 'Animal Nitrate' peaking at #11 and debut album *Suede* peaking at #8 in its second week in May 1993. Blur's first album to chart in New Zealand was *Parklife*, which entered at #27 in July 1994, with 'Girls & Boys' coming through as a minor hit, peaking at #16 in August 1994.

The New Zealand Herald - Definitely Maybe review, Russell Baillie[15]

entertainment

2 PUMPKINS   **3** WAYNE TOUPS   **4** FILMS

THE Mancunian candidate

A T THIS end of the world we can be allowed our natural cynicism. Another year, another English band which has commanded cover stories and slavering uncritical comment by a fickle, desperate London rock press in search of the Next Big Thing.

Oasis with Noel Gallagher (third from left) ... "we're definitely the best band in England since the Stone Roses."

The debut album by OASIS entered our charts at number eight last week and they are the best new band in Britain — at least according to their guitarist-songwriter Noel Gallagher. We've heard this one before, says GRAHAM REID.

'The Mancunian Candidate' from *The New Zealand Herald*, Graham Reid[16]

No radio airplay charts exist from the 1990s. Data from APRA (Australasian Performing Right Association) only indicates the percentage of New Zealand artists on the radio for royalties' purposes, a figure as low as 3%. The majority of artists on the radio were foreign. The clear dominance of pop and USA Alternative in the New Zealand charts throughout the early 1990s was also peppered with domestic hits from artists such as Supergroove, The Mutton Birds, Crowded House and Shihad.[17] Deregulation of New Zealand Radio in 1989, led to a range of new radio stations launching in the early 1990s. Many of these were youth oriented with pop and rock music a staple on the airwaves. The Rock started in Hamilton in 1991, gradually expanding across the country to become a nationwide network by the end of the decade. Channel Z launched in 1996 in Wellington, offering alternative music with a youth to adult target audience. Channel 91ZM operated with the slogan 'Rock of the Nineties' across Christchurch and Wellington. Combined with other long-standing networks such as student radio bFM and Radio Hauraki, there was plenty of opportunity for Alternative Rock music to flourish in the 1990s.

The ascent of rock music in the New Zealand charts coincided directly with the rise of the Big Day Out music festival, which started in Australia in 1992. Auckland hosted its first line up in 1994, with Soundgarden topping the bill. The success of *Definitely Maybe* saw Oasis selected to play Big Day Out the following year, which would have been their first visit to New Zealand and Australia. Due to perform alongside The Cult and Primal Scream, the tour never eventuated as Oasis cancelled, without reason, according to Big Day Out promoter Ken West.[18] This was the first of a few run-ins West would have with the band. In all probability, the band cancelled as they opted for a more lucrative tour of the USA which would build the band's popularity in a larger market. The success of the American tour helped propel 'Live Forever' to #2 on the Modern Rock Tracks chart (now the Alternative Airplay chart).[19] As it turned out their gig at DV8 in Seattle on January 28, 1995, fell right in the middle of the Australian Big Day Out dates.

An early version of the Big Day Out 1995 poster with Oasis on the bill. Artwork by Richard Allan of Soap Studios[20]

Chapter 2 – Morning Glory

'People are always going to be cynical of a band with one album out, but I think with Morning Glory being a better album, people are coming around…We're not sprinting now but settled in for the marathon. We're out in front and just taking it easy.' Noel Gallagher, November 1995[21]

In New Zealand at least, the first half of 1995 remained quiet on the Oasis front. In the UK the band achieved their first #1 single with 'Some Might Say', sacked drummer Tony McCarroll, headlined Glastonbury, and took on Blur in 'The Battle of Britpop'. In amongst all the drama, Oasis' sophomore album (*What's the Story*) *Morning Glory?* was recorded. Ahead of the October album launch, the first single to make its way onto the Australasian airwaves and charts was 'Roll with It'. As an Australasian-specific release, the track list differed from the UK release, containing B-sides, 'Acquiesce', 'Talk Tonight' and 'Headshrinker'. Released in October, 'Roll with It' initially charted at #24, peaking at #17 two weeks later, on October 29. The release of *(What's The Story) Morning Glory?* shattered records in the UK on its way to #1, with first-week sales of 345,000, making it the number two fastest-selling album in UK chart history, at the time. The record made a quieter debut in the New Zealand chart, first appearing on October 29 at #4.[22]

Several New Zealand-based reviews of the album ran in a variety of publications, with contrasting opinions.

Oasis

(What's the Story) Morning Glory?

Sony

You can't help but find the Oasis success story enormously appealing. God knows the English music press have made it their bread and butter and helped create the stumbling media monster that is the brothers Gallagher. Their garish rock 'n' roll bravado could have been disastrous if this, their sophomore album, hadn't lived up to all the hype. But the proof is in the trousers, and these boys must now be wearing oversized briefs. With little or no fuss, Noel and Co. knocked out in 10 days what can only be described as *the* definitive British rock 'n' roll album of the 90s, barely pegging out their good friends, the sadly defunct The Verve. Steeped in the musical history of their land, Noel has crafted 50 minutes of melodic elegance, using Liam's unique tones as if they were his own, tempering tales of ecstatic confidence (*Roll With It*) with prudent perceptive advice (*Don't Look Back in Anger*, *Cast No Shadow*) and blind devotion (*Wonderwall*). Most bands take four or five albums to exhibit the kind of historic depth that *Morning Glory* radiates from every groove. Let's hope the jubilant lifestyles fuelling their art don't push the self-destruct button prematurely. Cheers! ***Geoff Wright***

Pavement - (What's the Story) Morning Glory? review
– Geoff Wright/Barney McDonald[23]

Liam Gallagher, Oasis

albums

FINNS

Neil and Tim Finn
(Parlophone)

If the walls could talk in the Finn family home in Te Awamutu, this is the album from the boys' bedroom. Its relaxed, spontaneous feel captures a childhood spent playing acoustic guitars together, working out a few chords after a session with *A Hard Day's Night* on the mono radiogram. Recorded quickly, it benefits from a natural sound and unlaboured approach. It's a charming album full of melodic colour and sonic surprises, as if they've grabbed whatever was in the air and thrown it onto tape.

It may sound as if the session was yesterday, but this album has been threatened for years. This is the second time the Finns have got together for a diversionary bit of brotherly music-making. The first time, the songs were so poppy they were requisitioned for *Woodface*, the breakthrough album for Crowded House in Europe. But the five years since then have made all the difference to the way this album sounds. Neil and Tim are now much more in charge of their musical destinies. With *Together Alone* Crowded House cut the apron strings with Mitchell Froom, and found a more Pacific voice. *Before & After* saw Tim Finn in complete command of his songwriting skills, and the album quietly captured a committed audience. But producing Dave Dobbyn's *Twist* put the final stamp on the flavour of Finn.

This isn't the Everly harmony album many were expecting, but a glimpse at the Finns' musical vocabulary before the production craftsmanship adds its polish. The language they grew up with is, of course, the Beatles. But it's the period that matters: this recalls *Magical Mystery Tour* and the 'White Album', when they were having some fun experimenting in the studio after the hard pop graft of *Sgt Pepper* was completed.

Just as clear, however, are the distinctive Finn touches: the Enzy paranoia of 'Eyes of the World', the swampy 'Suffer Never' that could be recent Crowded House. Their voices are often indistinguishable, with the unique harmonies which always result when siblings sing together. 'News Travels Fast' and 'Where is My Soul' in particular are glorious acoustic duets, the latter with a soaring middle eight that belongs in a Crowdies' hit. The songs seem like works in progress, with verses and choruses that might fit elsewhere, and dodgy lyrics left in to retain the spirit of creativity. Giving the minimalism some flavour are the "found sounds" taken from whatever was at hand — wooden drums, scratched piano strings, muffled drums and tea-chest bass, a ukelele and backward tape loops.

Only 38 minutes long, with 11 tracks (and a couple of those could go), *Finn* bubbles with musical textures and gestures. It's a captivating insight into the brothers of invention.

CHRIS BOURKE

OASIS

(What's the Story)
Morning Glory?
(Sony)

I'm not going to rave about Oasis' melodic brilliance or their Beatlesque catchiness. I'm going to refrain from going on about Noel Gallaghers's mouth watering array of tunes, about his brother Liam's much improved vocals, about new drummer Alan White keeping the whole thing together better than Tony McCarrol ever did. There'll be none of that here.

It's not all brilliance and ease. 'Hey Now' is a lazy dirge that sounds like Noel was down the chippy when they were recording. And while it's just as well they had to remove 'Step Out', the horrible Stevie Wonder 'Uptight' rip off, it's absence has left an imbalance in the highs and lows.

Noel must have had a melancholic 1995 because *Morning Glory* is Oasis developing their delicate and intricate side. If you were a fan of 'Live Forever', 'Slide Away' and 'Supersonic', you'll love it. There are fragile hopes in their next brilliant single, 'Wonderwall'. The fizzing enormity of their finale, 'Champagne Supernova', will take up residence in your soul. 'She's Electric', akin to 'Digsy's Dinner', is a silly pop thing that'll stick in that part of your brain that makes you hum. 'Don't Look Back in Anger' has Noel on vocals (saving one of the best tracks for himself), and 'Cast No Shadow', about the Verve's Richard Ashcroft, is a sad, string section assisted number.

Looking at the wider picture, Blur's *The Great Escape* may well be a Brit-pop masterpiece, but *Morning Glory*, is a masterful piece of rock and roll — twice as easy to get into and twice as rewarding once you're in. It's full of what makes classics, erm, classic — crafted, mood swinging guitar melodies, vocals that pace you up and slow you down, a supportive rhythm section and, most importantly, a sense of magic that transcends the hype.

JOHN TAITE

SONIC YOUTH

Washing Machine
(Geffen)

This is where smart guitars go when they transcend this plane — to a sonic jam store in the sky, where they get to play not only with

Sonic Youth

Rip It Up - (What's the Story) Morning Glory? review – John Taite/Simon Grigg[24]

16

Blur
THE GREAT ESCAPE
(Food/Parlophone)
Oasis
(WHAT'S THE STORY) MORNING GLORY?
(Epic)

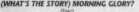

Imagine this as a thought experiment… Take two bands. Genetically endow each of them with the very best strains of assorted quirky English pop sensibilities. Name one band Blur. A few years later, name the other band Oasis. Hothouse each of them and grant rapid success. Allow each the freedom to grow. Nourish each of them well with a balanced five-star mixture of the late sixties (Beatles, Kinks, Barrett-era Pink Floyd), lots of seventies (Electric Light Orchestra, Status Quo, Steve Harley & Cockney Rebel, XTC, The Jam, Magazine, Madness, The Specials etc) and the early eighties (some more XTC, Soft Boys, Robyn Hitchcock & The Egyptians). Resist the temptation to prescribe predetermined growth paths – just leave each band alone and allow their true natures to keep developing. Oh yes – hire top-notch visual designers to create some mighty fine graphics packaging, cultivate a bit of attention-grabbing sibling rivalry and mild bickering in public, engage the media… etc.

Oasis: Status Quo '95?

Now imagine that you are not imagining… and that today you have two albums released within weeks of each other, to be listened to as progress reports on the no-longer-imaginary experiment. Strange – how two bands can find nourishment in basically the same places and yet still sound so distinctly different.

With *The Great Escape*, Blur – with the songwriting talent of Damon Albarn at their core – have now released four official albums (or five, if you count a Japan-only B-sides compilation). All the influences listed above are present and accounted for. But the overall tone leans towards the semi-detached cleverness of The Kinks, Cockney Rebel, and McCartney-style Beatles, with keyboard and orchestral colours never far from the front. For example, *It Could be You* sounds not unlike our very own Split Enz covering The Kinks. *Ernold Same* slips unashamedly into a Sgt Peppery music hall waltz. *Yuko and Hiro* would feel quite at home on Eno's early vocal albums.

Meanwhile, *(What's the Story) Morning Glory?* is only the second Oasis album, following on from last year's much-hyped *Definitely Maybe*. Double and triple guitars trip and jangle their way through the same catalogue of influences as above. But unlike Blur, Oasis – with the Gallagher brothers as mainstays – tend to scour history for rock (rather than pop) sensibilities. *Roll With it*, for example, evokes seventies-era Status Quo blended with *Revolver*-era Beatles (think of the George Harrison song *Taxman*). *Wonderwall* (nothing to do with Harrison's solo album of the same name), revives memories of XTC (dear God!) merged with Robyn Hitchcock. There are keyboards and orchestral colours here too, but they sound more Lennon than McCartney – for example, on *Don't Look Back in Anger*. This track also manages to capture, en passant, at least Bowie, Mott the Hoople's *All the Young Dudes* and XTC again. *Some Might Say* reminds us that Matthew Sweet is also interested in the same chapters of the musical past.

So… Blur and Oasis – same heritage, different personalities. Despite the differences, the family resemblances are unmistakable, especially in the structural nuances and lyric gestures. Notice the almost identical sense of what's funny and the shared "guess-where-you've-heard-it-somewhere-before?" hipness. But does it make sense to compare? As the Syd Barrett song says – *Apples and Oranges*.
– Ilmar Taimre

Blur: Semi-detached

Real Groove - (What's the Story) Morning Glory? review – Ilmar Taimre[25]

17

annoying.

Example: the first single, 'Country House' – naff. 'It Could Be You' is brilliant, though, as is 'Best Days'. It lacks the depth of 'Parklife' and feels like a bit of a rush-job, but including the guitar chords with the lyrics on the sleeve is a nice touch.

KATY

end of 'She's Electric' is the same as the end of 'A Little Help From My Friends', and a few lines are from Fab Four tunes.

A great album, with the most forced rhyme in the history of rock: 'And god only knows I've missed her/On the palm of her hand is a blister'.

PAUL

her previous albums, but a few tracks stood out like 'One Sweet Day', which features Boyz II Men. You know what that means – mushiness mushy mushy mushy.

And 'Long Ago', a cool, cruisy, '90s hip-hop sort of feel which shows that she is moving in a slightly different direction musically.

'Daydream' gets the thumbs up.

Whether you love her or hate her, her voice is just simply amazing. She can sing for me anytime.

ROBBIE

OASIS
Morning Glory

Oasis are back with another guitar-driven album. The unique sound remains, mellowed a bit.

Beatles homages abound! The opening chords of 'Don't Look Back In Anger' (the title perhaps a homage to David Bowie's 'Look Back In Anger') are straight from 'Imagine'. The chorus harmony at the

MARIAH CAREY
Daydream

We first heard this woman in 1990 with her first Number One single, 'Vision Of Love', from her debut album.

Now, five years and six albums down the track, Mariah still manages to pop out a Number One hit from 'Fantasy', the first single of her new album.

This album sounds a lot like

TEARAWAY also reckons...
VARIOUS DUNEDIN
('Disturbed'):

A good introduction to the scene.

South-facing juke box of primo Dunedin acts from the old skool (Martin Phillipps) to the fresh (Chug), which leaves you wanting more.

TWINZ ('Conversation'):

Street meets R&B – real live identical twinz meet Warren G (he produces).

New homies off the old block (Snoop, Nate Dog, Warren G).

Tearaway - (What's the Story) Morning Glory? review[26]

Music
with Matt Greenop

Oasis
What's The Story (Morning Glory)
Epic

This is obviously what Oasis were trying to achieve with their debut album *Definitely Maybe* - that time around, they didn't quite get there. Veritable demi-gods now back home, Oasis have been reaping profit-plus with what has been described as the best pop music Britain has produced for a really long while. It's a fair call too, if *What's The Story* is any indicator. There are no two ways about it - the brothers Gallagher are pretty talented when it comes to writing guitar music.

There are the inevitable weak spots, such as the pathetically limp *Roll With It*, but other bits verge on the brilliant. Swelling violins aren't the normal pop accompaniment, unless, of course, there are four of you and you're pretty fab. It works big time on *Wonderwall*, which starts off as a mellow, laid-back acoustic outing but rocks out towards the end. *Some Might Say* is another high, but *Champagne Supernova* is the one! Its swelling and ebbing makes it a very appealing listening experience - a top quality pop epic.

This is strangely reminiscent of several well-known British pop invasion acts - it's Beatlish, Stony, sometimes Creamy. Awesome.

The Strip – (What's the Story) Morning Glory? review – Matt Greenop[27] overloaded brain.

That's from the grand sweep of the title track, the *Ashes to Ashes*-style funky angularity of *Heart's Filthy Lesson* (featuring a neatly thorny Garson solo) and *I Have Not Been To Oxford Town*. There are major kickdrum stompers in *Hallo Spaceboy* and the similarly industrial *No Control*, vertiginous moods above Robert Fripp-ish squalling guitars on *The Voyeur of Utter Destruction* and *I'm Deranged* and suitably menacing moments like the foreboding *Wishful Beginnings*.

Some of this, especially the late-in-the-piece likes of *Thru These Architects Eyes* and the closing *Strangers When We Meet* do leave you wanting less. As do those character monologues.

But as Bowie sings on *Motel*: "There is no hell like an old hell." The old confounding hell of Bowie's best work has its echo here.

Oasis, (What's the Story) Morning Glory? (Creation/Sony)

Oasis are a very big deal in Britain right now as their second album does battle with Blur's *Great Escape* — and they do verbal battle with Blur via a UK media eager to revisit a modern variation on the Beatles v Stones rivalry of the first golden age of Britpop.

It was the brawling brotherly

Oasis frontline Liam and Noel Gallagher that got them much attention in time for last year's debut, *Definitely Maybe* (a brilliant/vastly overrated effort depending on what it says on the front of your passport).

So this time round it's a slanging match with the smarter, craftier Blur which backfired when in a recent interview Noel was quoted as saying he hoped the other band's singer and bassist caught Aids.

Yes, well ... not that any of this really affects a colonial perspective on *Morning Glory*. Especially as Oasis' world domination for any part of the planet except Britain is still a long way off.

So this is another album of lumbering ringing guitar pop given character by the Lennonish vocal scowls of Liam Gallagher on many an anthemic melody. It has its moments, even if quite often they aren't its own — like the Gary Glitter bit in opener *Hello*, the piano chords from *Imagine* which start *Don't Look Back in Anger* ...

There's convincing raucous stuff in the likes of the title track and fine crafted string-accompanied quiet moments on *Wonderwall* and *Cast No Shadow*. But ordinary rock plodders *Roll With It*, *Hey Now* and *Some Might Say* seem the dominant flavour here (and curiously resembling the

Electric Light Orchestra). And here they are enough to make you consider Oasis second-division material that mystifyingly has made it to the top of the Britpop league.

AC/DC, Ballbreaker (Albert/EMI)

The umpteenth (okay, 14th then) AC/DC platter is notable for two things.

It marks the return of Phil Rudd, owner of the Bay of Plenty's Mountain Studios, to the drum stool. It also has Rick Rubin as producer, a man who likes to focus on essential strengths as he's done before with the likes of Tom Petty, Johnny Cash and solo Mick Jagger.

While with those singers it was a case of getting the best out of those voices, with AC/DC it's a matter of getting those curiously stunted riffs humming hard without the bloated production of recent times.

So you get some gritty guitar interplay between the brothers Young that actually makes it sound like they — and not a hangar-sized Marshall stack — are doing the work. And combined with the vocal sandblast of Brian Johnson and Rudd's caveman grooves, this turns out a really big primitive blues rock thrill.

As expected there are not a lot

The New Zealand Herald — (What's the Story) Morning Glory? review — Russell Baillie[28]

Another single, 'Morning Glory', was released in December 1995, meaning more radio airplay and TV coverage for the band. Options included free-to-air music channel Max TV, launched in 1993, broadcast across Auckland. There was little music programming on local TV stations in the mid-1990s and Max TV filled the sizeable gap in the market. Juice TV, which launched in 1994, was another outlet for the band for those subscribed to Sky TV. Despite the two singles, *(What's the Story) Morning Glory?* was on its way out of the top 20 by the end of the year.

Reverse of CD single, 'Morning Glory'

The mediocre chart positions achieved in New Zealand didn't accurately reflect the genuine interest New Zealand was developing in the band. In December, *The New Zealand Herald* published an interview between Noel Gallagher and music reviewer Graham Reid, who'd flown to the UK to meet him and report back to the ever-increasing New Zealand fan base.

As with most things in New Zealand at Christmas and New Year, the music charts shut down. No figures were issued between December 24, 1995, and January 14, 1996. The release of a third single from *(What's The Story) Morning*

Graham Reid interview with Noel Gallagher, *The New Zealand Herald*[29]

Glory? 'Wonderwall' saw Oasis graduate from UK indie chart toppers to global rock 'n' roll superstars. A ten-week run at #1 on the USA Modern Rock Tracks chart propelled the song to #8 on the Billboard Hot 100, their biggest hit in America to date.[30]   In January 1996, the single began to rise steadily in the Australian chart, reaching top 10 status and eventually topping the chart on February 11.   No doubt this success in Australia led to an increased push for the single, and album, in New Zealand.   'Wonderwall' debuted at #3 in New Zealand the same week the single topped the Australian chart.   For the next few weeks, the song hovered around the top four alongside OMC's 'How Bizarre' and Peter Andre's 'Mysterious Girl'. *(What's the Story) Morning Glory?* reached the #1 position in the album chart on January 21, and remained there for an eight-week run, culminating in double chart domination on March 10, when both the album and 'Wonderwall' made it to #1. The band's debut album *Definitely Maybe* made a return to the chart late in 1995 and gradually found a new peak of #5 in April 1996. Two further singles from *(What's the Story) Morning Glory?* 'Don't Look Back in Anger' and 'Champagne Supernova' ensured steady sales for the album for the remainder of the year, eventually going on to become the second biggest selling album that year behind Alanis Morrisette's *Jagged Little Pill*.[31]

Due to their rising popularity, and their antics off stage, Oasis was no longer confined to the music press. The tabloid stories generated in the UK often made their way into the New Zealand papers. Coverage of the Brit Awards and the band's jibes towards Michael Hutchence was reported in the *Evening Post*.[32] Speculation that Oasis was to shirt sponsor Manchester City appeared in the *Sunday News*.[33] Any possible link with New Zealand was exploited in the pursuit of creating a news story out of it. *The Sunday Star Times* interviewed Wellington's Onslow College alumni Alec McKinlay, of Ignition Management, the company that looked after Oasis, using the headline 'Kiwi behind Britain's Biggest Band'[34]. Thanks to the success of Oasis, the door started to open for other British acts, but not with the same fanatical reception. *Moseley Shoals* by Ocean Colour Scene charted for 10 weeks on the album chart and the revitalised Manic Street Preachers made a New Zealand chart debut with their 4th album, *Everything Must Go*. Even Northern Uproar got a review in the *Evening Post*, but it didn't translate to any chart success.[35]

Spring and summer in the Northern Hemisphere were dominated by what could only be described as Oasis mania. A series of large-scale outdoor gigs cemented the band's position as the biggest act in the land and the hottest concert ticket in the world. A homecoming at Manchester City's Maine Road in April was a huge success. But that was soon surpassed by the most closely anticipated concert series in UK music history, two nights at the iconic Knebworth Park. Pink Floyd, Queen, and the Rolling Stones had all performed at this musical mecca. Over two million people applied for tickets in May 1996

Rip It Up – Noel and Liam quotes – Simon Grigg[36]

for shows to be held on August 10 and 11. Fans in New Zealand were keen to get a slice of the mania and see them in the flesh, hoping they would make the trip down under. In July, it was announced that Oasis would be heading to New Zealand for the first time to play a one-off show at the Auckland Supertop on Friday November 15, hosted by tour promoters Lees and West.

Adverts for the gigs popped up in all the usual media channels, *The New Zealand Herald*, *Rip It Up* and posters plastered on the streets. Ongoing coverage of the band's exploits on and off the stage added to the hype and ensured sales were strong. The band's every move regularly filled the columns of New Zealand's papers, be it their appearance at the Cannes Film Festival, the all-conquering Knebworth gigs or Liam Gallagher's relationship with Patsy Kensit, everything was newsworthy when it came to Oasis.

After the showstopper at Knebworth, the band performed two gigs in Cork, Ireland, and a slot on *MTV Unplugged*, where Noel had to take on lead vocals with Liam pulling out with a sore throat minutes before the show. Memorably, he still had enough energy to heckle his brother from the balcony. This was an unfortunate sign of things to come. A short USA tour was scheduled prior to visiting Australia and New Zealand, which saw the wheels start to fall off the Oasis machine. Liam missed the first gig to go house hunting, famously declaring he needed somewhere to live just as the band boarded their USA-bound flight. Liam did re-join the tour in time for the second gig in Auburn Hills, Michigan. However, nine gigs into it, mounting tension within the band saw Noel fly home to London and that was the end of the USA visit.[39] New Zealand fans watched on, still hoping their idols would turn up in November. Local promoters The Sequel remained confident the tour would still go ahead.

It wasn't to be, and the tour was cancelled. Fans, promoters and the music press were incensed. This was a band at its commercial and creative peak, barely holding it together, and for the second time, fans were left in the lurch. Ticketholders had to return them to the place of purchase to receive a refund. The positive press generated throughout 1996 was superseded by outrage and the feeling that Australasian fans were being taken for granted.

Oasis booked for Supertop concert

By Graham Reid

The British rock band Oasis have been confirmed for an Auckland concert on November 15 at the 13,000-capacity Mt Smart Supertop.

The band — in the vanguard of the Britpop revival of the past five years — established an early reputation for indulging in the excesses of the rock'n'roll lifestyle.

While the British music press took them to heart, there was understandable cynicism abroad until this year when their second album, *What's the Story Morning Glory*, broke them into the United States.

In this country that album has been at the top of the charts intermittently since its release nine months ago and has sold over 70,000 copies. The band's debut album, *Definitely Maybe*, has sold 20,000 copies here.

Led by the brothers Gallagher from Manchester — songwriter/guitarist Noel and singer Liam — Oasis are aware they have some work to prove themselves in this part of the world.

"There's always going to be cynicism about us," said Noel in an interview with the *New Zealand Herald* late last year, "so we've got to go out [to New Zealand] because until people can see us in the flesh we are still going to be a figment of the press' imagination."

Tickets go on sale on Monday.

The New Zealand Herald story on Supertop gig – Graham Reid[37]

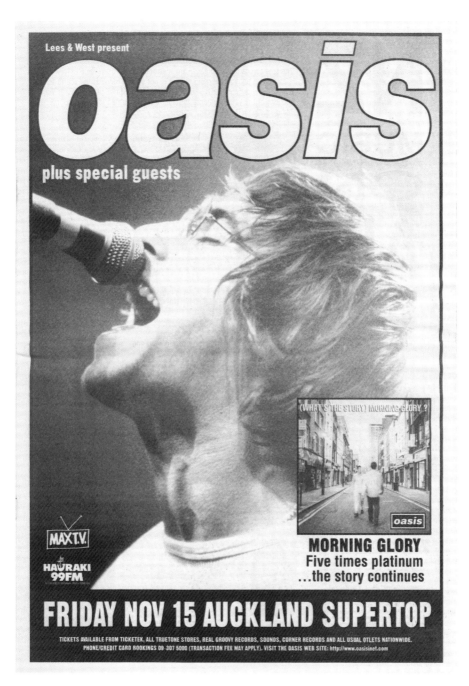

Rip It Up, featuring the 1996 tour advert – Simon Grigg[38]

The New Zealand Herald article – 'Stormy Oasis'[40]

EAMS935	LEES AND WEST	96172341641
960723 A1641	PRESENTS	
4798	OASIS MT SMART SUPERTOP FRIDAY 15 NOVEMBER 8PM	TAUKL6 CHA
ADMIT 1	50.00 General Admission ADULT	ADMIT 1

Daniel Phillips' ticket to the cancelled 1996 show[41]

The (What's the Story) Morning Glory? tour was over and so too was the band's chance of reaching stadium act status in Australia or New Zealand. The remainder of 1996 saw even more negative press with the Waikato Times nominating Oasis as turkeys of the year, and local rock magazine Rukkus naming Oasis the worst band in the world in their annual readers' poll.[42]

OASIS SOAP OPERA

The Gallagher brothers, small guys with attitude, have returned to England after walking out on their USA tour and cancelling their Pacific tour. In Australia alone, 80,000 tickets were refunded.

But whether there's a crisis in the brotherly love stakes or whether the pressure of touring has made them both spit the dummy, is not at all clear.

When questioned by reporters in Chicago before their first USA gig Noel was understanding when facing Liam's absence, "You have to support people when they're going through a personal crisis. So, no, I don't feel like slapping him."

Media have sort to identify friction between the brothers, painting Patsy Kensit as a Yoko Ono like figure seeking to destroy Oasis and stories highlight the difference in the Gallaghers' incomes. Noel as chief songwriter collects 70 percent of Oasis royalties. Does Liam want Noel's money. Does Noel want the attention the singer gets?

With their touring cancelled, Noel has made it possible to achieve his mid-year plan to record a new album in October. Maybe the events of the last few weeks were designed just to clear the Gallaghers' calendar of unwanted committments.

• **August 24** — Liam is Unplugged for *MTV Unplugged* at Festival Hall, London. Liam loses it, hunched in a corner, in a foetal position, crying. *Once he regained his composure, Liam refused to go on stage. Noel took over the vocals but MTV do not plan to screen the million dollar production. NME* found such phrases as "half-cocked" and "debacle" to describe the churlish event.

• **August 26** — Liam does not board plane to Chicago, leaving Heathrow Airport 15 minutes before the plane's departure to go flat hunting with girlfriend Patsy Kensit. A UK tabloid read, "PATSY'S GOT HIM BY THE WONDERBALLS."

• **August 27** — Liam-less Oasis play Chicago. The large signs outside the venue read, "Liam Gallagher is ill and will not perform this evening. Noel Gallagher, song-writer & guitarist/vocalist will be performing all vocals & show will go on. Should you wish a refund, do not enter the building. Return your full untorn ticket to the point of purchase."

• **August 29** — Liam rejoins the Oasis tour in Detroit. He performs the following night just outside Detroit, then it's on the road, next stop is a Festival near Toronto with Screaming Trees, Gin Blossoms and Neil Young headlining over Oasis.

• **September 4** — Oasis play MTV Music Awards in New York. Performing 'Champagne Supernova', Liam spat, added "up yer bum" to the lyric and threw a beer can into the audience. There was booing when the song ended. He told a journalist "They're all here for one reason, to see the greatest rock 'n' roll band in the world."

• **September 12** — Noel returned to London looking shagged. An official statement said the cancellation of the tour was a decision, "taken solely by Noel Gallagher on behalf of his four friends."

Rip It Up – 'Oasis Soap Opera', October 1996 – Simon Grigg[43]

PETULANT prima donnas like Oasis' Gallagher brothers Liam and Noel are bad news for the music industry so let's hope their much publicised bust up isn't just a publicity stunt.

Oasis have never been far from controversy since bursting onto the pop scene three years ago. Noel publicly hoped that fellow British band Blur's Damon Albarn and Alex James would "catch Aids and die". Then Noel disappeared in the middle of their first American tour claiming that drugs and drink were wrecking the band. He was at it again this year when, on receiving a Brit award from former INXS singer Michael Hutchence, he came out with "Has-beens shouldn't give awards to gonna-bees". Liam and fiancée Patsy Kensit were blamed for last month's decision to pull out of the band's US tour. Liam complained he couldn't go househunting with the former wife of Simple Minds singer Jim Kerr if he was "trying to perform to silly ****ing Yanks". He eventually joined the tour which got anything but rave reviews. His biggest contribution in the US was spitting and throwing things at the MTV awards audience.

The bust up between the brothers in North Carolina eventually saw the band return to London without completing a world tour which was to include a New Zealand concert in November. Before then Noel had endeared himself to nobody when he was quoted as saying "We have sold more records than The Beatles, we've played bigger gigs than The Beatles and we're bigger than The Beatles."

Whatever.

Just for the record, according to the Guinness Book of Records, The Beatles sales to date are estimated at more than one billion discs and tapes. Oasis have sold around 15 million copies worldwide. What's the Story Morning Glory has sold 9.5 million copies worldwide since its October 1995 release while their debut album Definitely Maybe has been in the British top 40 for more than 100 weeks. In New Zealand, Morning Glory has been in the charts nearly a year, selling over 60,000 units.

The sad thing is that plans for a third album in the New Year have not yet been scrapped. The album could be great, but do we really want to put up with more from this dubious duo? Why can't they have the same type of class as someone like New Zealand's leading lady of music, Annie Crummer? Okay, Oasis and Crummer shouldn't be compared musically but both have high profiles in their parts of the world and both are supposedly role models.

While Oasis continue to lose credibility, Crummer is oozing class. After a two-year hibernation, she has stormed back onto the New Zealand charts with her second album, Seventh Wave. She's broke but she's happy. She's excited about the state of New Zealand music. In fact, she goes out of her way to sing the praises of potential chart rivals OMC and Emma Paki.

Maybe the world would welcome back Oasis with open arms if the Gallagher brothers had a little, just a little bit of Crummer's MPressive class.

JOHN MATHESON

Music Press Magazine – October 1996, John Matheson[44]

Chapter 3 – Be Here Now

'It's a great album, and it will be massive, but no way is it the major progression some have claimed. The sound is Oasis Classic.' – Noel Gallagher, 1997[45]

Speculation surrounding the third Oasis album was mounting in the press. With the remainder of the *(What's the Story) Morning Glory?* tour cancelled the band retreated to Abbey Road studios to record some new material. Meanwhile, Oasis continued to fill the columns of *Music Press Magazine*, a free product available at record stores across New Zealand. Stories on everything from the music to Liam Gallagher's caution for drug possession and war of words with George Harrison featured in early 1997. The TV landscape was in the midst of a battle of the channels, between independent Max TV and TVNZ, who had signed a deal to introduce MTV to the New Zealand market. Max TV had built a decent following of teenagers and twenty-somethings across Auckland, since launching in 1993. The introduction of MTV, broadcast free to air on terrestrial TV, was an attempt to persuade the audience to switch allegiances. While Max TV had local hosts, programmes and music that catered to the demands of their audience, the agreement between TVNZ and MTV Europe was for MTV to be a direct feed from the UK on a 12-hour delay.[46]

MTV launched in New Zealand on July 2, 1997, on the old Horizon Pacific channel. New Zealand was the only country in the world where MTV was free to air with Oasis the very first MTV act to appear with a re-run of the band's *MTV Unplugged* performance from 1996. In the channel's first weekend of operation, over six hours of material dedicated to Oasis was broadcast, a signal of the mania still generated by the band back in the UK.[47] Though mostly a carbon copy of the feed, the channel did introduce local content to appeal to a Kiwi audience, most notably *Havoc*, launched September 15, 1997. Hosted by musician and media personality Mikey Havoc, the show initially aired at 9.30 pm each weekday, featuring interviews with musicians, actors and local music video content.[48] Other local programming included the hip-hop show

Wreckognize. TV4, launched on June 29, 1997, offering content that appealed to a youthful audience. The Sky TV-owned The Box and Juice TV, channels playing music videos 24 hours a day, were the other choices for music video consumption. Initial viewing figures for MTV were disappointing, with the channel losing out to TV4 in the youth audience bracket. For fans of British music, MTV, however, remained a blessing. The rise of New Zealand music programming coincided with the release of 'D'You Know What I Mean?', the first single from Oasis' third album *Be Here Now*. Launched on July 14 in New Zealand, the song peaked at #4 in the chart.[49]

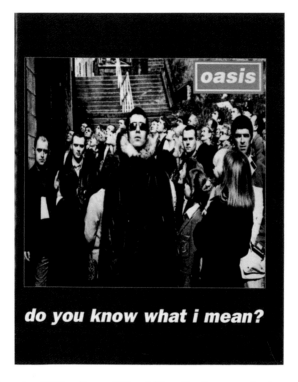

Music Press Magazine 'D'You Know What I Mean?' ad – note the incorrect spelling of the song title[50]

Music reviewers and journalists had limited access to *Be Here Now* ahead of its release, adding to the huge anticipation that was building for the album. Press coverage in New Zealand appeared in a wider range of publications than ever before, and numerous reviews were on offer when the album finally did become available.

Be Here Now

WHEN THE highly-anticipated third album from Oasis arrives in late August, fans may be treated to more than they bargained for.

The group's latest effort, Be Here Now, features the band in a windier mood than usual, as some of the songs clock in well over the norm for pop songs.

"We don't really set out to make long tracks, but we do like a long intro and a long outro in the balance," says guitarist and primary songwriter Noel Gallagher. "It wasn't planned that way though."

While one of the new tracks weighs in at over 11 minutes, the band fully realises the pitfalls of running long.

"You might fall asleep halfway through," says Gallagher.

According to Gallagher, the band's first video, for the song D'You Know What I Mean, set the tone for an elaborate collection of videos.

"They're quite cool. Apparently it's a take on some... they've come up with some Vietnam idea. There's lots of military helicopters floating about in a couple of them."

If Oasis seems to be overdoing things a bit, it may be because the group is eager to get back to what they do best.

"We're just looking forward to getting back and being a band again, really, 'cause we've had a lot of time out of the spotlight, if you like, so it's good. We're looking forward to it."

MPress can confirm Be Here Now clocks in at over 70 minutes. All 12 songs were written by Gallagher and produced by Gallagher and Owen Morris, the same team behind the eight times platinum (What's the Story) Morning Glory?

This is the official running order of the album which is due out on 25 August.

1. D'You Know What I Mean – Is it our imagination, or does Liam actually sneak the F-word into the intro of this first single? (Check out the :35-second mark of the CD). Those weird-sounding words before the first verse turn out to be the Beatles catch phrase "yeah, yeah, yeah" played backwards. The background vocals that kick in just before the chorus are just the first line of the chorus – "All my people, right here right now" – sung backwards. Finally, Noel has been quoted as saying that the song's sampled drums are taken from NWA's rap classic, Straight Outta Compton.

2. My Big Mouth – One of two new songs the band performed last year on tour. An aggressive rock tune.

3. Magic Pie – Lead vocal by Noel.

4. Stand By Me – This string-heavy ballad features the chorus, "Nobody knows the way it's gonna be/Stand by me."

5. I Hope, I Think, I Know – Apparently a rant against the press.

6. The Girl in the Dirty Shirt – A reference to the first time Noel met his now-wife, Meg, who was apparently caught ironing a dirty shirt at the time.

7. Fade In-Out – Features actor Johnny Depp on slide guitar.

8. Don't Go Away

9. Be Here Now

10. All Around the World – This was written three years ago, prior to the sessions for (What's the Story) Morning Glory?

11. It's Getting Better (Man!!) – Performed last year on tour, the live version was every bit as Beatles-influenced as its title would suggest.

12. All Around the World (Reprise)

Music Press Magazine – Be Here Now speculation[51]

BE HERE NOW
ALBUM AUGUST 25

SEE OASIS LIVE!

The new OASIS album BE HERE NOW is released on August 25. Between now and then, if you go into any specialist music store and fill out the entry forms provided, you and a friend could be flying to London to see OASIS live at Earls Court.

Win return airfares for two, accomodation for two nights, $500 spending money and 2 tickets to the greatest show on earth. Pre-order your copy of the OASIS album BE HERE NOW today. BE THERE NOW with OASIS.

Rip It Up – Be Here Now competition – Simon Grigg[52]

Oasis graced the front cover of *Rip It Up* in September 1997, inside Liam and Noel Gallagher were interviewed by Gareth Evans.

Rip It Up cover, issue 241 – photographer Stefan De Batselier[53]

NOEL

What was it like making this album through the media madness of the last 12 months?

"It wasn't that difficult at all really. We're in the business of making records. That's what we do, and we enjoy doing it. It took us two or three weeks to get into it, because we hadn't been in the studio for a year and a half, but we'd never let people outside the band influence the way we work."

Who produced the album and what did they contribute?

"I produced the album with Owen Morris. Owen's contribution was a lot of shouting and a lot of drinking. It's quite difficult to remember who done what really, cos I was half-pissed most of the time. I think Owen can get the best out of the rest of the band really. I can play the same thing on the guitar 50,000 times, if I was asked, but some of the others need to be pushed now and then. I think he's good at that. He's a mate, he's like one of the band, and we've always worked well with him — I don't know why. And he gets it loud. He's good at spotting if there's something wrong with an arrangement, or if a song's too long."

You're particularly pleased with Liam's singing. How do you get him to perform?

"Shout at him really. Call him a cunt. It depends what sort of songs he's singing. For the songs that need belting out, you just wind him up really. So you call him a cunt, tell him he's shit. If you tell him he's shit, he goes out of his way to prove you wrong. Sometimes we do it on purpose. Sometimes we don't."

It's a great album, and it will be massive, but no way is it the major progression some have claimed. The sound is *Oasis Classic*.

"We tried to make it a bit louder, put a few more guitars on it, but I don't see this big progressive leap that people have been talking about for the last couple of weeks. To me it's not really a progression. This takes the best elements of *Morning Glory* and *Definitely Maybe*, puts them together, and out comes a new album."

I thought that, after working with the Chemical Brothers, you had different things planned for Oasis.

"There's a few breakbeats on 'D'You Know What I Mean' and 'Fade In-Out', but the songs didn't call for much technology. They will do on the next album. I don't think we can keep on making records like this for the rest of our career. It would become a bit boring after a while. The production on the next album is going to be better. The production on this album is a bit bland, a bit safe, a bit commercial. I wanna make a really mind-blowing record next time, but we'll see what happens."

Who's your mystery celeb pal on 'Fade In-Out'?

"Johnny Depp. He plays slide guitar. We were on holiday at the same time in Mustique. I was writing the album and I had a little digital eight-track studio with us. He happened to be staying at the same place I was staying, so we got drunk one night. I was trying to play a slide guitar solo — not very well at all — and he asked could he have a go. I said yeah. It's no big deal really, but he's a brilliant guitar player. He's a mate more than anything, but he's a top guitar player."

Do you know what you mean, because I certainly don't?

"Not a lot really. I don't say much. The people will know what it means. I can't put it into words, and nor would I want to. But I think the kids will know what it means. I hope they do anyway. It's just an expression, 'd'you know what I mean'? I dunno what it means. Fuck all really."

What do you say to people who say your lyrics aren't ever about anything?

"I tend to agree. I go out of my way to try not to say anything really. I get myself in enough shit with my fucking mouth anyway, without me writing subliminal messages in the lyrics. I don't consider myself a great lyricist, but while the words may not say much on paper, in the context of a song they say quite a fucking lot. I don't actually know what that is, but it must be saying somethin' to someone. I like the lyrics to 'Magic Pie', because I don't even know what a magic pie is, but I wrote a song about one. 'D'You Know What I Mean' is a brilliant title for a song."

Why did you start recording in Abbey Road?

"We only recorded three songs there anyway. It was all right, but everyone was staying in hotels or going home every night, so there wasn't really an atmosphere — they were all doing their bit and getting off again. We're best if we piss off to a farmhouse together for six months. It was all a bit fragmented at Abbey Road."

Are drugs a big part of your creative process?

"I can't do anything when I'm off my tits. I usually hammer myself into the ground and fall over or fall asleep. I can write stupid lyrics when I'm out of it, but I can't play guitar, I can't make records and I can't perform. You've got to have your wits about you. You have to wait until after the gig."

What's touring going to be like now that Liam is very clean-living?

"He's very clean? Clean living? Where did he get that from? First I've fucking heard. Married life, you see. What's it gonna be like being out on the road again? Well, Liam will probably be in bed at eight o'clock every night now, saying that. Me, personally, I'll be 'avin' it fuckin' large every night on that tour bus, and getting it wherever I am. It'll be the same as it was last time: wake up wherever you are, hang around all day, do a bit of a soundcheck, do a load of interviews, get something to eat, do the gig, go and get fucking trashed off your head afterwards and go on to the next place, where you wake up with a hangover. You've got to have a night off sometimes, days off to stay in bed, but you have to unwind, let off a bit of steam. A few things might get damaged, but we pay for our damage."

Where do your exploits score on a scale from Rick Astley to Led Zeppelin?

"Rick Zeppelin or Led Astley. We're definitely not up there with Led Zeppelin yet, though Bonehead was making a valiant effort years ago. But he's 33 now, he's going through the change, so he's calmed down a bit. Compared to them we're probably a right bunch of fucking pussies. Probably a little bit above Rick Astley."

What have been the best and the worst bits of the ride?

"Looking back, I wouldn't change a single day. The worst experience was when I got fucking smacked in the mouth by some Geordie bastard in Newcastle."

The best ones have been being onstage at Knebworth and Earls Court and Maine Road. I'd say — that was a bit of a spiritual homecoming. Just seeing the crowd getting into it, jumping up and down. Top!"

Can you possibly still have any unfulfilled ambitions?

"Playing Australia, playing South America. I wouldn't mind a No.1 album in America. Oh, there's plenty yet. Bomb the White House and No.10 Downing Street. Well no, not No.10 Downing Street any more, cos my mate [Tony Blair] lives there now."

What do you do with all that money?

"Fuckin' spend it mate, that's what you do with it. A couple of houses, cars. My missus takes care of my money for me, and you've got no trouble spending it with my wife. I don't know anyway, I don't spend it anymore. The trouble is, being in a band ... when you're on the dole you got to buy all your fuckin' clothes. By the time you have become a millionaire, everybody gives you everything. I don't think I've paid for one item of clothing I'm wearing today. Stop giving me clothes! I wanna buy me own. I dunno, stick it in the bank account it. I haven't got that much money, anyway. I've only got about £40,000 in the bank."

How's the 2 million country seat turning out?

"I haven't moved in yet. The woman who's living there moves out on August 1st, so it'll be quite soon. I'll be able to play a bit of croquet on Sunday afternoon with the wife, bit of horse riding (laughs). Can you imagine? Few laps of the pool, get out, fuckin' puke up probably."

I hear you're not fond of videos.

"That's because they're shit. I like the new one, and I like 'Wonderwall', but I think they're the only two I like. The rest are dreadful, to be quite honest. The one for 'Don't Look Back In Anger' is particularly appalling. It's just disgraceful. Have you seen that bit with that fucking square magnifying glass? What the fucking hell was I up to there? Why did I agree to do that?

Do you have much creative input on your videos?

"No, the less I have to do with that the better. It's usually Marcus (Oasis manager), he's the video expert. I just turn up and fucking mime for three days, get pissed-off and go home. I don't watch videos anyway. I don't even watch MTV, except when we're on it."

The cover artwork of *Be Here Now* is said to contain a whole heap of hidden messages and visual clues. Is that true?

"Well, people were making up their own hidden messages really. There's absolutely nothing, no hidden meanings on the album sleeve at all, apart from we put a rolls Royce in the swimming pool that's got a registration plate off one of the cars on the back of Abbey Road. That's it really. It's just a white Rolls Royce drove into a swimming pool, and us lot stood round looking like cunts basically. Everyone seems to think it's got these hidden Beatles references, but it hasn't really."

Why is it called *Be Here Now*?

"Which explanation do you want? I've got about 10 for you, all true. It doesn't mean anything really. It's just a good title for an album."

What songs are you most proud of having written?

"I'm proud of writing 'Champagne Supernova', 'Don't Look Back in Anger', 'Wonderwall', 'Cast No Shadow', 'Magic Pie', 'Fade In-Out'. All of them really. There are ones I'd like to re-record and some of the early B-sides, cos they were just demos."

What song would you have liked to have written?

"Can I have more than one? 'Anarchy In The UK', 'My Generation', 'Jumping Jack Flash', 'Paperback Writer', 'I Am The Walrus', 'Search And Destroy', 'Redemption Song' — loads mate!"

GARETH EVANS

> I can't do anything when I'm off my tits
> NOEL

Rip It Up - Noel Gallagher interview – Gareth Evans/Simon Grigg[54]

LIAM

Was there a lot of pressure following-up the success of *What's The Story*?

"No. It goes where it goes. We just go in and make it, then the people take it where they're gonna take it. They either like it or they don't, and if they don't, I'm not mithered."

Why did you start recording in Abbey Road?

"We wanted to go there because we had the money to go there, and we thought we'd check it out because people we liked had recorded there before us. Then, when we got there, there were all the loudmouths on reception who were telling stories to people, and all these knobheads with violins and that, and orchestras saying shut up and keep it down. So we thought, fuck you! We're going away. But we had a lot of fun in there. Late at nights, when we'd finished recording, we'd put the Beatles on, turn the lights down and walk around the studio where they'd recorded it, and just feel the vibe."

Were there any bizarre incidents during the recording?

"There were bizarre incidents every day. In Abbey Road there were people everywhere, in studios all around us, so we decided to go to Ridge Farm in the country, where it was just us. We can make as much noise as we want, tell as many dirty jokes as we want, and no one can bother us. We can stay up all night and do what we gotta do, and no one can complain. So we did."

What worked for you best out the three studios you used?

"I only sang one song in Abbey Road — 'It's Getting Better Man' — and I weren't ready for it. You've got to wait for the cloud to disappear. It's no use singing while the cloud is there, and there was a bit of a cloud there, so I couldn't really get it together. I couldn't be arsed basically, it weren't the right moment. When I got to Ridge Farm, it weren't the right moment either. When we got to Air Studios, it all kicked in. I don't prepare for it. I just drink a load of lager, smoke a lot of cigarettes and talk a load of bullshit — and it sort of goes where it goes."

One song is called 'My Big Mouth'. What's the biggest trouble yours has got you into?

"My big mouth makes me a load of money! My big mouth is important, because nobody else has got a big mouth."

You recently described the media's intrusion as a good thing for you. Surely not?

"The more I get relaxed into my world, the more I can do what I want to do, then I reckon I get lazy. I think fuck it! But if people are slagging me off, saying I've got a four-grand-a-week cocaine habit, then it makes me want to go in and show them that I'm not like that, that I can work and I can sing a good song. It does give me a kick up the arse. But I'm not happy with the tabloids. They're slags, and your gonna get what's coming to you — one day. It may be soon, may be a long time, but you'll get it! I like pressure though, that's what I'm trying to say."

Does media interest cramp your style when you're out and about?

"No. I've got to do what I've got to do. I'm 24, I'm in the best band in the world, the most important rock 'n' roll band in the world. I've got a load of fucking money. What else am I supposed to do? Sit at home all fucking day? Walk around with a halo on me head? I'm a little devil, and I like life, and I like spending my money, and I like getting up people's noses. I can't go to Manchester much though, because there are people there who have a problem with me, who read too many papers and think I'm mad for it 24 hours a day. And sometimes I'm not. I'd like to have a cup of tea with my mother, meet my aunties and do what I used to do, but I can't cos everyone knocks at the fucking door. They should fucking respect a person's wish to spend fucking a bit of time with their mother and their maker."

Don't you get that attention in London?

"London is just like Manchester only bigger. You can get lost in London. In Manchester you can't, everyone knows your business. That's why I like it here, cos you can float about, join the Japanese tourists going round Big Ben going Haaa! Big Ben, and no one gives a fuck."

And you can't hit people anymore for fear of being sued.

"That's the journalists though. When you're skint you can knock 'em out for fun, can't you? But no, I'm not going to hit people any more. But then, you never know. I might do. Depends how many snake bites I've had."

What incidents in your youth shaped the person you've become today?

"No, just my mam. My mam shaped me. Mam learned me to give respect to people. And I do. People think I don't, but I do. Basically I don't give a fucking shit what people think, to tell you the fucking truth — here, there and everywhere. Cos I know I'm doing something worthwhile. And that's it — simple. If anyone's got a problem with me, then fuck off!"

Is being a celebrity couple worse than being just a celebrity?

"I'm not a celebrity. People try to make me one, but I'm not. I'm just Liam Gallagher, twit first and ... (totally incomprehensible) ... who's married to a beautiful wife. Fame is bollocks! It's not important, is it? It's making a great record that's important, and making your life the way you want to live it, and wearing the right pair of shoes. I think people should write about more important things, instead of me getting married. I'm sure the public don't wanna hear about it. It's only important to me and Patsy. I wouldn't give a flying fuck if anyone else was getting married."

> **I don't need drugs. I just like lager and cigarettes**
> LIAM

There was a time last year when you were threatening never to play liveagain.

"Yeah, but we were fibbing, telling lies because we needed some time off. We knew we would play live again. I needed time off to find a house, cos you need somewhere to live, otherwise you end up in McDonalds' doorways, eating Burger King."

What expectations should we have of the new tour?

"Rock 'n' roll! We're playing to 20,000 each night, which is big, but it's not big when you've done Knebworth. I'm proud of Knebworth. It wasn't too big for me, too big for us, and we're gonna do it again. But now we've got to go indoors and capture the fucking minds and souls of people, and give them a good kicking with this new album."

After constantly rubbing people's noses in your coke-taking, were you surprised that the police — given the chance to nail you — let you right off?

"Well, I got caught with a gram a coke, and it was my first offence, so the law says they have to let me off. If it had been three or four grams, I'd have been charged. And if I get caught again with a load of coke, I'm going down — which I won't, cos I don't do it anymore. I don't want to go to prison. People will say that I do it, but I don't and I don't care. Anyway, it's bad for you. You get arrested and banged up in the cells with all the pooftahs. I meditate now. I've learnt to do it in the last year. I meditate, I relax and I don't need drugs. I just like lager and cigarettes."

What do you think about when you meditate?

"Me."

I don't suppose you spend much time wondering why you re so popular?

"Cos we're important, and we're saying something that nobody else is saying — which is get off your arse and do what you wanna do! And don't listen to anyone else. Don't listen to fucking me! Don't listen to Noel! Listen to yourself and get on with it. Cos you can have everything you want, if you want it. And, if you don't, see you down the dole office."

Is there a definable Oasis look?

"I wear what I want. I'm not a fashion victim. Fashion is for knobheads. I just wear what I wanna wear, and it fits me well. It's what you say that's important, and what you're singing about, and what you do that's important, not your fucking clothes. There are people out there who've not got a load of money, like my mates in Manchester, but they wear it well, whatever they can afford to get. They wear it well, and they look smart. There's people out there with loads of fucking money, and they buy all these smart clothes, but they wear them like a bunch of fucking teds. They wear their keks wrong, their shoes wrong, their shirts wrong. All of it's wore wrong. But people who've got no money, they wear their clothes well. And when I was on the dole I wore my clothes well. I might not have had the best gear, but I wore it fucking well."

What was it like supporting U2?

"It was great. I didn't support anyone though. We just played with them. I'm not a support band. I just loved playing a gig again. It was the first gigs we've done, and it was great just being on the stage again, playing them old songs — and the new ones."

How do you feel about the art of video-making?

"I don't like them. I don't like these dicks who turn around and say you've got to jump around when I'm standing still. Well, fuck off and go and make a video of fucking Blur or some'at, where the people are gonna be clowns. I'm not a fucking clown. I don't wanna dance. I want to stand still. The new one's good, but the last ones I've not enjoyed. It's a waste of time, a waste of money 'Wonderwall' was alright, I suppose, not bad. The rest of 'em are fucking shit. If anyone buys our records because of seeing the video, you're missing the point, dickhead! They're not that important. It's only for fucking MTV, and I don't like MTV. It's about time someone fucking said it. Music's more important than a fucking square box in a room."

What have been your best and worst experiences onstage?

"I don't know that I've ever had a bad time onstage. A lot of the gigs we've played have been really fucking special. Then there's a few that have been really great and a few that have been alright. I don't think we've done a bad gig, never ever. D'you know what I mean? I think we've gone on there and done the business."

Are there any elements of what you do that are too British to travel?

"Americans don't like being stood and looked at, they like that whole showbusiness side of it, and we're not showbusiness. If they have a problem with that, that's their fault. They like a big show, and you don't get a show from us. You just get music. And if you don't like fucking music, you shouldn't be going to a gig. It's really important to me. I'm not a dancer and I'm not an entertainer. I'm a vocalist. I was born one and I'll die one. It's simple."

Don't the fans deserve a show — something more than just playing the record?

"You entertain them ... on a record you don't see the people, do you? You just see a black thing spinning round. There's a fucking buzz of going on and seeing a fucking bunch of five lads going on and hitting that sound. It's a different sound every time. It's not the same sound as a record. And that's all I want out of a band. I don't want a fucking show. All that leaping about, it distracts you from the music."

Are you still influenced by your earlier idols like Happy Mondays and Stone Roses?

"Nah. You take a bit out of people, and you get on your own plane, don't ya? You know what I mean? You buy your own ticket, and then you fly your own plane."

At what point did you first feel you'd made it?

"You've never made it, have you? You're only ever happy in your own garden, aren't ya? What's making it? I don't believe I've made it. I don't want to make it. Making it's boring. Making it's for knobheads. I just want to keep on making music for us, and for the people who like it. Once you've made it, you might as well go and blow your head off. I just wanna keep on doing what I do, and keep on getting bigger and better — for me."

You've come so far in five years. Are there any dreams left to fulfil?

"Nah. Having a couple of kids would be nice — the normal things in life."

What's a day at home with the Gallagher family like?

"Eat loads of pickled onions, man! Just chilling out and doing what you wanna do, listening to music. I'm not going to tell you, cos it's private, innit?"

What words would you use to describe your personality?

"Clever, enterprising and real."

What's next for you?

"I'm mad for getting out there and playing the new songs, getting out there and being a band again, and seeing what it brings. We'll go to different countries see what happens. Play the new album and see if they like it. I hope they like it, but if they don't, they don't. We'll just come back and play it for people who do ... (adopts sarcastic tone again, clenching hands in prayer mode) ... but I really love you, honest! I really care for you. I hope you're all well and fit and just doing what you wanna do."

Are there any records you wish you had made?

"Yeah. 'Across The Universe' — John Lennon."

GARETH EVANS

SEPTEMBER 1997 ripitup 21

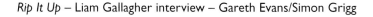

Rip It Up – Liam Gallagher interview – Gareth Evans/Simon Grigg

Fashion and youth culture magazine *Pavement* photographed Oasis in London with an accompanying interview by Cameron Adams.

BIGMOUTH

Taking it up the nose and on the chin, Oasis head honcho Noel Gallagher talks candidly about drugs, making millions of dollars, getting into dance music, piracy on the Internet, causing scandals and his turbulent times with "our kid" Liam

Noel Gallagher interviewed in London by Cameron Adams   photography by Davies & Davies

Pavement interview – Cameron Adams/Barney McDonald – Photography Davies & Davies. Design by Glenn Hunt.[55]

38

STRIKES AGAIN

Noel Gallagher
"Fuck that shit, man!"

WHAT CAN I SAY? WE'RE NOT AN EXPERI
BAND. WE'RE DERIVATIVE. I DERIVE MY

In the UK, *Be Here Now* was released on Thursday August 21, 1997. Over the course of just three days, sales rocketed to 663,400 copies, making it the fastest-selling album in UK chart history. In New Zealand, the album was released four days later on Monday August 25. Demand for the album was so huge that, at the request of Sony Music New Zealand, several record stores

MENTAL BAND; WE'RE NOT AN INNOVATIVE
SONGS FROM MY RECORD COLLECTION"

opened their doors at midnight. The release was such a big deal that it generated stories on mainstream media platforms such as Radio New Zealand's *Morning Report*, the midday news on TVNZ and in a wide variety of newspapers. The album debuted at #1 in the New Zealand chart for the week

NOEL GALLAGHER IS TRACKING THROUGH the new Oasis album in his head, trying to remember the genesis of a particular song he's been asked about. He hums the lyrics to himself: "Get on the helter skelter… You've got to be bad enough to beat the brave…" But it's to no avail. An explanation escapes him. "It's just a bunch of songs I've written," he says. "They're just fucking songs, man. Journalists get frustrated because I say, 'It's just a song; it doesn't mean anything; I can't remember writing it, so can we move on'. They want to know what it all means and it doesn't really mean anything, to be honest with you."

Oasis songs may not mean anything to Noel Gallagher but millions of people around the globe beg to differ. Gallagher has mastered the art of songs that simultaneously mean everything and nothing, writing immediately familiar tunes with suitably vague lyrics that neither amaze nor offend you. Showcased on just two albums — *Definitely Maybe* and *What's The Story (Morning Glory)?*, his songs have sold over 30 million records in just three years. And the singles have become radio station staples, in the process attaining a status as anthems for this generation and plenty to come. The band who always aimed for world domination may not quite be there yet but they can certainly see their goal from the pedestal on which they've been perched.

"I wouldn't say we were the biggest band in the world but we're one of them," states Gallagher."

The guitarist is nothing if not blunt. A millionaire many times over, Gallagher remains suitably down-to-earth, free of the usual rock star baggage or attitude. He is refreshingly candid and thoroughly charming. Of *Be Here Now*, the third Oasis album, he states: "I'm as pleased as you can be. It's not perfect but it's getting there." A half hour later, Gallagher is less modest. "The album sounds fucking fantastic. I think it's the best album I've ever written but I'll do better. I'm convinced of that. If people say it's shit, they obviously don't know shit about music. And if it's critically acclaimed, well, fucking hell! Wait until you see what we're going to do next."

Be Here Now is certainly the most pondered-over Oasis album. While many bands lose their way after releasing a critically and commercially successful album, Oasis stick to what they do best. You don't sell 15 million copies of one album for nothing. And you certainly don't try to sabotage your success unless you've got a Nirvana-style career death wish.

"The music business is there to give you money to make your records, then it chews you up and spits you out," reasons Gallagher. "You just have to be sure you've made enough money by the time it spits you out to not have to work again. That was our aim — and to leave behind a load of fucking good records in the process. We don't have to worry about the financial side of things now. That's all taken care of. As long as we're given the freedom to do what we want in the studio and play how we like, of course we'll enjoy it."

Be Here Now wasn't an easy record for Oasis to make. In fact, it almost never got made. Then it was going to be the last Oasis album, their legacy after a nasty split that never actually happened. But Gallagher is clever enough to know that their antics and inner turbulence "sell[s] newspapers". Since kicking off their world domination with the single *Supersonic* in 1994, Oasis have been responsible for clearing several forests in the name of journalism. And never more than the "Oasis to split" rumours that arose after a disastrous American tour last August. The tour was doomed from the start. Gallagher's younger brother and Oasis singer, Liam, had stayed in England to look for a house with now-wife Patsy Kensit. To compensate, the band performed as a four-piece, with Noel on vocals. Liam rejoined a band stressed out and under the spotlight. After a "two year schedule squashed into a year, so everyone could make money out of us", Noel had had enough. Band and crew were complaining and, with no end in sight, they took the brave option of deciding to halt a tour that still had a leg in Asia and Australia to go, as well as European dates. Oasis had a crisis meeting in middle America. They all wanted to stop touring but didn't know how to do it.

"I said, 'I'll show you how easy it is to go home,'" explains Gallagher. "I phoned for a taxi, got on a plane and went back to London. That was it. We talked about packing it in for a while but after you take some time off, you realise you're in the best band in the world and it's the best job in the

world, why would you stop?"

With the band back on track, Gallagher started working on demos for the album in the tranquil settings of Mustique. Recording spread over many studios, including Abbey Road until fans and tabloid photographers hounded the band out of the studio used to create many of Gallagher's favourite albums. The end result keeps the faith and presses a few new buttons.

There are four songs on *Be Here Now* which Gallagher is especially proud of. There's the rocky first single, *D'You Know What I Mean?*, the anthemic, heavy closer *It's Getting Better, Man*, the almost bluesy-swagger of *Fade In/Out* (featuring Hollywood actor Johnny Depp on slide guitar) and the psychedelic *Magic Pie*. These were the last four tracks recorded for the album and signal a new, harder Oasis sound that the guitarist is keen to pursue in the future. Elsewhere, *Be Here Now* exhibits a more familiar Oasis sound.

"The rest of the album is pretty much the same as it's always been," admits Gallagher. "It's the same pub rock bollocks, basically. Good songs recorded well, played well, sung well, written well, with a nice cover. What can I say? We're not an experimental band; we're not an innovative band; we're derivative. I derive my songs from my record collection."

And that collection features every scrap of music The Beatles ever made. Gallagher is a walking encyclopedia of Beatles information and trivia and grins furiously when talking of his recent acquisition — a Mellotron that only four other people in the world own, including Paul McCartney and Beatles producer George Martin. The instrument features on not only *Be Here Now* but The Beatles' seminal *White Album*, a fact which pleases Noel no end. When he got the new toy, Gallagher pressed a button to hear the exact intro to *Bungalow Bill*. "I thought Paul McCartney had played that tricky bit on guitar but it came straight out of this Mellotron. Bastard!"

So far Oasis have legitimately covered four Beatles songs: *I Am The Walrus* (often a closing song in their live show), *Come Together* (Gallagher with Paul Weller and Paul McCartney for the *Help* charity compilation), *You've Got To Hide Your Love Away* (widely available on bootlegs from a radio performance) and *Helter Skelter*, originally planned as an upcoming b-side to a single but now being held back for the next Oasis album. Oasis have also paid some serious homage to Lennon and McCartney in various songs, from the theft of the opening bars of *Imagine* for *Don't Look Back In Anger* to the Beatlesque ending of *She's Electric. Be Here Now* continues the trend. One track features the line. "Sing a song to me, one from *Let it Be*", while another mentions a certain long and winding road. When I joke that there's an obligatory Beatles reference in a song on the next album, Gallagher immediately remarks: "I think there's one on every song. I didn't mean it, honestly. It's just that The Beatles seem to have the best lyrics and the best song titles, so it just so happens that I pinch a few here and there. Sorry, can't help it."

Push a little further, like *Magic Pie*'s identical ending to *A Day In The Life*, or the lush reprise of *All Around the World* that closes the album in severely Liverpudlian mode, and Gallagher becomes less reverential. "We don't sound like The Beatles," he declares.

Pardon me?

"We're more of a punk band than The Beatles."

But there are countless reference points to Beatles songs.

"Of course there are. But we don't *sound* like them. *Live Forever* doesn't *sound* like *Hey Jude*. I mean, the *sound* of it. Of course we've been influenced by them; of course we've ripped them off left, right and centre. Why wouldn't you? We weren't expecting people not to notice. It just annoys me when people say, 'What do Oasis sound like? Oh, they sound like The Beatles'. I think The Beatles sounded far better than we do."

It's a rare display of humility for Gallagher. Although he wants his band to sell millions of records ("to decimate every other shit band in this country that fucking annoy me"), he freely admits he no longer needs the money. "None of us have to work ever again." And while he wants his band to continue their climb to the top, he's not going back to playing the kind of huge stadiums that saw the band enter the *Guinness Book of Records* for playing to the largest audience of people (almost 300,000) over just two shows last year.

beginning September 7. The delay in charting was due to the manual way in which charts were still counted at the time. This involved allowing for the full seven days of sales, then returns from physical stores being collected and sent to the Recording Industry Association of New Zealand (RIANZ), now Recorded Music NZ. This would all happen by post or fax, followed by a final

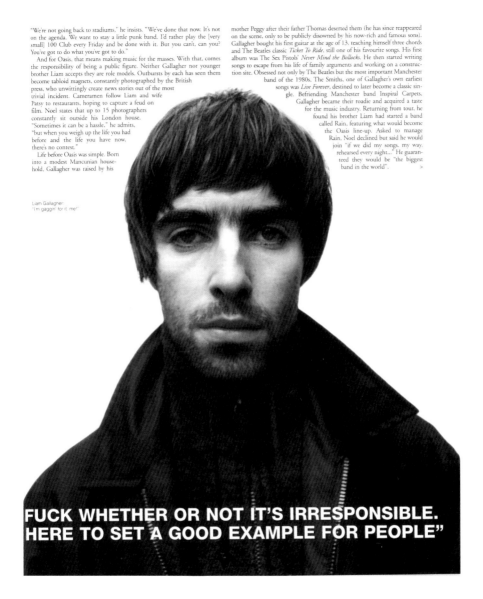

"We're not going back to stadiums," he insists. "We've done that now. It's not on the agenda. We want to stay a little punk band. I'd rather play the [very small] 100 Club every Friday and be done with it. But you can't, can you? You've got to do what you've got to do."

And for Oasis, that means making music for the masses. With that, comes the responsibility of being a public figure. Neither Gallagher nor younger brother Liam accepts they are role models. Outbursts by each has seen them become tabloid magnets, constantly photographed by the British press, who unwittingly create news stories out of the most trivial incident. Cameramen follow Liam and wife Patsy to restaurants, hoping to capture a feud on film. Noel states that up to 15 photographers constantly sit outside his London house. "Sometimes it can be a hassle," he admits, "but when you weigh up the life you had before and the life you have now, there's no contest."

Life before Oasis was simple. Born into a modest Mancunian household, Gallagher was raised by his mother Peggy after their father Thomas deserted them (he has since reappeared on the scene, only to be publicly disowned by his now-rich and famous sons). Gallagher bought his first guitar at the age of 13, teaching himself three chords and The Beatles classic *Ticket To Ride*, still one of his favourite songs. His first album was The Sex Pistols' *Never Mind the Bollocks*. He then started writing songs to escape from his life of family arguments and working on a construction site. Obsessed not only by The Beatles but the most important Manchester band of the 1980s, The Smiths, one of Gallagher's own earliest songs was *Live Forever*, destined to later become a classic single. Befriending Manchester band Inspiral Carpets, Gallagher became their roadie and acquired a taste for the music industry. Returning from tour, he found his brother Liam had started a band called Rain, featuring what would become the Oasis line-up. Asked to manage Rain, Noel declined but said he would join "if we did my songs, my way, rehearsed every night..." He guaranteed they would be "the biggest band in the world".   >

Liam Gallagher:
"I'm gaggin' for it, me!"

FUCK WHETHER OR NOT IT'S IRRESPONSIBLE. HERE TO SET A GOOD EXAMPLE FOR PEOPLE"

tally and the chart being printed. *Be Here Now* knocked *Pieces of You* by Jewel off the top spot in the New Zealand chart and prevented local star Bic Runga from returning to #1. *Be Here Now* remained at #1 for a second week before being relegated to #2 in its third week by the soundtrack to the movie *Spawn*.

Within months, Rain became Oasis and the band set about playing suitably arrogant shows to small crowds. One portentous night, Alan McGee, head of independent British label Creation Records, stumbled into a gig in a little Manchester pub after missing a train back to London. He saw three songs before deciding his life had been changed and offered the band a deal on the spot. A recording of early Rain songs (they sound like The Stone Roses before they lost the plot) is freely available on a bootleg in the UK called *Oasis: The Untold Story*. "That'd be our ex-drummer [Tony McCarroll, sacked after the release of the single *Some Might Say*] selling his practice room tapes," says Gallagher, referring to the bootleg. McGee is now one of the biggest players in the UK music industry, selling a large share of Creation to Sony, using Oasis as the very tasty carrot.

That's the Oasis story. But since the band became famous, it's been much more interesting than simply "rags to riches".

The Oasis attitude to drugs ("stick it in front of me and I'll take it, at least once," Gallagher tells me) has seen Gallagher slated in the press and in parliament for stating that, for him, using cocaine was like having a cup of tea. Keeping it in the family, Liam was arrested for possession of the substance, while their hit *Cigarettes and Alcohol* talks repeatedly about white lines. "Everybody knows what I think about drugs," says Gallagher. "We've hardly been anything other than forthcoming on our attitudes about drugs. I still do loads of drugs. People say it's irresponsible. I don't give a fuck whether or not it's irresponsible. I'm not here to be responsible; I'm not here to set a good example for people. The police don't give a shit about pop stars doing drugs. I'm not a drug dealer. If they wanted to arrest me, they could stand outside our house every night and kick the fucking doors in, there's enough people in there doing it. I'm sure they fucking know that anyway, so what's the point."

And the tabloids?

"They like to have a good scandal and we sell newspapers," scowls Gallagher. "But, god almighty, how is anyone going to damage a Gallagher brother's character? 'They take drugs!' Oh, shock! Gosh!"

One area Gallagher has been less than blasé about is in his attitude towards the Internet. With the rise in his band's popularity, hundreds of unofficial Oasis web sites have sprung up, many with lyrics and photos of the band which breach copyright laws. Although these sites were created by fans as some kind of virtual scrapbook of the band, earlier this year Oasis made history and headlines by cracking down on the fledgling phenomenon, circulating a legal letter stating that unauthorised use of photos and lyrics would incur legal action.

"As far as I'm concerned, it's bootlegging," explains Gallagher. "I'm all for free speech and all that shit but, at the end of the day, the Internet is only a way for fucking cunts with a lot of money to make more money. By law, they're not allowed to reprint any lyrics. If there was someone outside now doing it on the street, they'd get arrested. Anyway, they shouldn't be sat in front of fucking computer screens, they should have fucking guitars. Fuck them. And they're the ones saying they're going to take *us* to court."

Gallagher refuses to accept that these people may be doing it out of love for the band.

"Are they fans when I get a thing off the Internet where some smartarse in California is taking a load of money off my fans by saying they can get the new Oasis single two weeks before it comes out?" grumbles Gallagher. "He's getting a load of money in, putting it in his bank, and who the fuck is he? He's not authorised to sell my fucking single. It's modern day bootlegging, man. They tape it off the radio and play it down the Internet at a cost to someone. Fuck that shit, man! It's fucking wrong! I don't consider people like that fans. I don't mind bootlegging. I've bought bootleg CDs. I've bootlegged stuff myself. It's just that everyone I met on the Internet is a real twat."

Technology *has* entered the world of Gallagher of late, though. His collaboration with The Chemical Brothers on the landmark single *Setting Sun* reached number one in the UK, introducing him to a world of samples, drum loops and keyboard-based sounds. *D'You Know What I Mean?* even samples rappers NWA. "I got bollocked for saying that by my manager," laughs Gallagher. "We'll have to pay them now. It's an NWA loop from *Straight Outta Compton* but I can't recall them ever having a drummer, so I'm sure it comes from somewhere else." The dense sound of *D'You Know What I Mean?* is deliberate. "Listening to the Chemical's stuff, when it came time to mix the single, I had to go back in and do the drums again because their drums were louder than ours," says Gallagher. "Can't have people being louder than us."

The Chemical Brothers were rumoured to be shaping the sound of *Be Here Now*. They weren't directly involved but Gallagher admits they might play a part in the next record. Keeping the fans (and himself) on their toes, Gallagher has also recorded a song called *Temper Temper* with drum 'n' bass luminary Goldie to feature on the Metalheadz man's forthcoming album. Meanwhile, Goldie has remixed the Oasis track *My Big Mouth*.

"Goldie is a genius," enthuses Gallagher, also placing Prodigy (Oasis hired them as a support for their Knebworth shows), The Beastie Boys and The Chemical Brothers in the same league. "Working with The Chemical Brothers and meeting those kinds of people in the dance field, it has opened my eyes. People think that if you can't do music live, then it's not worth anything. Fuck that! You have to find a way to do it live, like The Chemicals, like Prodigy... That's the way it's going with us." Gallagher pauses. "This is the end of the first period of Oasis. You'll have to wait until next year, until this album is finished, when we decide to do another one, if we decide to do another one, if we have another fucking year off. You'll have to wait and see. In my own mind, things are going to change; I'm not sure how drastically or if at all. We spend a lot of time talking about how we're going to change things, then we go in and do the same old shit."

A new album is still a long way off. There are still plenty more singles off *Be Here Now* to be released, with the *Wonderwall*-esque ballad *Stand By Me* next off the blocks, with an array of b-sides lined up for each, and more cover versions to come. "The thing about covers is: when we do a single, we always put a few new tracks on," explains Gallagher, "and things like *The Masterplan*, which was the b-side of *Wonderwall*, that should have really been on this album and not just a b-side. So instead, we're doing a few covers for a laugh."

There's a song called *The Fame* which didn't make it onto the album.

"I've still got that. It's about the fame but it's not about me. It's about a fallen rock star - not me!"

Anyone in particular?

"No. Yeah. But I'm not telling. It's about all fallen rock stars. I'm sure people are going to look too far into it but fuck 'em."

There were even rumours that Gallagher had recorded a blues album with Paul Weller and Paul McCartney called *Yr Blues*, named after a John Lennon song. "I couldn't name you Blind Dog Jackson fucking albums or whatever they call themselves," rejoins Gallagher. "I like 12 bar blues but I'm not a big blues fan. That album was an April Fools' Day joke by a journalist. But, having said that, I actually had to think when I read it. I'd been out on the piss for four days with Paul Weller when I read it and I thought, 'That can't be... No, it's not... I do remember having a guitar... No, surely not... Did I? I don't think it's true. It might be'. Sounds like a good idea, though."

And, of course, there's more touring. America isn't a priority ("We've already made enough money out of that country. They know what we're about by now") and, after two cancelled tours, New Zealand and Australia may finally get a look in ("If circumstances prevail, we will go. If it doesn't happen, what can I say?"). But less touring and more recording is the new Gallagher ethos. The driving force behind Oasis wants to capture the new songs filling his head. "I'm fucking itching to do it," gushes Gallagher. "But I've stopped myself writing because if I start writing I'm going to demand to go into the studio and record. I want to do justice to this album first."

Gallagher laughs when asked if he plans to build his own studio so he can record at his leisure. "Imagine our kid [Liam] living with us for six months a year? Fuck that for a game of soldiers! Oh no!"

While many consider *Wonderwall* his finest moment, Gallagher is not concerned about superseding the song with another, even more classic, track. "I don't think by any stretch of the imagination that I'm ever going to write another song as universally popular as that. I might do. Who's to say? To me, *Live Forever* is a better song. It just happens that there are many many many millions of people who will never hear *Live Forever* because they don't own *Definitely Maybe*. It depends on what terms you use. If we release *Stand By Me* and it sells more than *Wonderwall*, does that make it a better song? People may have said to John Lennon, 'You'll never better *A Day in the Life*', but, to me, *Imagine* is a far greater song. But I'll always write songs like *Wonderwall*. I'll just probably end up giving them away to other bands."

Are they easy to write?

"Yeah, they're a fucking doodle, mate. Start in G, bang some strings on, go to E minor for the guitar solo and you're fucking laughing. Million seller!"

Gallagher should know. ●

Cold start for album

by Margaret Agnew

Only 51 die-hard fans of British rock band Oasis ventured into the Christchurch winter night determined to be the first to own the super group's new album early yesterday.

Echo Records manager Garry Knight was disappointed with the turnout.

The midnight release of the band's third album, "Be Here Now", did not go as well as similar midnight promotions.

Only 51 copies of the album sold early yesterday, and just 22 more by midday during normal shop hours.

"We're used to doing bigger figures," Mr Knight said. "Usually we've sold 150 units in one hour. The Prodigy album ("The Fat of the Land"), for example, did 201."

He put the poor sales down to the lack of singles released from the album, the cold weather, and that it was released at midnight on a Sunday.

Other record stores were happier with sales. The assistant manager of ECM's Cashel Street branch, Alun Kirwan, said the album was doing extremely well.

"It's been good — better than expected, but the die-hard fans aren't going to be deterred by a little frost," he said.

"Everybody knows it's out," the manager of the CD Store Cashel Mall Andrew Waterson said. "It's a far better Monday than most other weeks. We've added quite a phenomenal amount to our usual takings."

Despite Echo Records' disappointing initial sales, Mr Knight believed the album would be the biggest of the year, and would knock New Zealand singer Bic Runga from the top of the album charts this week.

"Whether you love them or hate them, they're a really strong band," he said.

PHOTO: DEAN KOZANIC

Garry Knight, of Echo Records, hopes for an Oasis rush after a modest start.

The Press - Be Here Now release – Margaret Agnew/Stuff Limited[56]

Fans lose sleep to buy new Oasis CD

About 40 die-hard Oasis fans descended on a music store in central Hamilton last night to buy the British band's latest album before anyone else in the country.

But they were probably beaten by 70 other fans who were in Wellington's Manners Mall store at 11.30pm and ready to hand over cash as the clock struck midnight.

Sounds Waikato manager Wayne Lim said Hamilton fans were slow to queue for Be Here Now, the band's third album. But after an hour of fans filtering through, the Ward St store closed with 40 sales on the till.

"They just took a little longer to turn up than usual."

Mr Lim said the last midnight opening was for the Prodigy album Fat Of The Land and sales topped 100 in 40 minutes. Large sales from midnight openings helped that album to debut at No 1 on the New Zealand charts.

He said the 5.9°C night would not have kept people away. If they want the album they turn up with sleeping bags, he said. "They're die-hard fans, they want the album and midnight opening specials are part of collecting."

Waikato Times - Be Here Now release – Stuff Limited[57]

Early morning glory for fans

About 70 hardy souls braved a Wellington winter night to be the first people in New Zealand to buy the new album by British rock band Oasis.

Tandys, in **Manners Mall**, opened its doors at 11.30 last night, and started selling copies of Be Here Now, the band's third album, at midnight.

"We had a really good turnout of people," Tandys senior staff member **Michelle Brown** said today.

Trade was also brisk this morning on the other side of Manners Mall at Tower Music.

"We've sold six copies already and we've only been open five minutes," said Steve Clansey, Tower Music senior manager. "I think it will be as big as the Prodigy album."

The Prodigy album The Fat Of The Land debuted at No 1.

If Be Here Now grabs the No 1 album slot, it will be from Aucklander Bic Runga, another artist from Oasis' New Zealand record company, Sony Music.

Evening Post - Be Here Now release – Stuff Limited[58]

Nexus – Tracks advert[59]

On the eve of *Be Here Now's* release in the UK, a BBC documentary, *Right Here Right Now* was broadcast. The documentary included a handful of live performances, including 'It's Gettin' Better (Man!!)'. The documentary aired in New Zealand on TV4 on Monday September 22, with a prime time 7:30 pm slot.

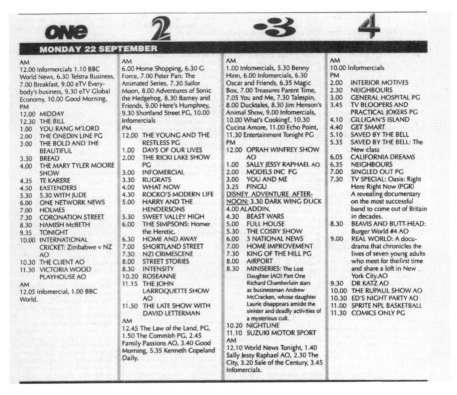

Nexus - TV Guide September 22, 1997[60]

Reviews for *Be Here Now* in the UK were more than favourable, and the same was true of most New Zealand reviews, bar a few that seemed less than impressed.

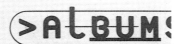

OASIS
Be Here Now (Creation)

Now the circle is complete. When I first heard Oasis they were but the learners. Now they are the masters of one of the most important rock 'n' roll sounds to emerge out of the 1990s.

Be Here Now doesn't need to skite or pander to the few non-believers who

ic pop of 'Welcome
plete with back tr
yet still profitable'
'Inside' are the
Andrew Brough's
powers in full bloom
gle tracks, 'Circus
and 'Save My Life',
that's 72% success

OASIS

still don't get it. This is the culmination of everything they said they were capable of. And forget all the easy Beatles comparisons, even when 'All Around the World' is championed as their 'Let it Be'. And ignore the mentions of the Stones when the American courtship of the title track and 'Fade In Out' are discussed.

This album is pure epic Oasis, with enough attitude and Hooj singalongs to level a salivating nation of millions. 'D'ya Know What I Mean' gave the real fans a terrace anthem. 'Stand By Me' will be a 'Wonderwall', though it's so much more in terms of soul squeezing glory with all these strings and harmonies and genius guitar riffery. The hairs on the back of your neck were invented for this song.

Noel has delivered 11 of the biggest, rockiest, emotionally depth-charged songs we've heard from him. And Liam's voice is in amazing form, with the disengaged sneer now becoming only one of the many vocal personas he has in his arsenal.

They'll create an absolute kicker like 'My Big Mouth', which makes your heart race with every chorus, and be able to change gear and create the equally credible beauty of 'Don't Go Away', a heartfelt ballad that shows a face we hardly get to see; vulnerability.

Be Here Now is a classic album of absolute mastery. It should be put on board every spaceship to show aliens what earth is capable of.

JOHN TAITE

release this month
ion piece to the Ste
pop thrills. *Take In*
its rays.

ECHO AND THE
Ballyhoo: The I

Hardly a coinc this *Best Of* j
Bunnymen's new what must be an at restoring McCu forefront of British

The 80s have l victed of being Liverpool's Bur Explodes, and ' enough heady, d intellectual mysti movement. The album, *Crocodiles* psychedelic rock ' lent *Ballyhoo* appro great drug anther and the revolution Jazz', as fitting r that timeless debut

From there it w epic sweep of *Hea* likes of 'Over The the metaphorical c and McCulloch ki on the otherwise Seas'. Their last *and the Bunnymer* ing and grandeur c but songs like 'L showed remnants The almost nar

Rip It Up – Be Here Now review – John Taite/Simon Grigg[61]

ECHO & THE BUNNEYMEN
EVERGREEN London

It's appropriate that the cover artwork on the comeback album by Liverpool's Echo & the Bunneymen recalls their debut, *Crocodiles*, released in 1980. That classic debut catapulted the band into both the new decade and the hearts of listeners throughout the Western world. It kept us interested in this band with the strange name through many years, numerous albums and countless singles, until Ian McCulloch, Les Pattinson, Will Sergeant and Pete de Freitas (Echo, the drum machine, was long gone) ground to an unceremonious halt. McCulloch, the singer, continued solo, while the others eventually drafted in a new singer and brought ill-repute to their own heritage by continuing under the old name. Then, McCulloch teamed up again with Sergeant to record as Electrafixion, releasing the album *Burned* and a couple of singles. They asked Pattinson to rejoin them (de Freitas died in a motorcycle accident in 1989) and Echo & the Bunneymen were doing it clean again. *Evergreen* (to all intents and purposes, the first Bunneymen album in 10 years) has rekindled the flame. Mac the Mouth hasn't lost that magical voice or the look that inspired a thousand boys to practice their pouts. And the songs, though more subdued, sparkle like silver. The singles *I Want to Be There (When You Come)* and *Nothing Lasts Forever* are gorgeous examples of the Bunneymen magic. And the artwork on the various versions of the CD singles is excellent. If the music's great, package it in greatness. I remember seeing Echo & the Bunneymen in early 1988 playing in a stunning historical building a couple of blocks from the Whitehouse in Washington D.C. They were great then, housed in a beautiful venue befitting their greatness. *Evergreen* reminds me of that moment. Welcome back. BARNEY

OASIS
BE HERE NOW Creation

By the time you read this review, you'll probably have already bought the new Oasis album and helped send it to number one (or thereabouts). And you'll also have bought into the biggest hype surrounding the release of an album in the last decade. Which would be fine if it was the best album released in the last 10 years, or even this year. But, beat me to a pulp if you disagree, it isn't. Sure, there are all the trademark Oasis characteristics that mark them as one of the most exciting acts to emerge from Britain in the '90s, such as the rollicking *D'You Know What I Mean*, with its wah-wah flutters and roaring beats. But is it necessary for it to be over seven minutes long? And while there's no denying that this is loud, proud, stand up and shout from the roof-tops, sing-along, stadium-rock, as *My Big Mouth* and *It's Gettin' Better (Man!!)* show, what happened to the three-minute pop treats so evident on *What's the Story (Morning Glory)?* or the cheeky wit of *Definitely Maybe? Be Here Now* may be the fastest selling British album ever, with over a million sales in its first week of release in the UK alone, but quantity doesn't always denote quality. And there's a big difference between proclaiming you're the best band in the world in the tabloids and actually proving it, as *Be Here Now* illustrates. As the saying goes: the proof of the pudding is in the eating. But judging by *Magic Pie*, *Be Here Now* isn't as fresh or wholesome as you'd expect or even wish for. DESMOND SAMPSON

HOWIE B
TURN THE DARK OFF Polydor

Who's a busy boy then? Björk's new boyfriend (move over Goldie!) and U2's leading dance music light, Howie B, that's who. A right little renaissance man. But the canny Scot has, perhaps, been too quick to the draw on this new album. Although undoubtedly more uptempo than his previous and wonderful album *Music for Babies*, *Turn the Dark Off* is, in parts, just so much snoozing on the settee. Take the opener, *Fizzy In My Mouth*, or even the lamentable *Take Your Partner By The Hand*, with chief "Boring Old Fart" Robbie (The Band) Robinson. Oh, how the mighty (and I mean Howie) have fallen. Now, don't get me wrong. There's great stuff on here. Check the beats on *Hopscotch* and *Switch* or the lilt of *Sore Brown Eyes*. But, kick me if I'm dreaming, some tracks, such as *Limbo*, sound like leftovers from the *Music for Babies* sessions and, taken as a whole, *Turn the Dark Off* has all the hallmarks of an album rush-released to capitalise on his current high profile. Standing in the shadow of *Music for Babies*, one just hopes it's just a shaky stepping stone to a blinding third album. JOCK LAURIE

PORTISHEAD
PORTISHEAD Polydor

After the phenomenal success of their debut, *Dummy*, Bristol's biggest export, Portishead, return with their second instalment of musical noir. And, rather than reinvent themselves after a three-year hiatus to combat the onslaught of copy-cat trip-hoppy bands they've spawned, such as Lamb, Moloko and Olive, they've wisely decided to stick with their tried-and-true formula. Opening track (and limited release single) *Cowboys* sees Beth Gibbons' demonic vocals competing with a *Hammer Horror* soundtrack, as Geoff Barrow brews an unsettling backdrop of church organs, tinkling piano, trip-hop beats and distorted scratching. It's one of the most disturbing songs Portishead have ever written. But the next track, *All Mine*, sees Portishead return to more familiar territory. With its loping beat, jazzy vocals and bursts of trumpet, it echoes former singles *Sour Times* and *Glory Box*. Unsurprisingly, it's the first wide-release single to be culled from the album. Elsewhere, the mood and tempo remain true to Portishead's

Pavement - Be Here Now review – Desmond Sampson/Barney McDonald[62]

50

LIMP
Pop & Disorderly
(Honest Don's/Global Routes)
From new Fat Wreck Chords offshoot label Honest Don's, Limp's debut plants them firmly at the lighter power-pop end of the punk spectrum, though does little to distinguish them from the rest of the pack. Great production, the band sound tight and would as per usual be worth seeing live. Lyrically moronic, the same old mix of I-am-growing-up/I-used-to-have-a-girlfriend bullshit coupled with the monotonous vocal style sent me straight to the dictionary – "Limp: to proceed lamely, lacking strength or wilting" couldn't be more to the point. **(5)**
Nick Anderson

OASIS
Be Here Now
(Creation/Sony)

When a creepy reviewer for my local urban weekly recently chided Oasis for being overly ambitious, I had to laugh: over-ambition is precisely what's made them my (and a few zillion other pop fans) favourite end-of-the-millenium rock band. Oasis weren't merely going to be the next Beatles, they were going to embarrass themselves doing so, and be fairly relentless about it; that Noel Gallagher was capable also of penning some classic tunes seemed almost an afterthought. Perfect.

A few listens in to *Be Here Now*, however, and I kind of see the creep's point. This album tries very hard to convey a certain type of pop mania (never a dumb thing to aim for), but is mostly just full of its own hall-of-fame-here-we-come back-patting. For instance, lest you ever happen to forget where you were the day the third Oasis album came out, the release date is plastered on both the front and inside covers; and if you listen real closely during the second chorus of "It's Gettin' Better (Man!!)," you'll hear Bonehead repeating, "August 21, 1997" over and over, like a mantra (first time I heard it I swore he was saying "could I get some more cranberry sauce over here, please?").

One thing's for sure: this disc *sounds* huge – if I could afford a mixing console large enough to lay down 18 separate guitar tracks, I'd sound huge too – but this is a mixed blessing at best. For one, it doesn't conceal the fact that most of the elder Gallagher's much-vaunted melodic gifts are barely negligible (on such "rockers" as "My Big Mouth"), or in remission altogether (witness "Fade In-Out," their first blues number, and some kind of creative nadir). And where the sheer volume of the thing is supposed to knock you out, too often it merely bewilders; it's less a wall of sound than a wash of sound. Drummer Alan White

laid down such a nimble (but brusing) beat all over *(What's the Story) Morning Glory*, that he became my favourite hip-hop drummer of '95 by default, but here he's pretty much just part of the (oops) blur. It's a pretty suffocating affair overall.

Having said all that, it's a very real possibility that mega-airplay will turn me around on some of these numbers (though I'm already dreading the album's fully-pronounced masterpiece-plus-reprise, "All Around the World," which makes "Champagne Supernova" sound like "Blitzkrieg Bop"), and there are two instant keepers: "I Hope, I Think, I Know" and the title track. Both numbers give singer Liam a chance to twist his larynx around some lovely hooks: when he sings, "You know I don't care" (on "I Hope, I Think, I Know"), you swear you're hearing Johnny Rotten all over again, only this time with tears in his eyes. Liam, in case you're wondering, is my favourite Oasis, one of those rare singers who sounds better the more affected he is. Believe me, without him there *is* no Oasis. **(6)**
Scott Woods

PRIMUS
Brown Album
(Interscope)

2046

The songs of bassist Les Claypool are generally fucked-up little stories from the landscape of natural born '90s America, ballads for the generation who've grown up with death cults, serial killers and Sideshow Bob. Most every song contains some kind of reference to decay through substance abuse, and quite a few contain references to dying in flames, arson, or murder. From this, it can only be assumed that it's an ugly, ugly world which glares at Claypool each day as he incessantly practices those mind-numbingly difficult bass riffs. There's also an element of laziness creeping into the music, cheap rip-offs like "Kalamazoo" and "Fisticuffs" are both very reminiscent of San Francisco's other demented (departed) substar, Snakefinger, but the sense of nasty humour so much a feature of the Finger's work is entirely absent here – probably the main reason why this album doesn't cut it like the earlier ones did. Still, there's definitely something weird and warped festering in this man's music, and from here it looks like it could go either way. Next record could be a killer, or it could be the death of them. Either way, hopefully it'll feature a

Real Groove - Be Here Now review – Scott Woods[63]

more stuff like that that would be better too. Like, say, on a Garageland b-side.

KATE HARDCASTLE, Kerikeri

Coolio is one of America's top, notable rap artists. He's released yet another genuine album, which features chart hit *C U When U Get There* and many others.

Although it contains explicit language, its message is 'sweet-as'. With expectations of selling it to teens, radio stations etc, it's looking very promising.

Rap/hip hop is the overall style. E-Z as beats to get down with, so enough talk... make the request for the album and 'shake-your-rump' to nearest music store and purchase... THIS ALBUM IS DA-BOMB!

BERNEE GRAY

This starts off like a *Sgt Pepper*-style concept album, and you find yourself thinking, 'who do they think they are? The Beatles?'

Oh, right. Of course they do. And this is a good thing and a successful thing for these guys.

By now they're so famous (they sing a song! They have a fight! They marry a star! They get drunk and talk about drugs!) that it almost wouldn't matter what they sing.

They've stuck to their old formula of brilliantly droney pop songs, and this album will probably do well. But I doubt it will be anybody's favourite Oasis album. But buy it, and collect the set.

KATY

Whatever else this might be (eg a sequel cashing in on the success of the first soundtrack, which was probably just cashing in on the success of the film...), this is an excellent compilation.

It has plundered more of the film's own sounds, and added the slightly dodgy area of music 'inspired by' the film. But the CD cover goes some way to justify this with quotes from main players in the film as to why, for example, David Bowie's *Golden Years* should be included, or Goldie's *Inner City Life*.

It's a list of great tracks, the time-honoured (Joy Division, Iggy, Heaven 17, Fun Boy Three) and the newly rising stars (Sleeper, Underworld, Leftfield).

I'd recommend buying, especially if you're in danger of wearing out your first compilation. And the record company does assure us there will be NO MORE sequels.

KATY

Björk has never been one to conform to commercial ideals or commit to any particular genre. This is proven by her latest album *Homogenic* which is refreshingly free of any distinct influence.

The first release is *Jóga*, a funky yet mellow blend of original beats and haunting vocals teamed with swelling strings and horns.

My favourite track is *5 Years*, opening with a bizarre blend of militant rhythms and climaxing with violins and soft, simplistic lyrics.

Homogenic can be heavy on percussion in parts, but it doesn't seem unnecessary and appears to highlight Björk's mellow, yet passionate vocals. Try before you buy – won't appeal to everyone!

JUSTINE

Tearaway - Be Here Now review[64]

Music

GALAXY RECORDS

Oasis

Be Here Now

Creation Records

Even from a quick glance at the sleeve of this album Oasis seems more self indulgent than ever. A brand spanking new Roller half submerged in a larger than average swimming pool in the grounds of some fucking huge house. The last thing we should do is buy this crap, and thus support the sport of rich folk (ie the "find the most expensive automobile you can and sink the fucker for a laugh" game), not to mention a certain unmentionable band member's £1000 a week coke addiction.

The overall production quality is slightly muddy (even by Oasis' standards) and the outcome is a handful of fuzzy 'Champagne Supernova' and 'Digby's Dinner' inspired tunes that all have their own merits, but are more often than not too long for their own good.

Unfortunately, this crap is great and, as much as I hate to admit it, everyone should at least make the effort to buy a blank tape and sit tight waiting for their favourite commercial radio station to murder every song *Be Here Now* contains. No surprises here, this album sounds pretty much the same as the other two.

Alex

Canta - Be Here Now review[65]

OASiS ⊚
Be Here Now

Sony

The headline on a recent British magazine featuring Oasis said it best: "Nice planet. We'll take it!" As they prepare to unveil their third album, Be Here Now, to a planet hungry for the rare thrill of great rock'n'roll, the world is theirs for the taking (as are platinum awards and sold-out arenas and scandalous headlines). Be Here Now will drop like an incendiary bomb onto a lethargic pop world that has been lulled into a stupor of diminished expectations by big bands who have recently muffed highly-anticipated releases (U2, REM, Pearl Jam).

It's hard to imagine anyone who still enjoys the charge of loud, proud pop being disappointed by Oasis '97. It starts with aerodrome sound effects and ends with an orchestral reprise of guitarist-songwriter Noel Gallagher's self-proclaimed masterpiece, All Around the World (already tagged to be the highly-prized Christmas UK chart-topper). In between, it's a great, big sprawling record, filled to the brim with more of everything that made its predecessors so great: Bigger guitars, rapturous melodies (many lovingly nicked from the Beatles), thunderingly epic arrangements, sneering and leering vocals – the lot.

You already know the opening salvo, D'You Know What I Mean? from radio and its layers of dense guitars and arena-ready chorus set the tone for the album perfectly. The turmoil that beset the group last year, when Noel's brother, singer Liam, went MIA just as Oasis was about to launch its biggest North American tour, is vaguely alluded to on My Big Mouth. It flips a middle finger at any number of foes, and mentions "walking slowly down the hall of fame" and "sleeping with the enemy". Don't Go Away sounds like a gentler rewrite of Slide Away, and Noel's lyrics ("Damn my education, I can't find the words to say all the things caught in my mind") are his most nakedly revealing yet. The shocker is Fade In/Out. With its droning slide acoustic guitar and chest-puffing vocals, it sounds like Bon Jovi's Wanted Dead Or Alive relocated to Manchester. I Hope I Think I Know gallops briskly and the lighthearted The Girl in the Dirty Shirt shambles along with barrelhouse piano. On more familiar turf is Stand By Me (not the Ben E King classic), with a glorious chorus that lends itself well to soccer terrace chanting. Noel Gallagher has said he has held All Around the World in reserve since Oasis' early days, waiting until the band had the wherewithal to hire a full orchestra. The result is an exultant epic but the lyrics have a wet-behind-the-ears exuberance that's at odds with the world-weariness and maturity found on the rest of the LP. The winning Magic Pie is the most overt steal from the Fab Four and Noel himself delivers his own lyrics about millennial anxiety and rock'n'roll dreams. "We'll have our time, we'll have our say, cuz my star will shine."

Music Press Magazine - Be Here Now review[66]

ɔ music music music music music music music music music music music music music mus
iic music music music music music music music music music music music music music mu
ɔ music music music music music music music music music music music music
iic music music music music music music music music music
ɔ music music music music music music music music music music
iic music music music music music music
ɔ music music music music music
iic music music music
ɔ music music
iic mu

tracs

Ho-hum, non-de-script, clang-clang music

Matchbox 20. Yourself Or Someone Like You (Lava Records). Reviewed by Gale Glasson.

If you want the definition of boring, miserable music, it's this album by MATCHBOX 20. They're a bunch of clang-clangs. If you don't know what that is, then say it out loud. Clang-clang. That's what they sound like: from the ho-hum, non-de-script, clang-clang music down to the annoying clang-clang vocals.

One could liken them to a demented version of Hootie and The Blowfish, in fact you could even give them points for trying to cash in on Hootie's style. It didn't work.

However there is one good track. It's the last one on the album, called Hang. Overlay someone crying onto it, and it sounds miserable enough to make you laugh at it. I give it 15 clang-clangs out of 10, and I'm collecting donations c/o NEXUS to help them break even.

Better than God and the Spice Girls

Oasis. Be Here Now (Sony Music). Reviewed by Gale Glasson.

Apparently there were a lot of people queuing patiently for the release of this album. They were probably expecting it to be an album of epic proportions, full of good old OASIS sound, some grunty helicopter noises like the last one. They would be right.

For OASIS fans, this highly publicised album is everything they could ever want. The opening track is the previously released "'Do You Know What I Mean?", and I have to admit, it's pretty good in my book (except for the helicopter noise).

As for the rest of the album, and the world, the helicopter noise is long past its use-by date, and it's hard to figure out where one songs ends and the next one begins. We're all totally sick of the never-ending publicity surrounding the Gallaghers, and I personally think that they should come up with something more original than claiming they're better than the Beatles, more important than God, etc. Better than the Spice Girls, perhaps? I'd sure like to be able to watch Oasis with the sound turned down. Forever.

I highly recommend this album if you brought and loyally listened to the last two. Otherwise, don't bother. Or you could use it as a cookie cutter.

Loud, aggressive, angry young man music

Sepultura. Blood-Rooted. Reviewed by Colin Dickson

SEPULTURA have made a career playing loud, aggressive, angry young man music with full distortion. This album promises nothing different.

The first half of this new release is "rare" material, ie shit that was omitted from previous albums or B-sides. To be blunt, the majority of the first half of BLOOD-ROOTED is bollocks, but War, Crucificados Pelo Sistema, Mine and Lookaway are excellent.

The second half of BLOOD-ROOTED is live, with all the songs coming from Chaos, AD and Roots, with the exception of Beneath the Remains/Escape to the Void. I don't remember these tracks being this fast on the aforementioned albums. It's truly extreme.

If you've never listened to SEPULTURA before, I would suggest you buy Chaos AD or Roots before buying this.

A menacing recording for fans only.

Sounds oh so good

The Magick Heads. Woody. Reviewed by John Needham.

They say good things come in small packages. Well it's true with THE MAGICK HEADS' second album WOODY. A pleasing mix of Robert Scott's (The Bats/The Clean) songs, Jane Sinnott's wonderful drifting folky voice and that famous Dunedin sound of rambling guitars, bass and drums. On paper it reads like more Flying Nun cliches, but out of the speakers it sounds oh so good.

27

Nexus – Be Here Now review – Gale Glasson[67]

THE ENGLISH BLATANT

Oasis' third effort *Be Here Now* is one of the most highly expected rock albums of the year. RUSSELL BAILLIE takes a long, hard listen.

Cover story

LAIDBACK, THINKING OF ENGLAND: Even Noel Gallagher's found some of those long songs a bit taxing.

Look down the back of the cover art of Oasis' third album *Be Here Now* and you can see Noel Gallagher peering down a telescope at a globe. Curiously, he seems to be looking at New Zealand.

Perhaps it's because — the international dateline being where it is — this is possibly the first country to have the much-expected album on sale, come its international release date on Monday. Though that poolside cover shot has a calendar showing "August 21 Thursday" among various inanimate objects, the band's foursome included.

Or it could be that the songwriting, guitar-playing senior Gallagher is pondering those parts of the world where last year they cancelled concerts after the famously fraternal tensions led to an abandoned American tour and had them virtually splitting upon their return to Britain.

Perhaps he's looking for real estate in faraway places, what with the inevitable

like that.

But seen from here, you might wonder whether all that is partly wrapped up in British national mood. After all, it's still summer there, they've a new nicer, kinder government, and Oasis are seen as the national team in a sort of World Cup of pop.

And one making a comeback from the brink of self-destruction, still playing rock music in traditional guitar-powered fashion and happy to wave the Union Jack while they're doing it.

Who would want to party-poop all that? "The biggest band in the world" they get labelled there, despite lack of off-shore statistical reinforcement. In Blighty, Oasis is the big band of the Little Englander.

On *Be Here Now*, Oasis certainly sounds bigger.

World to finish) stretching out to 70 minutes, the rockier tracks may have the initial momentum to carry them through their six-plus minutes. Until, that is, you notice many of the songs simply aren't very bright for all that extra wattage.

Sole songwriter and co-producer Noel Gallagher may have gained in attention span and still have an ear for the enormously catchy, but the biggest risk he seems to have taken on *Be Here Now* is the decision to include a lyric sheet.

Yes, in years to come when Sotheby's auctions off the Oasis paraphernalia, among the boxes of Beatles-made-easy books there should be found a much abused rhyming dictionary with the "me" page looking especially tatty.

Still, *Be Here Now* sure does have its rowdy Oasis-rock excitements and its occasional fetching ballads. Though there's not that much of the latter that comes that close to last album *Morning Glory*'s sublime *Wonderwall*.

However, there is the likes of the rather forlorn *Don't Go Away*, the laughably Beatlesque *Girl in the Dirty Shirt* that impress among the sensitive moments. Less edifying is Noel's single vocal effort, the vaguely psychedelic *Magic Pie* ("Cos you see me I got my magic pie/Think of me yeah that was me I was that passerby ...") and the *Hey Jude*-proportioned, orchestra-assisted *All Around The World*, the lyrical dippiness of which is only exceeded by its nine minute-plus duration.

Is there merit in pop songs that fade at a rate slower than your lounge curtains? In Oasis land apparently there is, and it's not just confined to those ballads.

That lengthy first single *D'You Know What I Mean?* opens this all up with its ear-raid of sounds, punchy slow rock and infectiously meaningless chorus.

Then it's into the uptempo guitar squall of *My Big Mouth*, a song neatly encapsulating the Oasis lippy attitude (as previously done on the likes of *Rock'n'Roll Star*)

across its Sex Pistols-like one-and-a-bit riffs.

Only *I Hope, I Think, I Know* and the trademark swagger of the title track sounds nearly as convincing so far as the loud and loutish numbers go.

And in between are a curiosity or two, especially *Fade In Out*, with slide guitar by one Johnny Depp giving this otherwise aimless number the result of Lennon fronting ZZ Top.

So Oasis' third album — it has its very, very long, occasionally very good moments.

But as a whole, it seems those Gallagher brows are just as low as they were the last two times through, even if their best tunes won't let go.

And despite the excitement no doubt raging right now about *Be Here Now* in Britain, listening to it here it feels a bit like looking up Noel's telescope the other way — it sure does cut 'em down to size. ★★★

'Despite the excitement no doubt raging right now about *Be Here Now* in Britain, listening to it here it feels a bit like looking up Noel's telescope the other way — it sure does cut 'em down to size.'

truckloads this one will sell, that lorry fleet having already kicked up a choking cloud of hype from recent weeks of revving hard with the handbrake on.

But listening to the new evidence you have to wonder: isn't this just another Oasis album, albeit a bigger, brasher, blunter, more bloated take on what Noel once quipped the "same old pub rock bollocks"?

According to the small heap of praise lavished on it in Britain before its release, apparently not. Music publication *Q* magazine awarded it five stars, the *Observer* dubbed it "a triumph" and there'll be more

It's an album that shows its hand quickly, which speaks highly of its frequently swaggering energy and anthemic melodies as delivered by Liam Gallagher's gripping Lennon/Rotten cross of a voice.

But once you've got your head around it, you soon notice it's not Oasis' own great leap forward — or sideways — that the likes of lesser-selling Brit bands have made already this year, whether it's been old rivals Blur (sideways), Supergrass (forward) or Radiohead (both forward and sideways).

With its 11 actual songs (there's a brief instrumental reprise of *All Around The*

Squid Top Ten

Wednesdays 7 - 8pm with your hosts "Fast Willy" and the cigar supplier "Side Kat"

1. (1) DLT - Poison Remix*
2. (5) KRS & Goldie - The Burial
3. (2) Darcy Clay - What About You*
4. (6) Dam Native - The Son*
5. (3) Apollo Delux - Good Lord Jack Lord*
6. (4) Bic Runga - Swim*
7. (10) Prodigy - Desiel Power
8. (7) Head Like A Hole - Wet Rubber*
9. (9) The Verve - Bittersweet Symphony
10. (8) Ovum - A Short Thrill*

As of 13/8/97 - 70% paua / 30% plastic
Compiled from listener request every Wednesday
Ring 9073 918, have your vote and maybe win a prize!

Monitor

And still they come. More spring tours are coming out of the international and domestic woodwork.

❏ Joining an already busy concert schedule during late September early October is Britrock outfit *Reef* who play the Powerstation on Tuesday, October 7, on the backs of their second

album *Glow* with its hit single *Place Your Hands*. Tickets are on sale from today.

❏ Those American weirdos *Ween* return to play the Powerstation on Friday, October 3. Tickets are on sale Wednesday.

❏ A reformed (therefore not quite living up to their name) *Suicidal Tendencies* are heading back this way the California punk-funk thrashers play the Powerstation on Wednesday, September 24. Tickets are already on sale.

❏ American exponents of that mod-

ern rock stuff *Matchbox 20* head to the Powerstation on Tuesday, September 30. It's actually an "industry showcase" but there will be a limited number of public tickets on sale from Monday.

❏ And on the local front, *Bic Runga* (she of the No 1 debut album) starts her national tour early next month, playing Hamilton on Friday, September 19, and Auckland's Powerstation the following night. On the latter date Runga will be supported by the *Stereobus* in the Christchurch outfit's long-awaited live Auckland debut.

ALBUM REVIEWS

OASIS
Be Here Now (Creation/Sony)
Sunday News rating: ★★★

OASIS is constantly likened to the Beatles. It is an unfair comparison, but one which Oasis has helped perpetuate.

Using the Beatles as a guideline, Oasis has passed the Help! stage and is somewhere between Rubber Soul and Revolver. In other words, their Sgt Pepper is still locked in Noel Gallagher's fertile mind. Whether it materialises is open to debate.

Be Here Now is frustratingly good. It delivers 11 well-constructed, inevitable pop-rock epics, but there are too many dollar signs where there should be substance.

Radio and MTV have played a big part in giving the first single D'You Know What I Mean rock anthem status.

It's certainly representative of the album. One instant classic after the other, but few songs with character. Standout tracks are the slightly more whimsical Magic Pie and the second single Stand By Me which drags you subconsciously into sing-a-long mode.

American music critic Jim Farber panned the album saying. "Every song seems to stitch together hundreds of tracks as if parodying the Beatles dense odes on Magical Mystery Tour."

He also says Oasis has imitated every act it has admired. This is evident on the title track, which raises Marc Bolan from the dead to add the sort of guitar riff he patented with T-Rex.

All Around The World is Oasis' Hey Jude, but at more than nine minutes (plus a two minute reprise) it is self-indulgence.

It is not the only song on Be Here Now which is overstated. Every one could be cut by at least a minute, often more, and not lose any character.

It would seem to be an offshoot of Noel Gallagher's increased confidence with his guitar playing and production nous which over-reaches for a full 71 minutes.

Fault-finding aside, Oasis knows what it takes to sell millions of albums (or move some units as the Yanks would say) and Be Here Now is as sure fire a hit as you'll get this year.

It topped the British charts within four days and is believed to have gone platinum less than 24 hours after its release. Sales are well passed the million mark making it the fastest-selling record in British history.

The formula is simple. Undeniably catchy lyrics (don't read the liner notes because – like Duran Duran – the words mean so much more when you don't know what they mean), based on verse-to-bridge-to-chorus, back to verse-to-bridge-to-chorus then, chorus, chorus, chorus until its as familiar as the times tables at school.

By that stage, Liam Gallagher's nasally vocals are firmly etched in your mind though Farber has a point when he says you cannot find any character for his voice beyond smug irony.

It will be interesting to see if Be Here Now stands the test of time. Definitely maybe, Oasis will be devasted to learn George Harrison doesn't think so describing its music as "not very interesting". What's the story?

– Dylan Cleaver

RATINGS
★ Ask for a refund
★★ Bearable, just
★★★ Worth a listen
★★★★ Almost fab
★★★★★ Fabulous

Sunday News – Be Here Now review - Dylan Cleaver/Stuff Limited[69]

RELEASES

OASIS
Be Here Now (Creation/Sony)

You can always tell when a reviewer doesn't like an album. They'll pick on things like song length and conduct a statistical analysis of the most used rhyme. Forget the fact that Oasis have made yet another of the three best rock and roll albums of the decade (guess the other two). It doesn't matter how good it is, if you don't like Oasis then you won't like Be Here Now and you'll find plenty of petty things to pick on. (If this is you, put on a Blur CD and turn to the sports pages because you won't want to read on.)

Oasis have again encompassed all things good in rock and roll so we (new generations) won't have to waste our money on poor-quality recordings dubbed "classics" for showing flashes of brilliance.

Listen to this: after the familiar-sounding D'ya Know What I Mean?, My Big Mouth kicks in, taking you back to Oasis of 1994 with thrilling fast changes and in-your-face lyrics. "My Big mouth, my big name, who'll put on my shoes while they're walking slowly down the hall of fame?" Where the message of Definitely Maybe was "I'm gonna be famous so stuff you!", the message here is "I'm famous, up yours!".

Oasis match this message with sonic optimism, although they do seem to love ballads these days and Stand By Me is a lovely, full-bodied song. This is half of the album's appeal. Many '90s rock writers glue melodies to rigid structures that move from verse to chorus like someone turning the lights on and off. But Oasis let their melodies take a more liberal journey, making for more fulfilling works which don't shy away from cliches for the mere sake of originality. If the tune fits, they use it.

Fortunately, the album is not as wet as Morning Glory, the lyrics are more light-hearted. But as usual, the best songs are the fast ones: My Big Mouth, I Hope, I Think I Know, It's Gettin' Better (Man!!).

Any bad tracks? With the album's blistering pace, a couple of tracks seem out of place. Magic Pie, with Noel's dubious vocals, begins well but has a tired chorus. Likewise Fade In-Out.

Morning Glory was soft. Oasis are back.

★ ★ ★ ★ ½   **Bede McCarthy**

Waikato Times – Be Here Now review – Bede McCarthy/Stuff Limited[70]

Oasis' Be Here Now shot straight to the top of the British charts. Mike Houlahan finds the crown slipping on the kings of rock, while Karl du Fresne checks out comparisons with The Beatles.

OASIS have always walked the walk and talked the talk. One of the main reasons these five working class lads from Manchester are now the biggest rock band in the world is because charismatic lead singer and songwriter Noel Gallagher said they were going to be.

Attitude can carry you a long way. And it certainly carried Oasis through the storm of (What's The Story) Morning Glory. They've ripped off The Beatles, carpers sneered. Oh yes? And The Beatles never borrowed an idea? For its glorious marriage of melody and rock, Morning Glory remains the best album released in the 90s.

Which means, you guessed it, Be Here Now doesn't reach that exalted peak. Many times Noel Gallagher's genius shines bright, but others, where he seems to have got the jitters, where compromises have been made, where judgments have not been backed.

Opening track and first single **D'You Know What I Mean** is not one of those. A stirring clarion call, it opens with morse code beeping and chopper blades whirring before dissolving into a chorus which speaks straight to the heart of Oasis' audience. It's the band's most exciting single since Some Might Say.

My Big Mouth, a searing guitar work out, is also fine. **Magic Pie**, Noel's single vocal effort, is a bit of a mess however.

Is **Stand By Me** this album's Wonderwall? No doubt the record company hopes so, but this big ballad isn't quite as good. **I Hope, I Think, I Know** reprises Definitely Maybe's Rock And Roll Star, with Liam's defiant "Cos baby after all, you'll never forget my name," a scream against anonymity.

The Girl In The Dirty Shirt is a bit of an oddity. Mike Rowe's keyboards lead the way on a song which meanders like some mid 70s US southern rock number. Probably the weakest thing after Magic Pie.

Fade In-Out is another big guitar track, with Johnny Depp, of all people, guesting on slide guitar. **Don't Go Away** is ballad number two, and it leads into the title track. As you'd expect, **Be Here Now** does the business. A cracker of a tune and huge racket of a riff, with Liam roaring he's been "Kickin'" up a storm from the day I was born". No arguments there.

All Around The World is a bit of a worry though. Noel's summoned a string section and seemingly attempted his own version of All You Need Is Love.

Luckily, Be Here Now finishes resoundingly. **It's Gettin' Better (Man!!)** is the best song here after the single. It's got a classic chorus and guitars by the score.

Matching Morning Glory was always going to be tough. Beating it may perhaps have been too good to be true, but that's what we should have expected, because that's what Oasis led us to believe they could do.

Be Here Now isn't a disappointment. It is, however, a little anticlimactic. At times Oasis has seemingly settled for second best, something they've never claimed to be. Oasis still wears the crown; but it's slipped just a bit.

– *Mike Houlahan*

Evening Post – Be Here Now review – Mike Houlahan/Stuff Limited[71]

The Oasis Wonderwall of sound

OASIS "Be Here Now" (Creation/Sony)
★★★★★
Phone 366-6644 enter **2721**

Bandleader Noel Gallagher reckons this is an out-and-out rock record, with "about 50 guitars on every track". He's not kidding.

The third album by Oasis, the Manchester group who have dominated British pop in the last three years with their outspoken ways and Beatles-inspired music, is an enormous-sounding stream of anthemic rock and roll.

Its 12 tracks clock in at an average of six minutes, no small part of it thanks to the preponderance of introductions and fade-outs. Here, in particular, the music is buffeted by atmospherics like backwards loops, sound samples, and feedback (check Fab Four influences somewhere between "Tomorrow Never Knows" and "Strawberry Fields").

The effect of this cyclone of six-string and assorted noise, with Liam Gallagher's Johnny Rotten-meets-John Lennon whine resonating mesmerically over the top, is almost head-spinning, but it also makes for an exciting listening experience. It is the aural equivalent of the space ships of "Independence Day" hovering overhead; it feels huge and loud at any volume.

Mind you, if all the din were simply to cover up a shortage of good tunes, its appeal would quickly fade. But if there is one thing that Oasis have built their reputation on, it is plain, unpretentious, good melodies that people can hum or nod along to. That's what makes timeless songs like "Don't Look Back in Anger" and "Champagne Supernova" appeal to mums, dads, and boppers, rather than just the fashionable few.

Noel Gallagher has got a fantastic touch as a rock writer, and this is where critics who accuse him of simply Beatles-filching get it wrong. OK, the sound is certainly borrowed and built on, but essentially it is the musical values that the Gallaghers adopt, not the music itself. If that were the case, Sir Paul McCartney would be in litigation, rather than patting Noel Gallagher on the back, and Noel would not be humorously sprinkling Beatle references throughout his lyrics.

Not surprisingly, especially at a time when Oasis's last disc, "(What's the Story) Morning Glory?", is assuming the status of a 90s rock classic, "Be Here Now" is brimming with Oasis's optimism, can-do attitude, and stroppy confidence, and there is a sense of community-embracing as well.

The latter is noticeable in "D'You Know What I Mean?", the droning, stadium-proportioned single that opens the album, and "All Around the World", a buoyant

Brothers Liam, left, and Noel Gallagher, of Oasis.

DISCS

singalong with a "We're gonna make a better day" sentiment that helps put it somewhere in the neighbourhood of "All You Need is Love".

An instrumental reprise of "All Around the World" brings the curtain down on the LP in grand, Pepperesque fashion.

Elsewhere, the album divides along the line of plaintive, guaranteed hummable ballads ("Stand by Me", "Don't Go Away", both featuring string arrangements) and roaring, exuberant rockers ("My Big Mouth", "I Hope, I Think, I Know", "Be Here Now", "It's Gettin' Better Man!!"). Either way, Liam shows that there is probably no stronger singer in rock.

Noel — who writes all the songs, sings one, and co-produced the disc with Owen Morris — also sees in a few variations.

There's a hint of Badfinger here ("Magic Pie"), the funky keyboards of the Small Faces there ("The Girl in the Dirty Shirt"), and a bluesy, twangy departure featuring slide guitar by none other than Johnny Depp ("Fade In/Out").

"Be Here Now" is a whopper of an album, accessible, exciting, and with lots to absorb. It will certainly be producing singles and rattling neighbourhood windows.

If it does not top its immediate predecessor, the least we can expect it to do is confirm in people's minds — and bring home to America — that this is currently the hottest rock and roll band in the world. —*Alistair Armstrong*

SMOG "Red Apple Falls" (Flying In)
★★★★★
Phone 366-6644 enter **2720**

The bare, emotional songs of Smog (aka Bill Callahan) are exquisitely bleak in the way of the Red House Painters' and Sparklehorse's music.

"Red Apple Falls" has an inherent sense of loneliness. Songs about strangers and solitude are saved from moroseness by the contented resignation that pervades Callahan's low, husky vocals.

Nowhere does he sound more resigned — or more content — than on "To Be of Use". "Most of my fantasies are to be of use," he sings, gently plucking an acoustic guitar, which, aside from an occasional lament on pedal steel, is the only back-up to his melody-holding vocal.

Not all the songs are as stripped of accompaniment. Callahan also makes understated use of Hammond organ, trumpet, and French horn, but "Red Apple Falls" is unlikely to be accused of being upbeat.

Smog is probably regarded by some as depressing, but there is a sparse, melancholic beauty here that will make perfect sense to those who like their music bleak sometimes. —*Sharon McIver*

Ratings: ★★★★★ Excellent, ★★★★ Very good, ★★★ Good, ★★ Fair, ★ Poor

The Press – Be Here Now review – Alistair Armstrong/Stuff Limited[72]

59

Hook, line and swagger

By Nick Bollinger

BE HERE NOW, Oasis (Creation/Sony)

Liam Gallagher looks as if he'd rather be watching *EastEnders*, and the rest of the band might have been picked at random from a Manchester football crowd, but don't be fooled; not since U2 has a band been so intent on world domination.

Even the name Oasis – which implies an island of inspiration in a musical desert – has an arrogant swagger to it.

Like its hit-laden predecessors, *Be Here Now* has the musical swagger to match the hubris of the group's name. When Liam Gallagher sang "Tonight/I'm a rock'n'roll star" in the opening song of their first album, he was nothing of the sort, yet his audible sneer conveyed an absolute certainty of what he would become. Now, whatever he sings sounds like "I told you so".

His brother, songwriter and guitarist Noel Gallagher, never aims for anything less than a rock anthem. No alienating spiky riffs or one-chord dance grooves;

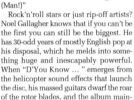
Oasis: if you can't be first, you *can* be biggest.

he concocts the type of generous tunes that defined 60s Britpop, sometimes borrowing entire melodic phrases from the writers of that era. The opening track and first single, "D'You Know What I Mean?", is typical, stacked with melodic hooks that seem instantly familiar. The first hook is the verse, which leads straight into a bridge so catchy that you think it must be the chorus, until the chorus finally arrives to grab you with the biggest hook of all.

Noel knows that the sound of a pop song is more important than any literal meaning one might extract from it. In fact, the sound *is* the literal meaning. So, if his lyrics seem to be no more than good titles fleshed out with vaguely related phrases, again it is those hooks that count. "D'You Know What I Mean?"; "Don't Go Away"; "Be Here Now": slogans that could sell Coca-Cola or rock'n'roll. Again, when he can't think of his own, he filches unashamedly: "Stand By Me", "It's Getting Better (Man!)"

Rock'n'roll stars or just rip-off artists? Noel Gallagher knows that if you can't be the first you can still be the biggest. He has 30-odd years of mostly English pop at his disposal, which he melds into something huge and inescapably powerful. When "D'You Know … " emerges from the helicopter sound effects that launch the disc, his massed guitars dwarf the roar of the rotor blades, and the album main-

tains that sonic scale through the punk-tempo "My Big Mouth" to the power-ballads of "Magic Pie" and "Don't Go Away". Just to make sure we get the message, many of these songs have outros that exceed "Hey Jude" proportions, running on for anything up to 10 minutes.

For the best part of three decades, British pop has lived in the shadow of the sacred 60s. But Oasis are far enough away from the epicentre of Britpop's first blast not to be overawed. Cocksure, and with a cunning sense of pop-craft, they simply grab whatever they require to make themselves the rock'n'roll stars of the 90s.

SHORT TAKES James McMurtry *It Had to Happen* (Sugar Hill): After three major label albums failed to win him more than cult admiration, this laconic guitar-pickin' son of Texan author Larry McMurtry (*The Last Picture Show*) retreats to the indies, his wry world view confirmed. Definitive verse: "Can you play 'Stairway to Heaven'?/Are you good enough?/Were those songs real/or did you make them up?" … **June Tabor** *Aleyn* (Topic): Tabor may be the singer's singer of English folk, but this powerful, dark collection finds her stunning voice in settings (accordion, clarinet, piano) that are closer to German cabaret. Great material by Richard Thompson and Ralph McTell rendered dramatically alongside ancient English ballads … **Guided by Voices** *Mag Earwhig* (Matador) Robert Pollard's usual jingle-sized fragments are interspersed here with more standard power-pop tunes, and the old eight-track is retired in favour of a cleaner studio sound. Otherwise, as obstinately oblique and sporadically superb as these prolific Ohio lo-fi-ers have ever been … ∎

NZ Listener – Be Here Now review – Nick Bollinger[73]

After an initial five-week run in the top 10 of the New Zealand album chart, *Be Here Now* soon faded into obscurity, slipping off the chart by the end of the year, with the release of the single 'Stand by Me' failing to reignite sales. Meanwhile in the Northern Hemisphere, the album went on to become the UK's biggest-selling album of 1997, most of these achieved within the first fortnight. Despite the initially positive reviews, opinion soon changed. *Be Here Now* was being described as a bloated, lengthy mess - a soundtrack of a band on drugs and out of control. The Oasis party was ending, just as albums by The Prodigy, Radiohead and The Verve all achieved critical and commercial success.[74] On the eve of launching the *Be Here Now* tour in Europe (a handful of gigs in the USA supporting U2 started the overall tour in June 1997), the death of Princess Diana signalled a change in the mood of the nation, and Oasis just didn't seem to fit the bill anymore. Despite selling over eight million copies, the album failed to live up to the great expectations set after the monster success of its predecessor. The European leg of the tour kicked off in Oslo, following a brief visit to the USA for *Saturday Night Live*, the tour continued across Europe culminating in a full UK arena tour. Liam was forced to miss two gigs in Dublin to rest his voice and one was cut short in Glasgow when a vodka bottle was thrown on stage, hitting Bonehead's leg.[75] A North American leg was booked in for January 1998 and on December 1 it was announced via the Oasis website that the band would travel to Australia in late February, but there was no word of a trip to New Zealand.

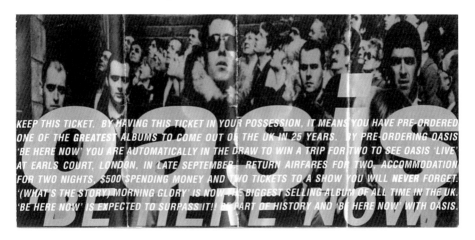

Pre-order voucher issued to buyers of *Be Here Now* – image courtesy of Ryan Holmes

Chapter 4 – Right Here Right Now

'I was doing this TV thing the other day for Australia and they said, 'When are you coming to Australia?' It's twice we've blown them out, and New Zealand too . . . it was all sold out last time, and we were really, really, really looking forward to going. We were supposed to do The Big Day Out with Primal Scream as well – we were like, 'It's gonna be like The Who and The Small Faces out there!' 'Hopefully, we'll get there before the band splits up. We'll probably start off the reunion tour there in 2007 when we've all got big colostomy bags like The Grateful Dead.' – Noel Gallagher, August 1997[76]

The Be Here Now tour continued to grow while the band was on the road, with new dates in the USA added. Tours of Hong Kong, Japan and Australia were confirmed and on January 6, 1998, an announcement on the Oasis website indicated dates for New Zealand would soon be announced. The big news came on January 17, when the dates and venues were confirmed. Oasis was coming for two gigs, one in Auckland and the other in Wellington. The local press soon spread the word with adverts and announcements appearing in *The New Zealand Herald, Dominion, Evening Post, Sunday News, Rip It Up, Tearaway* and *Music Press Magazine*. TV coverage also included segments on *One News*.

Oasis planning to be here soon

After a week of speculation, big-selling British rock band Oasis have been confirmed for two New Zealand concerts in early March.

The band — which was orginally scheduled to play in Auckland in November 96 but postponed that show after internal ructions — is riding on the back of the recent *Be Here Now* album. While it didn't do the sales figures expected, the record kept them at the top of the British charts and their arrogant behaviour in the tabloids.

Oasis have sold 25 million albums worldwide, won numerous awards and their *(What's the Story) Morning Glory* album is credited with six-times-platinum sales in New Zealand (around 90,000 copies).

Oasis have rarely been out of the news with their outspoken songwriter Noel Gallagher and brother Liam grabbing headlines for making outrageous claims for their abilities — all justified by the success of *Morning Glory* — and rock'n'roll excesses.

Noel Gallagher admitted last month *Be Here Now* wasn't a great album, "but I don't think anyone has written a great album this year," and said he was looking forward to getting out of England "because everyone seems to have a bit of a downer on us at the moment."

Oasis will play at the Queens Wharf Events Centre in Wellington on Tuesday, March 10, and in Auckland at the North Shore Events Centre on Wednesday, March 11. Tickets go on sale at the usual outlets on Wednesday.

The New Zealand Herald article announcing 1998 tour[77]

news

World first for rock fans

Rock supergroup Oasis will play its smallest ever concert on the North Shore. But that's good news for Kiwi fans.

The 4000-person capacity of the North Shore Events Centre has the intimacy that many overseas stadiums – which hold tens of thousands of people – don't have.

Oasis will play the venue on March 11.

Nicki Tysall of The Sequel, Oasis' agent in New Zealand, says the events centre gig will be of the best places to see Oasis anywhere in the world.

"It will be the smallest venue Oasis will play at this stage of their career. I'd always put my money on them to sell out in New Zealand."

Oasis has played to   crowds of 125,000 on two consecutive nights, at Knebworth, during a summer tour of England.

The crowd attendance at these shows set an all-time UK record for

North Shore bound: Liam Gallagher (left) and brother Noel

paid admission to a concert.

In comparison, the North Shore Events Centre will be the best chance for diehard fans to see the often feisty Gallagher brothers, Liam and Noel, up close and personal.

Ms Tysall says the band's popularity has increased because this will be

its first visit here.

Sales of Oasis' latest album, Be Here Now, have nearly reached double platinum (30,000 copies) in New Zealand.

Tickets to the North Shore Oasis show are $60 for general admission and $70 for reserved entry.

North Shore News article on the upcoming tour[78]

Music Press Magazine tour advertisement[79]

The Auckland concert was scheduled to take place at the North Shore Events Centre, a multi-purpose building more used to hosting sports fixtures and expos in amongst a few local and international music gigs. Blur used the centre for their Auckland concert on October 24, 1997, confirming its utility as a legitimate rock music venue. The Wellington gig was to be held at the Queens Wharf Events Centre (now the TSB Bank Arena). Again, another multi-purpose venue located on Wellington's waterfront. Tickets went on sale for both on January 21, with reportedly 'high demand' for tickets, particularly in Wellington. The next day articles in the *Evening Post* did offer a word of caution, stating that refunds would be available should the tour follow in the footsteps of the two previous failed attempts.

Evening Post – crowd queuing for tickets – Mike Houlahan/Stuff Limited[80]

MORNING GLORY: An elated Oasis fan Anthony Rickard displays a handful of tickets he bought after queuing for almost three hours outside Wellington's Opera House yesterday.

Fans had started queueing for tickets as early as 5am, and by late afternoon half of the 5000 tickets for the Wellington concert had been snapped up.

British band Oasis is coming to New Zealand in March and will play at Wellington's Queens Wharf on March 10 and Auckland's North Shore Events Centre on March 11. The band was to have played in Auckland in 1996, but canned the concert after frontmen Liam and Noel Gall-agher had a row, fuelling speculation that the band would fold.

By the time the ticket outlet opened at 9am yesterday more than 200 fans were queuing.

Auckland-based promoters the Sequel said that by 4.30pm more than half the tickets had been sold with Wellington sales much stronger than in Auckland.

Dominion – Oasis fan Anthony Rickard snaps up tickets – Stuff Limited[81]

Queue for Oasis tickets. Photographer unidentified. January 21, 1998. *Dominion Post* Collection[82]

Queue for Oasis tickets. Photographer unidentified. January 21, 1998. *Dominion Post* Collection[83]

Queue for Oasis tickets. Photographer unidentified. January 21, 1998. *Dominion Post* Collection[84]

The tour announcement reignited interest in the band. *Be Here Now* made its way back into the album chart on January 25, for a short run thanks to fans getting increasingly hyped for the shows. A new single released in late January 'All Around the World' outdid the previous single 'Stand by Me', peaking at #24 as part of a six-week run on the chart[85]. This would be the last Oasis single to crack the top 30 in New Zealand. Local papers promoted competitions to introduce the band live on MTV in London. Music magazines were gearing up for the tour too, securing interviews with the band early on. Noel and Liam promised their fans that all the shenanigans of previous years were now behind them and that the tour in New Zealand was going to be great.

Capital Times MTV competition advert[86]

Rip It Up cover, issue 247 – photograph by Brian Rasic[87]

Working Class Heroes

In the last four years Oasis have been in yer face. And fair enough. They've released two and a half great albums, a bunch of classic singles, offended all the right people, and stuck one or two digits in the faces of the smug middle classes. Sure, the Stones, the Pistols and even the Stone Roses have ruffled a few bourgeois feathers, but it was often publicity seeking art school prankster stuff. For Oasis it's different because here's a working class band who've made it mega and they haven't been prepared to compromise either their music or behaviour. Irvine Welsh, in January 1997's *Loaded*, reckons they get patronised because they're working class and successful. Liam agrees.

"The other side don't like to see us doing well. But you get a lot of that shit from all over, jealous people that like to keep you down. They don't like to see you running wild or having a bit of freedom, doing what you fucking want, saying what you want, getting into trouble, getting out of trouble. Years ago when we had no fucking money and you got into trouble it was hard to get out of it. And they don't like that. But I don't give a fuck what any cunt thinks, whether it's good or bad.

"We started a band because we like it, we didn't give a fuck whether other people liked it or not. It's nice to be understood, but it's also nice not to be understood so if a guy comes up in a fucking big cowboy hat and says, 'hey yeah, I understand you guys,' you think oh shit start again mate."

The Gallaghers are seldom out of the music press. Their 'couldn't give a fuck' attitude protects them from the hypocrisies of the music business. It also makes great copy. Noel has been getting a bit of flak recently for telling people to 'get over' Princess Di's death, and for his 'shoot the Queen' quote last December on Radio Milan.

"He's right though, keeps them on their toes, d' you know what I mean? Maybe he's been having a bad day and he starts fucking crowing. I think it's great, though. But when Princess Di got killed it really freaked me out. And I'm arsed when anyone says that it wasn't rock 'n' roll, what's fucking rock 'n' roll? It freaked me out that she died because I've been in that situation meself with the cars chasing an' all that. And I thought, right the press need a bit of a slapping for this one, and I look forward to them getting their limp wrist slapped.

"I'm not anti-royal, I don't give a fuck about them basically as they don't affect me that much. If you're anti-royal you're a fucking knob-head. What is there to be anti about? If that old bag of a Queen gets to young people then where the fuck's the young people's heads worrying about a fucking Queen? You can't give a shit about Queen Elizabeth."

Rip It Up issue 247 – Interview with Oasis – George Kay/Simon Grigg[88]

And late last year Noel, and an unscheduled and half pissed Liam did a live interview on Britain's Radio One. The phones are still hot. Did you get over the controversy that that stirred up?

"It never affected me, I was over it the day I did it. It was just two lads pissed up, not giving a shit and having the chance to have a rant. It's only as much as Chris Evans talks and he gets paid for it. He's a little cunt, the little bastard. We talked shit and I got drunk but why didn't they turn it off if it was that bad, which I don't think it was. I loved it, I might go back and do another one. I'll have plenty to rant about as soon as we've finished this tour."

In the interview you disagreed with the Richard Ashcroft of the Verve's song/sentiment that 'The Drugs Don't Work'?

"Course they do, they must fucking do for him to write that one. He must've been on some fucking come-down on that one. It's pretty much, 'they've all gone mate, but let's get some more but we can't because the shops are closed.' I think you're telling a little porky pie there Dickie."

Is the Verve's Urban Hymns still on your list as one of the best albums of last year?

"Fuck yeah, it was the best album, wasn't it, besides Be Here Now?"

Weeeeell, let's say that Be Here Now sees the band just holding the line. The first two singles off it, 'D' You Know what I Mean' and 'Stand By Me' are a touch predictable, but the huge heart of their 'Hey Jude' — 'All Around the World', points at what the album might've been.

"I don't give a fuck what anyone says, I think Be Here Now is better than Morning Glory. Morning Glory was a phenomenon, it was one of those bits of magic, but it was only 'Wonderwall' that sold it in America, and songs like 'Champagne Supernova'. And are you trying to tell me that 'Stand By Me' and 'All Around the World' aren't as good as any of them songs. They're as good if not better."

"I don't read our reviews, I don't need to. I got told Be Here Now got reviewed well at the beginning and the people who reviewed it like the NME thought it was great and now they're saying it's shit. I don't bother with that, Be Here Now is as good as it was when we made it and every time I hear it, it fucking turns me on, man. There was a time when everything was Oasis, Oasis, Oasis, the news was fresh and everyone bought it. Nobody's forced to buy Be Here Now and a lot of people have bought it anyway, but it's not something I'm gonna get grey hair about."

Live Dates

Oasis are in our desert paradise later this month. Their two dates here are their final live shows until the princely year of 1999. The band are going on the proverbial summer holiday — no more worries for a week or two. So how's Liam going to fill in the time?

"I haven't the fucking foggest. I'm gonna chill out basically, put me feet up for a couple of weeks and then I might start writing some songs which I've never had the time to do because I've been too busy up and down and fucking running around. But I must have a crack at it."

Take in the World Cup?

"I might have a bit of that an' all or I might have a kid. I'm tellin' ya mate!"

At the time of this interview, Oasis are a week into a three week tour of the States. Liam reckons it's been going fine, but how important is America to the band?

"It's important to get out and get your music played. For me it's not as important as playing England or Australia. It's not fucking life or death as some people think it is, we're just playing our songs to people who bought Be Here Now. We've been to America about 10 fucking times and it's doing me fucking nut in."

The American media have criticised you and the band for

Be Here Now is as good as it was when we made it and every time I hear it, it turns me on, man.

It was a bottle of vodka. We wouldn't walk off stage for something soft, we're not a bunch of girls.

-Liam

standing still in live performances.

"It's something I'm really fucking strong about, this standing still business. It's alright for others who dance and get into it, but when we dance we look like a bunch of cunts and it's not in us to dance anyway. Our music's not about dancing but you can dance if you want to or just stand there, I don't mind. And if I just stand there, it's not as if my vocal performances were shit or as weak as fuck because there's pure power coming out, so of course I'm into it. I give 100% every fucking night vocal wise . And fucking Weller does it while he's jumping around."

Your voice packed in for a while late last year.

"Yeah, in the last tour of England I got a bit of a... sore throat."

Noel didn't sound too happy about it.

"Because he had to do some fucking work for a change, didn't he? He had to do the singing, the hardest job of 'em all."

In early December of last year

the band pulled the plug on their concert in Glasgow after someone threw a bottle of vodka onto the stage. What's the story?

"Yeah, it wasn't a rubber duck or something fluffy or soft that didn't really hurt, it was a bottle of vodka. We wouldn't walk off stage for something soft, we're not a bunch of fucking girls. It was half of a big bottle of vodka and fuck that, I'm not taking that shit. Stopping the concert messes up people's night, but it's only music, innit? And I'm not prepared to lose me fucking eye and neither is Bonehead coz he's got kids, and I think he likes both his eyes. And it was like, fuck that you cheeky Scots cunt, see you later."

So that sort of thing has never happened to the band before?

"Yeah, it's happened a couple of times in America so we pulled it. Little things come on to the stage and if you don't see them then that's fine. But when things blatantly come at you, then you give them a warning and then you have to pull it. But when it happened in Glasgow it's like [Glasgow accent], 'ye cannae do that in Glasgow, man, they'll fuckin' kill ye man.' But I go, 'we've just pulled it.'"

So what have you heard of New Zealand, what do you expect?

"I don't really fucking know. I know that it's a place I haven't been to and I can't wait to get there. I've heard it's good. I don't know how Oasis stand there but I'm keen to go and play somewhere new and fresh."

So what can we expect live?

"Just a mixture off the albums. We'll probably do 'I Am A Walrus' which we haven't been doing, and since we haven't been to Australia or New Zealand before we'll probably be putting a lot of the old stuff in. But we've got to sit down and work it out. Most of this tour at the moment is mainly Be Here Now and a few from Morning Glory. It's a good set and down your way we might just play for a little bit longer. It's gonna be cool, it's gonna be top, I'm really looking forward to it."

GEORGE KAY

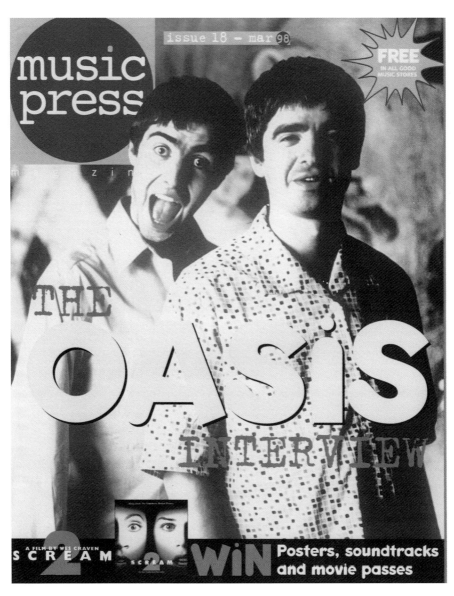

Music Press Magazine cover, issue 18, March 1998[89]

THE Liam & Noel SHOW

OASiS. Foul-mouthed rock gods to the lagered generation, Beatles try-hards and all-round stroppy buggers. Whether you think they are the quintessential nineties rock act or just a bunch of twats, there is never a dull moment chez Gallagher, as John Matheson discovered...

Music Press Magazine – Interview with Oasis, March 1998 – John Matheson[90]

THE MAN-CHILD was not happy. He couldn't sleep and he couldn't stop his mind from racing. It was heading towards dawn, a night in August a couple of years back. And there he was, sitting in a room in England, contemplating his unique place in the world, feeling restless and dreading the quickly approaching day that marked the beginning of yet another Oasis tour to the US. A few hours later, and 15 minutes before the plane was due to take off, he walked off complaining that he hated touring and in particular "silly f***in' Yanks".

History shows that Liam Gallagher eventually got on a flight to America three days later, only for brother Noel to instigate the cancellation of the tour, including a sold out gig in Auckland, 12 days later.

"We acted like a couple of c***s," Liam told ᴍPress as he prepared for Oasis' two dates in New Zealand this month. "I was sick of touring and I made sure that everyone knew about it. Noel was getting f***ed off with me and in the end we just packed it in. At the time it was the best thing to do 'cause we were going mad. We needed to take some time off. But looking back, we acted like a couple of twats. People were relying on us and we basically said, 'F*** this... we're off.'

"It's funny now 'cause while we didn't break up, we came as close as you can to packing it in. But I don't think we were ever gonna break up 'cause we're family. Family sticks together, do ya know what I mean? And we're still together and it's great. We're coming to New Zealand and it's f***in great. The whole tour has been f***in' great. When we got together to do Be Here Now after all the bollocks in America, we decided that if we were going to be in a band, we were gonna do it right. You know, instead of f***in' round, we were gonna be professional. And since that day Noel and I haven't had a fight... which is a bit disappointing because, between you and me mate, I'd like to take to him now and again."

Yes, believe it or not, the brothers Gallagher have matured... well, sort of.

Oasis' popularity in England is due as much to their Beatlesque lyrics and riffs and loud guitar sound, as to Noel and Liam's football-loving, working class roots and rebellious swagger... and they know it. So while they aren't insulting each other these days, everyone else is a target because unlike their carefully groomed and guarded contemporaries, they routinely and entertainingly lash out verbally without apology.

The latest target of Liam's wrath was none other than Sir Paul McCartney, after the former Beatle stated of Oasis, "They're derivative and they think too much of themselves. Really, they mean nothing to me." Liam promptly challenged McCartney, along

Liam, Noel and... the three other blokes

with George Harrison, Mick Jagger and Keith Richards, to a fight, telling a radio interviewer, "I will beat the f***in' livin' daylight shit out of them. If any of them old farts have got a problem with me, then leave yer Zimmer frames at home and I'll hold you up with a good right hook. They're jealous and senile and not getting enough f***in' meat pies. If they want to fight, I'll beat them up."

Cooler heads prevailed.

"Well, Paul McCartney was supposed to have said something in a French magazine about us. It's like, 'So what?'" says Noel. "And George Harrison's had a few digs in the press. But you know, Liam being Liam, I just said to him, 'Look don't even bother answering them.' You know what I mean? It's like they're all old men and past it. Of course, Liam being Liam doesn't see it like that. He has to have his little tuppence worth in there."

As far as Liam is concerned the threat still stands.

"Do ya know what? It's kind of sad that Paul and George are so f***ed up now. They used to be great guys. I mean, I'm still a Beatles fan. I like Paul and George as they were 25 years ago. But they've obviously got a problem with today's youth 'cause they hate us. They're very bitter old men. To be honest, I don't give a f***in' shit what those two old farts think. I'm glad they don't understand me. Look at the shit songs they come up with now. F***in' hell! It's hard to believe it's the same Paul and George that were in the Beatles. It must be embarrassing for them. F***in' old farts."

While Liam's ranting and Noel's knack of mastering the soundbite with quotes like "Taking drugs is as normal as a cup of tea in the morning" and "Oasis are bigger than God in England" continue to frustrate many, they just don't care.

"I try to get those words out: 'No comment'," says Noel. "I can say it at home in front of the mirror. 'No comment. I'm not at liberty to say anything.' Until I've had the first pint of lager, then that's it. But then you have to do that, really. You have to be honest."

Liam agrees. "I'm not here to bullshit the world. If I stood up there in front of a bunch of journalists and lied, then I'd be a f***in' sad git wouldn't I? I want people to know me when they meet me. I don't want the Liam Gallagher they see on TV to be totally different than the Liam Gallagher they're gonna meet on the street. Do ya know what I mean? They might think I'm a c*** or they might think I'm a nice guy. If they think I'm a c*** then at least I'm an honest c***."

It's an honesty that is a result of their childhood in Manchester. While both dabbled in shoplifting and street fights, they never forgot how to tell the truth. It was a childhood of love from their mother, hatred for their father, Tommy Gallagher. Along with Noel, Liam and her oldest son Paul, Peggy was regularly beaten by her husband, a womaniser who DJed in Irish clubs. After years of abuse, Peggy secured herself a new council flat and fled their home in the middle of the night, so she and the boys could start life over. Liam was 11 years old and escaped the worst of the violence. Still, one of his most vivid childhood memories is of seeing his father hit his mother on the head with a hammer.

"I stopped believing in God because of what happened to my mam. Her husband, which unfortunately is my dad, started knocking her about but she stayed in the relationship because of us. She thought she couldn't get divorced because that meant she couldn't take the body of Christ, which she'd been brought up to believe in. If she'd stayed with him and got battered she'd still be allowed to take the body of Christ. And does it taste good? Does it make you put on weight? Is it good for a meal? Is it f***. It's a figment of the imagination. If he died tomorrow, I wouldn't go to his funeral... and I want you to put that in. That's why I left him off my marriage certificate. Because as far as I'm concerned I don't have a dad."

One thing that will never change in the Gallagher households is their self confidence. After all, these are the brothers who along with guitarist Paul Arthurs, bassist Paul McGuigan and drummer Alan White, have given the world three of the most influential albums of the decade – 1994's Definitely Maybe, 1995's (What's the Story) Morning Glory? and last year's Be Here Now. Regardless of your opinion of Noel, there can be no doubting his genius. If Liam has the looks, then Noel has the brains. He's the one responsible for the Oasis sound, the man who inspires the dark, dirty, textured and layered sound that has seen Oasis become one of the biggest bands in the world.

Definitely Maybe was the fastest-selling debut album in British history. It stayed in the the charts for more than a year and the follow-up sold more than 12 million copies worldwide. Be Here Now is expected to eventually shift more than 14 million copies. They are the biggest British rock band since the Beatles and their earnings

Liam displays his legendary crowd management technique

reflect this. Liam is estimated to earn $NZ30 million annually, while Noel, with similar earnings, also holds the publishing royalties. With his catalogue wealth and accumulated assets his wealth is projected at $NZ90 million.

Noel may be the songwriter, the guitarist and the mastermind. But it is Liam, a cross between John Lennon and Johnny Rotten, who captures the imagination. Rock stars don't come much rougher or more charismatic. He has become both a symbol of the new lad culture – Loaded, lager, Vespas and V-signs... as well as a style icon. Thousands of young men now wear feathered haircuts and oversized anoraks and his oft-professed claim to be "mad for it" has become a national catchphrase.

While sales of Be Here Now haven't matched the massive numbers that hits like Wonderwall, Champagne Supernova, Roll With it and Don't Look Back In Anger helped (What's the Story) Morning Glory? generate, Be Here Now stands up as one of last year's best recordings. Readers of America's leading rock magazine, Rolling Stone, recently voted it Album of the Year. The singles D'You Know What I Mean? and All Around The World have hit No 1 around the world and tracks like Fade-In-Out and It's Gettin' Better Man are destined to follow.

Liam is convinced that Oasis are still the biggest band in the world. "I know that for a fact," he says. Noel believes they've lost that particular title... but only for a while.

"We were the best band in the world about a year ago but then we let it slide a bit by not turning up for gigs and various other things," says Noel. "I still have got an unswerving belief in the band but I've just decided not to ram it down people's throats any more. I plan to let the music speak for itself from now on. If every record I make is better than the last one, then to me that's all that matters."

Noel has been happy with the response to Be Here Now despite the slump in sales. "It's been brilliant everywhere around the world. Initially it was, how do you say, critically acclaimed but as soon as it didn't start selling as well as Morning Glory, then people started slaggin' it off a bit. So I'd say it's been 50-50. But reviews don't really interest me. When people come up to me on the street and say, 'Thanks for the music,' that's the only inspiration I need."

The inspiration for Noel's songs is another story altogether. He has a well-known habit of borrowing lyrics or chord patterns from

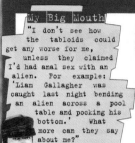

Noel revealing his sensitive side, just before massive lager consumption

other people's music. For Don't Look Back in Anger, he nicked a line from John Lennon and the opening piano part sounds like Lennon's Imagine. Some Might Say rips off Ooh La La by the Faces.

"It's easier than writing your own isn't it?" he says with a chuckle. "I'm getting sued left, right and centre but I wouldn't worry about that. Every song that's ever written has been ripped off by something else… I don't think anybody's done anything original for the last 30 years."

Regardless of where Oasis are on the charts, Noel and Liam continue to be the target of the notorious UK tabloids. In the last 18 months, they have delighted in covering any Gallagher story they can latch onto. In November 1996 it was Liam's drug bust on trendy Oxford Street (Noel says, "It's typical of Liam. Seven in the morning, two policemen ask him what he's up to and instead of being polite, he says, 'What's it got to do with you, c***ybollocks?'"), the cancellation of the US tour, marriages (Noel to Meg Matthews and Liam to Patsy Kensit) and fist fights with photographers. Not even last year's death of Princess Diana who was hounded by the paparazzi – even when she lay dying on a Paris street – has diminished the interest of newspaper editors.

"The thing about British people, they never voiced a concern about the treatment she [Diana] was given when she was alive," says Noel. "Soon as she's dead there's an outpour of f***in' grief that lasts for two weeks. It's like, 'What's the f***in' problem? The woman's dead. Shut up. Get over it.' It's not going to change anything, is it? I don't see anybody standing up for me. When a photographer's chasing me down the street, I don't see anybody getting out of the car saying, 'Leave him alone.'

I think people are more guilty because they bought the papers for her photograph more than anything else. It was an outpouring of guilt. It was not an outpouring of sympathy."

For Liam, whose house is constantly surrounded by the tabloid hounds, it is a case of preparing to face his enemies once again. Putting on his best Prince Charles voice, he rehearses the speech he plans to yell at photographers when he returns to the UK. "Have you got no feelings? I can't believe you're still doing this! You're wrecking innocent people's lives. Leave us alone! Murderers! You've taken one

life, do you have to take more? Brats! Rats! Leave us alone! Go away!"

While the press will still be knocking on their door, the other constant is sure to be success. While Liam will continue to woo the world with his powerful and unique voice (both on stage and in the odd attack on former Beatles or anyone else that manages to f*** him off), Noel will soon sit down to pen album number four.

"The next album is when the pressure's going to come," he says. "I think I've gone as far as I can with this sound, to be quite honest. The hype or the anticipation for the next album has already started to build and I've not even sat down to write the f***in' thing yet. So I would imagine the pressure's going to come then but you know, I've got pretty big shoulders.

"I've done Definitely Maybe, Morning Glory and Be Here Now in the space of four years, so I don't know any one person on the planet who could have pulled off three albums like that on their own in four years and produced all three of them as well and done the amount of touring and written the amount of B-sides I have.

"So, I'm not frightened. I'm looking forward to the challenge. I mean, we've done the loudest album and written the best songs, the longest songs, the best produced songs, blah, blah, blah. We've done the biggest gigs and the fastest-selling this, that and the other, so it's like, where do you go from here? And I don't know. But I'll have quite a lot of fun finding out." ◉

*Oasis play Wellington's Queens Wharf Centre on 10 March and Auckland's North Shore Events Centre on 11 March.

Two weeks out from the tour, on February 23, a press release announced a revised date and venue for Auckland due to a change in travel arrangements.

'23 February 1998

Oasis fans will now be able to see the band's first ever Auckland concert **two days earlier** *than expected. Due to a change in international flight schedules,* **Oasis will now perform in Auckland on**:

MONDAY 9TH MARCH

at

THE CARTER HOLT PAVILION

New Zealand Expo Centre, Greenlane, Auckland

ALL RESERVED AND GENERAL ADMISSION TICKETS THAT HAVE BEEN PURCHASED FOR THE MARCH 11TH PERFORMANCE AT NORTH SHORE EVENTS CENTRE REMAIN VALID FOR THE NEW VENUE AND DATE WITHOUT ANY NEED TO EXCHANGE TICKETS.

The Sold Out Wellington performance on Tuesday March 10th remains unchanged. *Oasis apologize for any inconvenience caused by the change of date and look forward to seeing their fans on March 9th. If unable to attend the new concert date ticket holders* **MUST** *obtain a* **refund prior to March 7th** *from the ticket agency at which they purchased their tickets.'* [91]

There wasn't time to reprint tickets and merchandise featuring the original venue. Tickets sold up to the day of the concert continued with the North Shore Events Centre label, but valid for the Carter Holt Pavilion. The *Be Here Now* tour programme, planned weeks in advance continued to list the incorrect venue. As the dates of the tour got closer, more interviews with the band started to appear in the press, including one with Paul 'Guigsy' McGuigan, not usually known for being interviewed – a true indication of the genuine interest in the band ahead of their maiden New Zealand tour. The documentary *Right Here Right Now* had a rerun on TV4 to add to the excitement days before the tour.

ONE (2) 3 4

AM

12.10 Home Shopping, 1.10 BBC World, 6.00 BBC World News, 6.15 Te Karere, 6.30 Telstra Business, 7.00 Breakfast, 9.30 Te Karere 10.00 UK Today,

| 10.15 | ONE WORLD OF SPORT - BNZ SERIES CRICKET - NEW ZEALAND V ZIMBABWE - SECOND TEST - DAY TWO |

PM

12.30	MIDDAY
1.00	BNZ SERIES CRICKET - NEW ZEALAND V ZIMBABWE
3.15	TE KARERE
3.25	BNZ SERIES CRICKET - NEW ZEALAND V ZIMBABWE
6.00	ONE NETWORK NEWS
7.00	HOLMES
7.30	MAGGIES GARDEN SHOW
8.30	RONNIE BARKER - A LIFE IN COMEDY

In his first television interview since bowing out of showbusiness, Ronnie Barker reflects on a career which spans over 30 years, and the memorable characters he has played.

9.35	TONIGHT
10.00	ALL RISE FOR JULIAN CLARY
10.35	THE LIVER BIRDS AO
11.10	MAD TV

AM

12.30 Martin, 1.00 Tropical Heat, 2.00 The Five Mrs Buchannans, 2.30 Movie, 4.10 White Fang, 4.40 Walker Texas Ranger, 5.35 Kenneth Copeland Daily, 6.05 Home Shopping, 6.35 Teen Wolf, 7.05 Animals of Farthing Wood, 7.30 Street Sharks, 8.00 Captain Planet and the Planeteers, 8.30 Barney and Friends, 9.00 Here's Humphrey, 9.30 Shortland Street, 10.00 Home Shopping

PM

12.00	THE YOUNG AND THE RESTLESS
1.00	DAYS OF OUR LIVES
2.00	THE RICKI LAKE SHOW PG
3.00	INFOMERCIAL
3.30	WHAT NOW
4.00	RUGRATS
4.30	THE TICK
4.55	AMERICA'S FUNNIEST HOME VIDEOS
5.25	MASH
6.00	HOME AND AWAY
6.30	THE SIMPSONS
7.00	SHORTLAND STREET

Rachel is forced to a reunion, Minnie is excited by a chance at romance

7.30	FRESH PRINCE OF BEL AIR
8.30	THE DREW CAREY SHOW
8.30	THE FRIDAY ACTION MOVIE: THE FUGITIVE

Action thriller as a Doctor wrongly convicted of killing his wife.

| 11.05 | WCW PRO WRESTLING INTERNATIONAL PG |

AM

1.45 Sally Jessy Raphael AO, 2.35 Homeward Bound, PG, 3.25 The Price is Right, 3.50 Infomercials, 5.00 Joyce Meyer Life in the Word, 5.30 Your Day with Benny Hinn, 6.00 Infomercials, 6.30 Oscar and Friends, 6.35 Magic Box, 7.00 Treasures Parent Time, 7.05 You and Me, 7.30 Off the Planet, 8.00 Ducktales, 8.30 Sesame Street, 9.30 Infomercials, 10.30 What's Cooking?, 11.00 Ansett Time of your life 11.30 Melody Rules

PM

12.00	OPRAH WINFREY SHOW PG
1.00	SALLY JESSY RAPHAEL PG
2.00	BEVERLY HILLS 90210 AO
3.00	YOU AND ME
3.25	THOMAS THE TANK ENGINE
3.30	CROCADOO
4.00	THE JUNGLE BOOK
4.30	HOGANS HEROES
5.00	FULL HOUSE
5.30	JUDGE JUDY
6.00	3 NATIONAL NEWS
7.00	HOME IMPROVEMENT
7.30	SABRINA THE TEENAGE WITCH
8.00	TEEN ANGEL
8.30	TEAM KNIGHT RIDER PG
9.30	FAST TRACK .
10.25	NIGHTLINE
11.05	AMERICAN ROULETTE AO

AM

10.00 Infomercials

PM

2.00	INTERIOR MOTIVES
2.30	NEIGHBOURS
3.00	SUNSET BEACH PG
4.00	MELODY RULES PG
4.30	GET SMART
5.00	SAVED BY THE BELL
5.30	SAVED BY THE BELL: THE NEW CLASS
6.00	CALIFORNIA DREAMS
6.30	NEIGHBOURS
7.00	SINGLED OUT PG
7.30	MODEL
8.00	DARIA: PINCH SITTER
8.30	OASIS RIGHT HERE RIGHT NOW PG

Documentary on the most suiccessful band to come out of Britain in decades as they return to their roots and visit their hometown of Manchester.

9.30	EGOS AND ICONS: ALANIS MORISETTE
10.35	RED SHOE DIARIES: LAUNDRYMAT
11.05	THE A LIST: BRETT BUTLER AND NICK DIPAO
11.35	COMICS ONLY AO

Nexus TV Guide – Friday February 27, 1998[92]

Oasis band members get on fine, specially the Gallagher brothers.
They are just all misunderstood or so says Oasis wild boy Paul McGuigan.
He talks to FLANN WILDE.

Geezers who know what they mean

Q. What's The Story has gone 12 times platinum in the UK and it's broken you in America. Are you surprised by that success?
A. It's a bit of both, without sounding arrogant. We sort of expected it to happen 'cos I suppose you have to otherwise you wouldn't bother doin' it. But when it happens it does surprise, you're surprised every time you release a record you never know do you? You're always thinking, will anyone like this?

Q. There were no worries within the group after the success of the second album that there was no way you could emulate it?
A. It's not really any pressure of thinking will it sell or not. The pressure is it any good? We think so ourselves, if we can impress each other. Noel's songs are always good, but if we can impress each other in the studio then hopefully everyone else will like it but if they don't, as long as we're 'appy with it then that's the main thing, originality.

Q. The new album is dense, very basic. There's not many strings.
A. Basically it's the usual gettin' on with it, just doin' what we do. I think the best way to look at it is as the last in a box set of three. The end of that trilogy and maybe we change a little bit from there.

Q. Last August was looking ropey for Oasis. Noel stormed off the American tour. Were you on the verge of splitting up?
A. Well it wasn't Noel storming off really, we'd just been on the road too long. Three years without a break and it came to a head but we had a chat before anyone went 'ome, we all had a chat about what we were doin' and the basic vibe was let's get back to England and get in the studio.

Q. Was it true Creation had an everlasting supply of cigarettes and alcohol on tap so you guys wouldn't abscond?
A. Ha ha. We wanted to go in the studio. Everyone was telling us to do these gigs and get back on tour but we wanted to go in the studio. It was us five and Owen Morris (Oasis producer) and a couple of our friends who just hung around and stopped us like from gettin' bored if we 'ad nothing to do, going down the pub and play pool or whatever.

Q. Now the third album is out do you think Liam has calmed down and realised he's got to be more professional? A. It's not calmed down, we're all just a bit older and we can't do it anymore. I'm 26 but I've got grey hair. Everyone still goes out and we still have a laugh but not as often. We concentrate on the music now but we have a good laugh when we don't 'ave to do anything but when we're doing something, that's the important thing.

Q. How do you think Noel and Liam's relationship has changed in the last year?
A. It's just everyone gettin' older and just getting on with things. It's changed with all of us over the years because we've been together for six years and we've known each other for about 15 so it's just when you first get put into a situation where you're livin' in each other's pockets for say three or four years there's bound to be ructions and there was between all of us but with brothers, one's the singer, one's the songwriter, it gets blown up. If you look back you'll see pictures of me or Bonehead with a black eye here or there so it went on. We got used to all that, we went through all that and it's something the press really picked up on but there was only a couple of ructions but we weren't smart enough to do it behind closed doors.

> 'If you look back you'll see pictures of me or Bonehead with a black eye here or there so it went on. We got used to all that, we went through all that.'

Q. Do you, Bonehead and Alan resent Noel and Liam get all the attention?
A. It's probably the other way round to be quite honest – with hair like that 'ow did he manage to keep in the background? Noel and Liam could do without havin' the media stood out on their doorstep every minute of the day and night and every single thing they say analysed to the last degree. But the press likes that and now it's an open secret the tabloid media are after us two now, me and Bone. They're given Alan another six months. I'll think they'll have a go at us but I've gotten nothing to hide.

Q. You had a nervous breakdown?
A. I never described it as a breakdown. Everyone keeps saying that to me. All that happened was I was ill one morning. I couldn't even stand or anything, no one knew what was wrong with me for a few weeks so I wasn't going on tour. It's that simple – I can't go on tour if they don't know what's wrong with me. I got diagnosed with irregular blood pressure, if my blood pressure was too low I couldn't walk or anything. It's a hereditary thing. I just had to take some betablockers and have an injection every three months.

Q. Noel claims he came up with the band name?
A. Nah. Noel wasn't in the band at first. He came in and said I'll 'elp you get a gig but he must 'ave seen something in us he liked so he said he'd write some songs for us.

Q. When Noel came in to take over, as he says, did you think, he's bossy?
A. Nah, I've known Noel for years. Noel's a double quiet geezer, he ain't bossy at all. He came to watch us rehearse and we didn't have any songs so we were just fiddling around so after about an hour he said I'll go and get me guitar' and he played a few riffs and jammed and that was sort of that.

Q. Do you think Be Here Now is your best album?
A. I think when we came out of the studio we couldn't have done any better. The day we left the studio we felt good. The whole vibe has changed and we came out of the studio totally happy about what we've done and I don't think we did that before because other things distracted us at times and we didn't have enough time and all sorts of different reasons. I think this time everyone got an extra 5 percent out of every little bit of it.

Q. What's your favourite Oasis song?
A. That's a damned good question. It might be the single at the moment D'you Know What I Mean? That single's got something a little bit different about it, it's like Wonderwall's big brother.

Q. Is there a side of the Gallagher brothers fans and the press don't see that you see?
A. Oh yeah, absolutely. It's the funniness of the pair, they're outrageously funny man. It's like watching The Fast Show. Noel's a top impressionist, you gotta get him to do some impressions. So people never see that. They see Liam as a loud geezer who goes round chinning the world and they see Noel as some sort of grumpy geezer who's got loads to say. When anyone ever gets near us, that's what they all say, 'Oh you're not like I thought you'd be.' I think they think we just go out and start smashing up the world.

Q. Are all five of you on an even cut?
A. We shouldn't be bashful about financial things but yes. The money I use to sort everything out, our mums and things. I just bought my mum's house, Noel and Liam have just sorted Peggy out 'cause she didn't want to move. Money's not everything. Obviously it's nice, I'd much rather have it than not. I've had none at all so I know what I'm talking about. Yeah, it's nice, it's great and it means you can live a nice life without worry, it takes stress out of your life.

■ Oasis plays the Auckland Carter Holt Pavilion tomorrow and Queens Wharf Events Centre, Wellington, Tuesday, March 10.

Sunday News Paul McGuigan interview, March 8, 1998 – Stuff Limited[93]

News Boys

While most bands are content with getting on and making music, Oasis are constantly in the headlines for less artistic reasons, sniffs Noel Gallagher to STEPHEN DOWLING

n O NEWS is good news, the saying goes. Except when Oasis happen to be touring. There should be drama. Fights. Walk-outs. A good-old-fashioned crisis. Drunkenness and foul mouths on airplanes, and ensuing behave-or-else warnings.

Let's face it – Oasis provide good copy. Before the most recent hour of laddishness, on the Cathay Pacific flight from Hong Kong to Perth, they were filling stadiums the length and breadth of the United States. Noel and Liam Gallagher were happy – and the rumour mill still flew into action . . .

A Friday edition of *The Sun* carried the story that the band would split at the end of this world tour. Noel Gallagher was bored with being a pop star. He wanted to call it quits, get out of the public eye. Perhaps the media intrusion, the fights, the soul-sapping slogs around America have finally proved too much.

But, in the grand traditions of tabloid journalism, all this talk was a slight exaggeration . . .

"I'm not even going to give the story credence by answering it," sniffs Noel Gallagher down the line from a hotel room in Dallas. "I've seen some twisted stories in my time, but this is a pretty good twist, I must say.

"We're playing in places that fit between 6000 and 12,000, and we've been playing those kind of venues for almost three years now, but no-one wants to write about that. They just want to write about the shit that goes down. I'm not going to sit here and gloat that we're playing bigger venues than any other British bands that come over here but we are! And I'm not going to sit here and say we sell more records than any other British band. But we do."

Despite the bravado, Noel Gallagher has every right to feel a little annoyed. Britain's biggest daily paper has just reported – inaccurately, as it happens – that the country's pre-eminent rock band are bailing out. The critical reaction to *Be Here Now*, somewhat inevitably after the hype and drama that surrounded its launch, has faded to grudging acknowledgement. And the zeitgeist defining qualities seem to have slipped, over-taken by the millennial malaise of Radiohead and, more importantly, The Verve's return from the brink.

But Oasis seem to be pretty stable. Now in their fourth year of genuine rock stardom, the brothers Gallagher still snipe and stir, but show signs of taking stock. The rest of the band – guitarist Paul Arthurs, drummer Alan White, bassist Paul McGuigan – seem happy with their job as the less famous faces behind the two frontmen. Oasis are doing what every big band does – learning to live with life at a very different level than it was four years ago.

But there are still traces of the bullishness of the past. For instance, the world tour is done the Oasis way, which means what might take two years for The Cranberries or REM takes them just three months.

"I'm never happy being away from England, but we'd decided that we were going to do the two-year world tour in three months," says Noel. "They've disappointed a few people by always seeming to cancel tours at the last minute but not this time. Oasis want to come Downunder. "Every day that goes by is another day nearer to getting to that part of the world. Everyone's well looking forward to it."

After Australasia, it's off to South America. Gallagher's quick to see the irony of the band on the loose in Brazil. "I wouldn't say they'd give us a couple of days to chill out down there, what with our reputation. I think everyone will be looking forward to getting home at that point." The thought of keeping Liam Gallagher out of the bar and – well, on the same planet – in Brazil makes you really feel for their tour manager.

And then that's it. A world tour which has taken in Europe, the States, the Far East, Downunder and South America in the time it would usually take U2 to travel from Pittsburgh to Portland. After that, Gallagher's not planning anything except a decent rest.

"I'm building my studio in my new house, I've just found a really old desk, and I'm trying to get planning permission to build something there. I'll be doing that and then – what will I be doing? I won't be doing anything! I'll be sat on the couch with the remote control to one 1000-channel television set and watching the end of the football, and getting ready for the World Cup. After that I'll probably go on a holiday with the missus, and then I'll start writing some new material."

On the eve of *Be Here Now*'s release, Gallagher said that Oasis fans – and there's still quite a few of those, even if the last album may not

TURN TO REVUE 2

Good news no news for News Boys

FROM REVUE 1

have sold as well as *(What's the Story) Morning Glory*, should build a box for the first three albums. The fourth installment in the Oasis story would be radically different.

And now? "I'm not in the frame of mind to be making decisions at the moment," he says, "cos we're on the road. We don't know who's going to produce it, which is not to say it won't be the same person as last time. Nothing's been decided except that Stage One is finished in April."

Certainly, a step away from the formula Oasis developed over the last two albums would be a healthy move – after the monumentally OTT (but still engaging) *Be Here Now*, Gallagher can't hope to add too much more to the bigger, brasher, bolder Beatles sound that's become their staple. So maybe that's why he's been collaborating with Goldie, and hanging out with Brit-Asian fusionists Cornershop, who have been supporting Oasis on the US tour.

He may miss England, but at least the world trip gives him a break from the English media. And though he's still genuinely friendly and easygoing with journalists, he's no fan of the tabloid treatment, and of the rather different influences on the band during their support slots, and has enjoyed the "you listen to my favourites, I'll listen to your" attitude as the dressing room after the shows. He's not writing on the road, merely concentrating on the gigs. He's even popped to the LA studios where the smashing Smashing Pumpkins have been recording and mastered with Billy Corgan.

So where do Oasis go from here? Who knows. Noel Gallagher isn't trying too hard to find that next direction just yet.

"At least that gives us a new set of parameters for the new album. The only thing I've decided about the next album is it will probably be done with eight-track, and the songs will be under four minutes long. Everyone from every c-rap to bombastic and pompous as All Around The World, you can't top it.

"What I'd like to do is a cross between *Raw Power* and some of the best things The Beatles have ever done. That's what I'd like to do, but whether that turns out the case is anyone's guess." He pauses. "It'll probably just end up like *Dark Side of the Moon*."

■ Oasis: Carter Holt Pavilion, Auckland, tomorrow, and Queens Wharf Event Centre, Wellington, Tuesday.

Sunday Star Times Noel Gallagher interview, March 8, 1998 – Stuff Limited[94]

In the background, unbeknownst to the fans, the wheels were actually beginning to fall off the *Be Here Now* tour. Three nights at the iconic Budokan in Tokyo and a single gig in Hong Kong went ahead without any drama, but the Australian leg that followed can only be described as the tour from hell. The brothers were mobbed at the airport in Perth, reflecting the pure excitement of the hundreds of fans waiting there to see them. Word soon spread of Liam's indiscretions on the flight from Hong Kong with accusations of smoking, throwing food and anti-social behaviour directed at air stewards, resulting in words between Liam and the pilot.[95] This was all strongly refuted by the Oasis camp in a press statement, but the Australian media had a bone to pick, due in part to the cancelled 1996 tour. In response to the fallout, Cathay Pacific issued a lifetime ban for all band members.

Cathay bans Oasis singer
Flint, John
South China Morning Post (1946-); Mar 12, 1998;
ProQuest Historical Newspapers: South China Morning Post
pg. 3

Cathay bans Oasis singer

JOHN FLINT

Oasis' Liam Gallagher has been banned from Cathay Pacific after he threatened to stab a pilot.

After the band's antics on a flight from Hong Kong to Perth last month, the airline said it would only carry it if it promised to behave.

But airline spokesman Kwan Chuk-fai last night said the position had been reviewed after executives saw television footage of Gallagher threatening the captain. He said all those who caused trouble would be banned.

Mr Kwan discusses the move in a letter to the *Post* today.

Staff unions are understood to have been pressing for a ban.

Mr Kwan said: "We have taken into account the welfare of our passengers and staff and the need to protect them."

Letter – Page 20

Liam Gallagher

Cathay Bans Oasis Singer – South China Morning Post[96]

This kind of media circus hadn't been seen since the infamous visit of The Who and Small Faces in 1968. Night after night and day after day Oasis ended up in the news or filling newspapers across the land. Shows in Perth, Adelaide, Melbourne and Sydney received mixed reviews, but in Brisbane, where the final Australian gig was scheduled, things really took a turn for the worse. Liam got into an altercation with a backpacker, and after being accused of head butting him, was arrested. The final gig was in doubt along with the remainder the *Be Here Now* tour. At a court appearance, where it seemed as if every single one of Australia's media outlets was in attendance, Liam was bailed for a $10,000AUD surety.[98] The case would later be resolved through the civil

Subjective
C. F. KWAN Manager Corporate Communication Cathay Pacific
South China Morning Post (1946-); Mar 12, 1998;
ProQuest Historical Newspapers: South China Morning Post
pg. 20

Subjective

In response to the letter head-lined, "Was safety rule ignored?" (*South China Morning Post*, March 9), I would like to address the questions posed by your correspondent.

First of all, passenger safety most definitely is a priority at Cathay Pacific. We go to great lengths to ensure our operations are safe and never hesitate to take any necessary course of action when safety is in question. The problem of drunk passengers attempting to board our aircraft is one that we face occasionally. We cannot possibly, nor would we consider, administering sobriety tests to every passenger. After all, the tired traveller who had a couple of drinks in the lounge and nods off to sleep after takeoff poses no threat.

It is the drunks who become abusive and confrontational after takeoff that are a problem.

Frequently these people show no obvious signs of impairment as they are boarding the aircraft and it is difficult for our staff to predict how a person's behaviour will evolve. While there are warning signs to look out for, there is no foolproof method because the entire process is subjective. It may also be of interest to your correspondent that since the incident, Cathay Pacific has taken the decision to refuse any further carriage to Liam Gallagher and people known to have been causing a nuisance on the flight in question.

C. F. KWAN
Manager Corporate
Communication
Cathay Pacific

Cathay Pacific discussing the Oasis ban – South China Morning Post[97] courts in the UK. The Brisbane gig went ahead with only half of the 14,000 tickets sold and received less than favourable reviews. The lack of an encore grated with attendees, and the Australian press and fans alike were glad to see the band depart for New Zealand. Oasis was no doubt relieved to be leaving Australia.

Fans watched on anxiously to what was going on in Australia. Although Air New Zealand refused to confirm or deny flying Oasis into the country, spokesman Cameron Hill said on the front page of the *Dominion,* that the airline would have no hesitation in calling police if alleged antics on the journey into Perth were repeated in New Zealand.[99] The story was also covered by *One News* and even New Zealand rock star Marc Williams publicly encouraged the band to get their act together. Nikki Tysall of local promoters The Sequel informed the *Evening Post* on March 7 that the tour would go ahead as scheduled. New Zealand fans were left worrying if their heroes would even land on Kiwi soil.

Singer on assault charge

BRISBANE — Rock star Liam Gallagher has been ordered to Be Here Now in June for an unexpected encore to his band's national concert tour.

Appearing in Brisbane Magistrates Court yesterday on an assault charge brought by a young fan, the Oasis frontman was bailed on a surety of $A10,000 ($NZ11,645) pending another court appearance in June.

Gallagher uttered only one word as he sat for his 45-minute appearance.

He answered "yes" to magistrate John Smith when asked if he was the Liam John Paul Gallagher mentioned in the summons.

The Manchester-born 25-year-old, whose group's sound echoes the Beatles, is on an Australian concert tour with the band.

The court was told he headbutted a 19-year-old backpacker fan from the United Kingdom who was taking his photograph on Thursday night on an inner-city Brisbane street.

Police prosecutor Roy Mientjes told the court Benjamin Russell Jones suffered a broken nose, severe swelling and pain as a result of the alleged blow.

"I'm instructed he is expected to suffer substantial discomfort during treatment and healing," Mientjes said.

It was unknown whether Jones would require further surgery.

Gallagher's barrister Kelly Macgroarty said his client would fight the charges.

The Oasis Australian tour has been controversial from the beginning, when the band and its entourage allegedly caused a disturbance on the plane flying into Perth from Hong Kong.

Mr Macgroarty fought for a reduced bail for Gallagher, whom the prosecution described as presenting such a "risk" of not reappearing, that he warranted the setting of a $A100,000 surety.

Mr Macgroarty described this as "extremely excessive", saying even alleged murderers were granted bail on a $A50,000 surety.

Gallagher, of Primrose Hill, North West London, was remanded on a $A10,000 surety for committal proceedings in the magistrates court on June 9, with three days set aside for the hearing.

Gallagher was scheduled to fly out of Australia tomorrow night for New Zealand and then South America, continuing his concert tour before returning home to London. AAP

OASIS lead singer Liam Gallagher is escorted into Brisbane Magistrates Court to face charges of assault occasioning bodily harm. REUTERS

Bay of Plenty Times, March 7 1998[100]

Bad Britpop boys told to grow up

By Andree Shelton

New Zealand singer Marc Williams believes the time has long passed since it was acceptable for pop stars to behave like little children as British rock group Oasis did last week on a Cathay Pacific flight to Perth.

The Britpop group, who play in Auckland on Monday, were accused of abusing other passengers, lighting cigarettes and generally behaving offensively while apparently drunk on the seven-and-a-half-hour trip.

Marc, based in Australia but in Rotorua to sing at last weekend's Lakeside '98, said that sort of behaviour was childish and inappropriate on a public flight regardless of who the band were.

"We've seen it once (this behaviour) and we don't need to see it again," he said.

Marc, part of the rock scene since the 1970s, said Oasis' petulance stemmed from the way bands in the 1960s and 70s behaved, particularly British bands.

"It's been a British thing since the

Marc Williams at Lakeside '98.

time I went travelling and touring with bands around New Zealand," he said.

Some performers remembered for this behaviour were Keith Moon and members of The Who — known for throwing TV sets out of hotel win-

dows, Marc said.

"I remember the very first time I went on tour in 1975 supporting Gary Glitter and (he was) very big."

Glitter caused all sorts of hassles during the tour while Williams said all he could do was watch with bemused interest.

"It's like an arrogance."

Williams said the "kerfuffle" on the Cathay Pacific flight could have been a publicity ploy by the band but also said the situation could have been blown out of proportion by the media, citing the fact that Oasis had been battling the tabloids "ever since they became huge".

Regardless, he said they needed to act appropriately on a plane where other people "who may not have a clue as to who they are" have paid good money to get to their destination in as orderly a fashion as possible.

"If you want to live it (the life of a bad boy) please live it away from us." **W**

Rotorua Daily Post, Marc Williams hits out at Oasis[101]

Chapter 5 – Auckland, March 9, 1998

Auckland gig advert with new date and venue,
published in the *Sunday News* -Stuff Limited[102]

New Zealand-based Oasis fans had experienced a rollercoaster of highs and lows, from number-one albums and hero worship to cancelled tours, but finally Oasis entered the country. They arrived on Air New Zealand flight 136 from Brisbane to Auckland, scheduled to land at 12:50 a.m. on Monday March 9, the day of the Auckland concert. The band crew travelled on an earlier flight, Qantas 141, arriving at 3.05 pm, providing adequate time for the crew to rest and familiarise themselves with their next assignment in Auckland. The early morning arrival helped offset the usual mob of fans that greeted the band, but some keen souls were still there to meet them.

Aerial view of Auckland Showgrounds. Building marked 'A' is the New Zealand Exposition Centre[103]

Elton and Billy face-off . . . while Brit bad boys arrive

Elton John, pictured at Ericsson Stadium on Saturday night, may not have been able to fend us any power generators – but hey, why don't we plug into his electric green suit?
PHOTO: ALAN SIMON

Oasis . . . arrived for their New Zealand gig with little fuss

By PHIL TAYLOR
staff reporter

Two of entertainment's most celebrated artists had 30,000 Kiwis in full flight at Ericsson Stadium on Saturday night.

The long-awaited Elton John (pictured above) and Billy Joel concert ended with the capacity crowd on their feet and singing along in fine voice to Joel's smash hit Piano Man.

These two may be old rockers, but they really do rock. They played and sang their way through hits old and new – the mainly older crowd particularly enjoying the older hits such as Elton John's Your Song, Daniel, Don't Let the Sun Go Down on Me, Goodbye Yellow Brick Road, and an especially rocking Honky Cat, while Saturday Night's Alright For Fighting had them on their feet en masse (despite the best efforts of the ushers who'd been instructed to keep everyone in seated areas in their seats). He also did a great version of Joel's song Uptown Girl – which Joel has sworn not to perform again because of its connection with his second ex-wife, supermodel Christie Brinkley.

Billy Joel and his band – who were clearly having a whole bunch of fun – also got the biggest cheers and applause for his older songs including Just the Way you Are. Joel is a real entertainer, and carries soulful ballads with aplomb, and handles rockier numbers like Angry Young Man, We Didn't Start the Fire, and Big Shot with panache.

One of the stunners of the set was a surprisingly good version of Candle in the Wind (the original Marilyn Monroe version), which the newly-knighted Sir Elton has sworn off since recording a re-written version in honour of the late Princess of Wales.

Before I went to the concert a friend told me to prepare for the disappointment of two tired old rockers who were past inspiring a full stadium to really rock. How wrong they were, and how glad I am that I was there. A top concert by two of the biggest stars in modern music history, face to face. Fabulous!
– Ruth Jackson

Manukau Daily News article on Oasis' arrival[104]

Noel Gallagher arriving in Auckland, March 9, 1998 – Murray Job/Shutterstock[105]

Liam Gallagher and Alan White arriving in Auckland, March 9, 1998 – Murray Job/ Shutterstock

Their home for the next two nights would be the Stamford Plaza Hotel on Albert Street.[106] Formerly the Regent Hotel, a change in ownership led to a name change to the Stamford Plaza in April 1996. Travel and accommodation arrangements were completed by Showtravel. To travel to New Zealand and perform, visas were required which were applied for in February 1998, while the band were touring the USA.

The venue for the first-ever Oasis concert in New Zealand was not what you would describe as an iconic setting. Set inside the grounds of the Auckland Showgrounds in Greenlane, the Pavilion opened in 1984, built by Fletcher Development and Construction.[107] A corrugated steel exterior greeted visitors as well as the name of Carter Holt Harvey on the side of the building, one of New Zealand's largest companies of the 1980s and 1990s that specialised in wood products and building materials. Inside, the largest of the halls was used to host exhibits such as houses, yachts and cultural activities. The Showgrounds were renamed the New Zealand Exposition Centre in 1989. The Carter Holt Pavilion was the largest of the three halls, occupying a central position, with a hall on either side where partitions could be removed to make a bigger venue. Inside, concrete floors and what was at the time to be believed, some of the largest indoor wooden beams used in the world.[108] The approximate capacity was 5,000, slightly bigger than the originally scheduled North Shore Events Centre which could only hold 4,000. Radiohead performed at the venue a few weeks earlier on January 28. According to the schedule of rentals on the Auckland Showgrounds website, the cost to use the venue was $4800 per day, with set up and stand down days at a 50% discount.[109]

Auckland wasn't spoilt for choice with venues in the 1990s. The Spark Arena didn't arrive until 2007 which is the indoor venue of choice for today's established acts. With the concert on a Monday, an outdoor venue was out of the question. Even if suggested, the likely destination of the Ericsson Stadium (now Mt Smart Stadium) wasn't an option with Billy Joel and Elton John booked in for March 8. The St James Theatre was hosting Joe Cocker on March 10 and 11. The Logan Campbell Centre was a frequently used venue, also at the Showgrounds, but the larger Carter Holt Pavilion was chosen. This was a step down from the 13,000 capacity Mt Smart/Ericsson Supertop when Oasis was booked in for 1996, indicating demand to see the band in Auckland had

The venue for the gig, the New Zealand Exposition Centre at the Auckland Showgrounds[110]

dropped in the 18 months from the cancellation. With the originally booked North Shore Events Centre hosting a Home Show from March 6 to March 8, offering little set-up time for a gig scheduled for March 9, there was no choice but to change dates and venues.

Having gone from crisis to crisis in Australia, they arrived at a city facing its own battles ahead of the concert. Starting in late February, Auckland experienced a series of blackouts. At the time Auckland CBD was supplied by four 110 kV power cables from Penrose Substation, connecting to sub-stations in Liverpool Street and Quay Street. The first cable failed on January 9, the second on February 9. The final two failed on February 19 and 20, sending Auckland CBD into a blackout. Generators propped up hospitals, central city businesses and hotels.[111] The workforce and vibrancy of the city centre disappeared overnight as workers were redeployed to areas outside of the blackout. International students at Auckland University were sent on a weeklong camp to avoid powerless halls of residences in the CBD. Elton John and Billy Joel's co-headlining *Face to Face* concert went ahead powered by generators, including those from the steamship *Union Cargo*, sent in by Mercury Energy to provide more power to the CBD.[112] The five-star Stamford Plaza Hotel where Oasis stayed was in the middle of the blackout zone. At the peak of the crisis, the hotel was 90 per cent full with no lifts, computers and a limited meal service. With Oasis and Joe Cocker arriving on the same day, General Manager Graeme Goldberg had his hands full:

'We just thought this is going to be an absolute nightmare, especially given the reputation Oasis has. I thought they would come in and look at the power situation, look at me, and then rip my jugular out. But what happened was it seemed to pull everyone together. It wasn't them against us; it was us against the power company'[113]

There appeared to be few complaints about the band's behaviour at the hotel, other than a quick telling-off and a confiscated ball for playing football in the hotel lobby.

The Stamford Plaza Hotel, Auckland[114]

The gig, as published in the updated advert, was scheduled for an 8:15 pm start. There was no support act. The tour itinerary produced by Michael Coppel Presents pencilled in Australian band You Am I for the Auckland support slot. They had already supported Oasis in Japan, Hong Kong and Australia. However, they never did fulfil the support slots in New Zealand. To perform in New

Zealand, overseas acts required work visas which often required support from the New Zealand Musicians' Union. Part of the deal to gain support from the Union was that international acts would use a local artist as a support act. In turn, the Union would inform Immigration New Zealand they had no objection to the tour. The final decision on visa approval was from Immigration New Zealand, but the recommendation by the New Zealand Musicians' Union heavily influenced the decision. Local promoters The Sequel indicated a local band would be used as support and the visas for the band were granted. The local band scheduled to support Oasis was The Stereo Bus but according to Bridget Darby of The Sequel, in an interview in *Rip It Up*, the change in date and venue for the Auckland gig led to their cancellation:

'There was a problem with us even having the shows in New Zealand, the Auckland concert date changed at the last minute, and at one point it looked unlikely that the shows were going to go ahead. The reason that we didn't end up using a local band, is that we shifted the venue from the North Shore Events Centre to the Expo Centre. The contract with that venue determines the amount of time we can make noise for, as the Expo Centre is right opposite Greenlane Hospital. At that point, that was the only venue available to us to shift the Oasis show to, so rather than cancel the Auckland show, we agreed to go to the Expo Centre and play a reduced amount of time. And rather than asking Oasis to trim their set back by half an hour, which I'm sure would have disappointed the Oasis fans, we chose not to put a New Zealand act on.'[115]

As part of this project, an application was made under the Official Information Act (1982), to the Ministry of Business Innovation and Employment, the government agency that manages the border and immigration, to access any surviving visas for Oasis. The following information was supplied:

'Prior to travelling to New Zealand in 1998, the members of Oasis applied for work visas under instructions for Entertainers and Performing Artists. These applications were submitted in paper form and processed at the Immigration New Zealand (INZ) office in Washington D.C., United States of America. The Washington D.C. office of INZ is now closed and the paper applications have been destroyed in line with INZ's retention and disposal schedule.

At the time when these applications were processed, INZ's electronic Application Management System (AMS) recorded the fact that visas were granted to the band in 1998 but the considerations that led to the decision on the visa applications are not recorded in electronic form. A copy of Liam Gallagher's record from AMS is attached as Appendix One as a sample so you can see the information that is held by INZ in regard to Oasis' 1998 tour to New Zealand. Some information has been redacted under section 9(2)(a) of the Act to protect individual persons' privacy.'

While in Auckland, Noel Gallagher took on media duties. *Havoc*, on MTV NZ, had turned into a one-hour weekly show that aired on Thursday nights. Noel Gallagher was interviewed by Mikey Havoc, but the episode in which the interview appears seems lost forever. No copies exist with Nga Taonga Sound and Vision, TVNZ, NZ On Screen or Mikey himself. All episodes of Season 2 of *Havoc* do exist, bar the one containing Oasis. In a surviving snippet, Mikey refers to the mental behaviour of Liam in the public eye and asks if Noel likes a bit of 'gentle mental' time on his own away from the others. To which Noel responds he's laid back in both his public and private life and that Mikey needs to talk to the others about their behaviour, though Liam aside, the others are 'boring bastards who got nothing to say'[117] Another interview with Marcus Lush on 91ZM has also fallen foul of inadequate archiving in the 1990s. NZME confirmed that radio shows from this era were not retained for archive. A brief summary of Noel's conversation with Marcus appeared in the *New Zealand Herald*.

Being the first performance in New Zealand, the setlist was a good mix of classic hits from the first two albums as well as *Be Here Now* tracks. There wasn't much variation in the setlist from the point the band toured the USA in January 1998. In the European leg of the tour in late 1997, Noel Gallagher introduced an acoustic set in the middle of the gig on occasion. This became a staple of the set from January 1998 onwards. Derived from attendee recollections, reviews in the press and seeing a copy of the setlist used in Wellington, assuming the same was used in Auckland, this is the setlist from the performance at the Carter Holt Pavilion:

Be Here Now

Stand by Me

Liam Gallagher

Application Number :	2607744 — Visa, Work, Entertainer/performing artist & support

Principal Applicant :	Gallagher, Liam			
Held At :	Hard Copy Destroyed (Purged)			
File Number :	**Section 9(2)(a)**	Case Manager :	Choy, Andrew	Change
Type :	Standard	Location :	Not Allocated	Change
Date Tendered :	03/Feb/1998	Date Accepted :	03/Feb/1998	Status
Date Decided :	03/Feb/1998	Date Completed :	03/Feb/1998	Accepted ☐
Decision :	Approved			Decided ☐
				Completed ☐

AMS - View Label details

Label Details

Label Number :	1134138		
Type of Application :	Work Visa		
Place of Issue :	Washington DC	Client Number :	**Section 9(2)(a)**
Start Date :	03/Feb/1998		
First Entry Before :	N/A	Expiry Date Travel :	26/Mar/1998
Number of Entries :	Multiple	Visa Expiry :	27/Mar/1998

Label Holder Details

Name :	Gallagher, Liam		
Travel Document Nbr :	**Section 9(2)(a)**	Date of Birth :	21/Sep/1972
Sex :	Male	Citizenship :	Great Britain

Label Endorsee Details

Endorsee Name	Sex	Date Of Birth

The holder may travel to NZ and on application may be granted a permit for/to 27/Mar/1998 Funds waived Outward passage waived The holder may work as Oasis Tour Group for The Sequel Limited in Auckland/Wellington

Identity	Gallagher, Liam 21/Sep/1972 Great Britain	▼

Date/Time	Arr/Dep	Flight	Disembarkation Port	Ref.	Embarkation Port	Travel Doc.	Visa	Expiry	Statu
09/Mar/1998	Arrive	NZ136	Auckland		Brisbane	**Section**	Work	27/Mar/1998	R
11/Mar/1998	Depart	AR1881	Buenos Aires Airport		Auckland	**9(2)(a)**			R

Liam Gallagher visa[116]

The New Zealand Herald – summary of Noel Gallagher interview on 91ZM[118]

Supersonic

Roll with It

D'You Know What I Mean?

Cigarettes & Alcohol

Don't Go Away – Noel Acoustic

Setting Sun – Noel Acoustic (The Chemical Brothers cover)

Fade In-Out – Noel Acoustic

Don't Look Back in Anger

Wonderwall

Live Forever

It's Gettin' Better (Man!!)

Champagne Supernova

Encore:

Acquiesce

I Am the Walrus (The Beatles cover)

Mission accomplished. The band turned up, they held it together and performed a full set with an encore. Now it was time for the press to write up their reviews, and overall impressions were positive.

Oasis' bad reputation a mirage

By KEITH PERRY

The British pop group Oasis appear to have gone from wild to mild after leaving their bad-boy behaviour across the Tasman.

The band played at the Carter Holt Pavilion in Greenlane last night.

Fears that the Gallagher brothers would cause trouble on a flight from Brisbane to Auckland proved groundless.

The pair were even praised by fellow passengers for their "gentlemanly" behaviour.

Air New Zealand passengers told how Liam quietly tuned his guitar in the airport waiting lounge while brother Noel practised his soccer dribbling skills to wile away time.

The hellraising duo even posed for photographs and signed autographs for fans before boarding the flight, which arrived in Auckland about 2.30 am yesterday.

The brothers slept for most of the four-hour journey.

"We saw Noel and Liam sitting in the Brisbane airport lounge," said passenger Mike Puru, aged 22, who works for a radio station.

"Liam was practising a few chords and Noel was tapping a football around. They seemed perfectly sober and well-behaved," he said.

"I was a bit nervous of approaching Liam because of his reputation but he was really pleasant and chatty."

Liam Gallagher is on bail for allegedly headbutting a 19-year-old English fan outside his hotel in Brisbane last Thursday night.

But the singer was all sweetness yesterday.

Passenger Xeina Williams, aged 17, said: "I couldn't believe it when Liam and Noel posed for a photo with me.

"I really like Oasis' music and asked if I could shake Liam's hand.

"He said, 'no problem, love' and stood next to me while I had my picture taken. He was great."

Only a handful of fans were on hand to greet the band at Auckland Airport.

Liam, wearing his trademark sunglasses, waved briefly to admirers before being whisked away with his brother to their city-centre hotel.

NO TROUBLE: Oasis frontman Liam Gallagher in concert in Auckland last night. The hellraiser was "really pleasant" on the flight from Brisbane, says a fellow passenger. HERALD PICTURE / GLENN JEFFREY

The New Zealand Herald cover story with an image of Liam Gallagher by Glenn Jeffrey. Article by Keith Perry[119]

Whine and loud song

Oasis
Expo Centre
Review: Russell Baillie

Well, it happened. After one cancelled Down Under tour and a turbulent time in Australia which seemed to threaten this one, Oasis finally made it to our manor on Monday night.

And while Aussie reports suggested the Auckland show was but a Liam Gallagher mood-swing or croaky voice away from turning farcical, it ran its full 90 minutes.

So the 5000 or so who endured the comfort-free acoustic nightmare of the Carter Holt Pavilion at the Expo Centre probably feel they got what they paid for.

Yep, Liam was suitably lippy between the songs (though a Mancunian phrase dictionary would be required for accurate quotation here) and gave good whine during them.

His brother, guitarist and songwriter Noel, certainly cranked that instrument as if there was no tomorrow, or no such thing as premature deafness — he being the main offender in dishing out the ringing-in-the-ears feeling from an often brutally loud sound mix.

And the other three, well, they turned up and seemed to know what was going on.

But it sure did limp along as a show, all the way to the closing encore of *I Am The Walrus*. You could blame that on the sound. But much of the fault lay with the overwrought, underfed numbers off the most recent album, *Be Here Now*, which dominated the set.

Live, they seem more time-consuming platforms for Noel's guitar excursions than much cop as songs.

Even with the sonic power of the likes of *Do You Know What I Mean* — featuring two additional keyboardists — the show emerged as a long finesse-free plod.

No, ironically, for a band with their own five-fingered reverence for rock's past, they, too, seemed to suffer from a case of the older, the better.

On tried-and-true tracks like *Cigarettes and Alcohol* (which took in a bit of Led Zep's *Whole Lotta Love*), *Wonderwall* and *Don't Look Back In Anger*, Oasis mustered real brash pop power.

So did Noel in his traditional mid-gig solo acoustic set, giving good ciggy lighter opportunities on the forlorn *Don't Go Away*, cleverly "covering" (he guested on the recording) the Chemical Brothers' *Setting Sun*, backed by conga and hurdy-gurdy, then into a Zeppelinesque *Fade In/Out*.

But overall it was a concert to remind one of the gap between money's worth and magic.

This might have achieved the former by going to full time, but wasn't within headbutting distance of the latter.

The New Zealand Herald review by Russell Baillie[120]

Not a tantrum in sight as Oasis boys turn up the charm

By KERI WELHAM

SINGING SUPERNOVA: Oasis' Liam Gallagher, left, sings at the top of his lungs while brother Noel strums through the band's hits. PICTURES: Kent Blechynden

Rock bad boys Oasis put their tour mischief on hold to play nicely for an audience jammed into the New Zealand Expo Centre in Auckland last night.

The five British men from the world's most infamous rock band hugged each other as they exited the stage before the encore, smiled at the crowd and threw friendly comments about.

"How about you, you having fun?", frontman Liam Gallagher asked. This suggestion that he cared was a change from the band's last tour stop, Brisbane. He is on bail for allegedly headbutting a 19-year-old fan outside his hotel last Thursday.

All eyes were on Gallagher and his brother Noel as fans watched for squabbling. But there were no tantrums and none of the tension reported after a Brisbane concert where fans stormed out of the venue in disappointment and the band apologised for terrible singing.

In humble little Aotearoa, the band restricted themselves to playfully pulling the fingers at photographers and poking tongues at young girls in the crowd.

The band played hits from their three albums including Live Forever, Supersonic, Wonderwall and Stand By Me.

Noel Gallagher, who took centre stage with his guitar and sang ballads partway through the concert, teased fans by offering to exchange his guitar pick for "two quid".

Waikato Times review by Keri Welham/Stuff Limited[121]

Oasis blokes aren't so bad

BY PHIL TAYLOR AND NZPA

They came, they saw, they played. Britain's biggest pop group of this generation, Oasis, flew out of New Zealand yesterday after a whirlwind visit to our shores, which included playing sold-out concerts in Auckland and Wellington.

Monday's show at the Carter Holt pavilion in Greenlane had been well anticipated by fans of the group who have waited four years to see them.

It was apparent from the first song that Oasis are not the dynamic stage performing types.

They prefer to rely on sound, of the powerful variety, and audience attention tends to concentrate on the volatile, stage-wandering, tambourine-tapping singer Liam Gallagher.

At the end of song four, "Know what I mean", the latest of the band's living anthems, Liam found exception with the behavior of one of the band's road crew and was hurling some pretty thick Mancunian abuse cross stage.

The gig could have deteriorated at that point and the audience must have wondered what had provoked Gallagher. It seemed that the liquid contained within the plastic bottle he was escorting around the stage was the prime subject of concern.

But, soldier-on he did, to his credit. Gallagher's been in an uncomfortable mood since arriving for concerts in Australia and New Zealand and his behaviour may be reflecting his longing for home in England. This particular Oasis tour has taken on some pretty mad dimensions, which hasn't allowed the band to breathe in the places they've visited. But, it's been an important tour for the band, an opportunity to deliver to fans.

Monday's gig showcased the band's blockbusting back catalogue of hits and anthems, and rousing versions of "Roll with it", "Wonderwall", "Cigarettes and alcohol", and "Don't look back in anger", were supported by a chorus of fans singing.

The set was closed with an extremely loud and stirring rendition of "Champagne supernova", which high-lighted the driving and influential sound of the rhythm section, bassist Paul McGuigan, guitarist Paul Arthurs and drummer Alan White.

For the boys, it was another day at the office and they didn't offer much in the way of expression, or even, physical leg movement. What they did provide was a lock tight foundation for lead guitarist Noel Gallagher to layer his memorable licks and twists.

Noel Gallagher plays with a variety of distortion and effects, which enhance his total understanding of what is required in a popular song. His playing may not be a clinical as a Clapton, or as quick as a Beck, or as dynamic as a Townshend, but in the fine tradition of great British pop guitarists and song-writers, he knows what it takes to write a tune that people will remember and sing in the street.

Gallagher also recognises pop history. He knows the sounds offered through certain guitars and amps and responds to each songs requirement.

For an encore, Oasis roared out of the pavilion with John Lennon's "I am a Walrus", ringing through the rafters and hissing in the ears of fans.

Oasis have been, they may not have been "magic" as some critics have reviewed, but they came. And, that's something in these days of the big corporate entertainment rip-off.

While in New Zealand, Noel Gallagher spoke about his hobby of collecting tropical fish, renovating his home and fatherhood, and the singer admitted he had been selfish and had acted arrogantly in the past.

The musician showed a quieter side to his personality, unlike his brother Liam, who stayed up until 4am drinking in his hotel bar after the band's concert the Carter Holt Pavilion in Greenlane on Monday.

"I've been a bit of a w**ker. I have been arrogant boasting about how much money I have got," he told radio DJ Marcus Lush.

But the musician said he had no regrets about his controversial views on the late Princess of Wales and the monarchy.

Gallagher, who attacked Diana as a "lazy cow" and sneered at the masses who turned out for her funeral, said: "My wife got a letter the other day from a 53-year-old British housewife who said she thought I was right what I said about Lady Diana."

"The tabloids in England say I am out of touch with what English people think, but I don't think I am."

"Most young people don't like the royal family."

"Admitting he had not written any new songs recently, the band's songwriter added: "I have not been writing for a while now. I've got a bit of writer's block at the moment. I need a rest, which is as good as a change."

Gallagher said he already had some experience of New Zealanders before this tour as a couple of Kiwis worked in his London office.

"The Kiwis who work with us are fairly mad so I expect that's what the rest of the country will be like."

And he said the band had no problem with travelling to New Zealand playing to smaller audiences because it gave loyal fans the chance to see Oasis rather than just reading music magazine reviews about concerts.

Manukau Daily News review by Phil Taylor[122]

98

The Northern Advocate review by Mike Dinsdale[123]

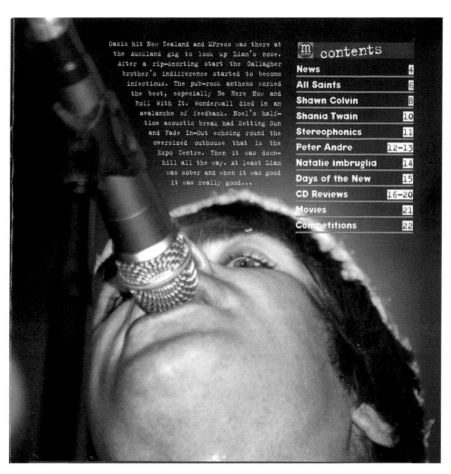

Oasis hit New Zealand and MPress was there at the Auckland gig to look up Liam's nose. After a rip-snorting start the Gallagher brother's indifference started to become infectious. The pub-rock anthems worked the best, especially Be Here Now and Roll With It. Wonderwall died in an avalanche of feedback. Noel's half-time acoustic break had Setting Sun and Fade In-Out echoing round the oversized outhouse that is the Expo Centre. Then it was down-hill all the way. At least Liam was sober and when it was good it was really good...

Music Press Magazine review. Image by Niels Schipper[124]

Thereafter, gentle versions of 'There Goes God' and 'Four Seasons in One Day' drew proceedings to a halt, almost two hours after Finn made his cagey promise to play the odd old tune.

Understandably, there were a few nervous moments tonight — it being one of Finn's first outings with his new songs and new band. But on the strength of what was on offer at Tabac, and with his debut solo album on the way, Neil Finn, with over two decades in the biz, is going to be one to watch!

JOHN RUSSELL

OASIS
Expo Centre, Auckland, March 9.

Rock 'n' roll. Oasis. Liam's sneering, well fed ego, the acoustic 'Setting Son', the deafening 'I am the Walrus', Noel's smart arse guitar improvisation — it was a night of extreme highlights for anyone who loves this band. This was the night we finally got to experience the band who've often been described as the perfect live contradiction. While Oasis do very little in terms of 'jump around entertaining' on stage, they manage to generate this massive compelling performance.

Tonight was a night of back to basics, a stadium band in the livestock shed. No huge lights, pretty minimal backdrop, it was like the early intense Oasis performances, before they started to play to hundreds of thousands of punters. Liam prowls around like a coked up gorilla, eyeballing the crowd, tapping his tambourine, and chucking in the odd one liner; "This one's dedicated to me 'cause I'm Supersonic." You're constantly drawn to him while he's on stage, and his live voice is more powerful than anything heard on record.

True, it wasn't all brilliance from the start. The first couple of songs were pretty lethargic, with 'Stand By Me' plodding along. But by the time 'Roll With It' raced out and revved up the crowd, there was more of an anthemic atmosphere. The rock monster was in full effect with 'Cigarettes and Alcohol' with crowd going appropriately apeshit, and Noel mucking about with the riff to Led Zep's 'Whole Lotta Love'. Forty minutes in, Noel comes on with his infamous acoustic set, just to

remind us that while our kid might be getting all the attention - he's the real mastermind behind it all. With 'Don't Go Away' a couple of thousand saddos thought they were up for a Noel duet (me included) and sang along with all the finesse of a football crowd. An acoustic version of the Chemical Brothers' 'Setting Sun' (which Noel guested on) sparked up everyone who recognised it, all sitar drones and bongos, and then it was on to 'Fade In Out' and a pretty triumphant 'Don't Look Back in Anger'.

Liam swaggers back for 'Wonderwall', which sounded average up against the unstoppable might of 'Live Forever'. Then they climbed even higher, starting 'It's Getting Better Man' with the opening riff to the Pistols' 'God Save the Queen', and turning out an epic 10 minute 'Champagne Supernova'.

The encore of 'Acquiesce' and the double top, excruciatingly loud version of the Beatles' 'I am the Walrus' were such rockin' behemoths, you were left deaf and gasping, and blinded by strobes at the end of it. Thousands of people wandering out like zombies into the cold night air - the smell of Oasis rock forever burnt onto their consciousness.

JOHN TAITE

SPELLING MISTAKES
aLuna, Auckland, March 7.

For most of the full-to-overflow crowd, the Spelling Mistakes reunion show was a big deal, and a good one at that, as the $10 door charge included a 22-track CD of rare and classic Spelling Mistakes material. While a New York Dolls doco played on the video screens, a sort of old school reunion of the prime movers and fakers of the late 70s Auckland punk scene was taking place. Surely the last time that Simon Grigg, Rena Owen, and Barry Jenkin all attended the same rock 'n' roll show, Muldoon was PM and a jug was under two dollars.

Since then, everyone's grown up, but no one's admitted growing old. And though the room was full of teenage rebels approaching middle age, the vitality of the Spelling Mistakes (who apart from a couple of rehearsals and a private party hadn't played for 18 years) still came as a shock — even if it appeared initially that guitarist Warwick

Rip It Up review by John Taite/Simon Grigg[125]

Auckland concert ticket – courtesy of Ian Ryberg

As part of this project, many attendees were interviewed for their recollections of the concert as well as their general interest in Oasis before and after the concert. Now, twenty-five years on certain details no doubt fade away, but as with anything Oasis-related, opinions are divided.

Alan

'I owned their albums, and particularly loved *(What's the Story) Morning Glory?* and I looked forward to new releases. It had been a while since there had been proper guitar bands, so I'd sat up and taken notice when I first heard them. I'd bought a ticket for the Auckland show when it was originally scheduled, but then the tour had been cancelled, as Noel and Liam had had a falling out, and months went by with no word about the tour. I think they offered people their money back. I didn't think I'd get to see them. Then the tour was back on again in 1998, so I was mostly glad they were coming after all and that I would get to see them.

I went with my brother, who was also a fan. We were both born in England and had been living in New Zealand for about 20 years by then. New Zealand is a bit remote from the centres of rock, so we missed out on a lot. The venue was packed and the crowd was squashed. I had to squeeze past some bigger guys to be able to see the stage. The band was very confident and tight. I dabbled with the guitar (badly), so I was mostly watching Noel's guitar playing. I don't remember the detail of the show now - it's so long ago. But I remember wishing they'd played a few more songs from the first two albums. 'Morning Glory' was my favourite song and they didn't play it.

I kept buying and playing their albums but never saw them live again. I've separately seen Noel and Liam play live and would definitely go to an Oasis gig if they reformed. It's madness that they've let sibling rivalry break up the band and consign the pair of them to bit parts and supporting acts instead of the headliners they could still be together.'

Amanda Slade

'During the 1990s I was (and still am) a fan of British music; The Smiths, The Stone Roses, Suede, New Order (who we went to see in Spain a couple of years ago) and The Cure. I liked Oasis at the time. The first album was great, refreshing sound although obviously influenced majorly by the Beatles. Britain had its groove back and there was some great music coming from there at that point in time.

My partner of the time (now husband) is English and he moved over here in the 1980s where we met working in television. I then went to work for Virgin Records and Dave went on to become Paul Holmes' Producer at TVNZ. Auckland is not that big a place and working at a record company you know all the other record company people. They give you new releases, you give them yours. Tickets to gigs the same. So, we had free tickets to see Oasis at the Expo Centre.

For a start, the venue was pretty terrible. We left halfway through the Oasis gig. Liam looked bored. There was obvious tension on stage. The sound was shit. We looked at each other and said, 'let's go.' Perhaps we would have stayed to the end if we had paid for the tickets, I don't know.

I still like Oasis and have them on my playlist... especially good when driving a long distance... keeps me awake.'

Andrew B. White

'At the height of Oasis' popularity, around 1995, I was not what you would call a fan. Of course, I'd heard all of their hits on the radio – 'Wonderwall' et al –

but I largely ignored what I thought was 'whiny rock' from a bunch of English prats trying to emulate the Beatles via the Stones. I drew the line at British acts like Radiohead and preferred my rock Americanized from the likes of R. E.M.

In August 1996, I found myself in London to visit my sister Andrea who was living there. In addition to an impromptu posh dinner with a certain New Zealand musician and music lawyer with some Sony Music execs on Portobello Road and a side trip to Paris, my sister had bought us tickets to a big outdoor concert in a field featuring Oasis at some place I'd never heard of. Since she'd already bought the tickets and booked the coach to get there and back, I couldn't really say no. Oasis wasn't on my bucket list, but everyone in the UK seemed to be extremely excited about this event. Oasis mania was at full peak, so it wasn't hard to get swept up in it. Besides, the concert would also feature The Prodigy and The Chemical Brothers (two acts I liked), along with The Charlatans, Kula Shaker, Manic Street Preachers and Ocean Colour Scene (all acts that I was indifferent about), plus novelty act The Bootleg Beatles. Something for everyone and loads of lager and fish and chips. After riding the tube and then onto the hour and a bit coach trip to Stevenage, we arrived at the outdoor venue with half of the population of the UK all wearing Oasis merch. Despite the numbers, we managed to find a decent spot with enough access to the nearest beer tent. It was a fairly pleasant day despite the organised chaos. The other acts on the bill were great – The Prodigy and The Chemical Brothers were both great to see but the day was all about Oasis. When they hit the stage, I was surprised to find myself immediately impressed. Of course, the crowd were both buzzed from the anticipation and nicely liquored up and that created an electric atmosphere.

As it turned out I actually liked the songs and pretty much became a fan from that point onwards. Sometimes seeing what a band can do live can have that effect. After the show and the inevitable trek with hordes of people, we found and waited in our coach for what seemed like hours, inhaling diesel fumes from idling buses, before finally heading back to London. We had no cameras or cell phones to document our day, but it was a bloody good outing that turned out to be one of rock's biggest. Given the scale of that event, I approached my friend John Russell, then editor at *Rip It Up* magazine, and asked if I could

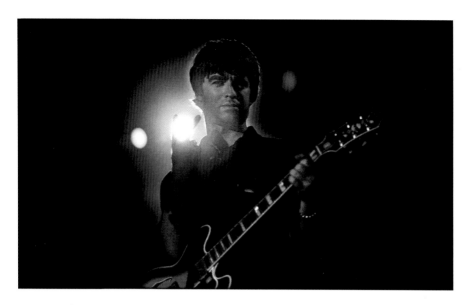

Noel Gallagher at the Carter Holt Pavilion. Photograph by Kent Blechynden

write a review of the show, so I was able to put my thoughts down in print at least. Thanks for the tickets sis!

When I arrived back in New Zealand later that month and back to my job as a graphic artist at Revolver Design, I was excited to learn that one of our clients The Sequel (headed by Doug Hood and Bridget Darby) were going to be the promoter for the New Zealand leg of the Oasis world tour. The Sequel handled local live shows and international tours for Australian outfits Michael Coppel Presents and Lees & West. Part of our work was creating promotional art for live concerts – posters, ads and promotional material. This was great as it meant one of the perks of the job was free tickets in addition to the buzz of getting to work on artwork for artists I liked. The Oasis show was scheduled for November 15, 1996, at the Supertop in Auckland, a giant circus tent in Penrose where Guns 'N Roses, Michael Jackson and Pearl Jam had played previously.

As was often the case, tour artwork was supplied to us from Australia that was suitably boring and with crappy typography, but we weren't allowed to redesign it or change it much. As a designer, I'd never liked the Oasis artwork that Brian Cannon's Microdot studio had created to begin with. The logo

Liam Gallagher performing at the Carter Holt Pavilion, Auckland.
Photograph by Kent Blechynden

seemed too simple and Microdot's typography and layout was always all over
the place (they butchered the Verve stuff too). Though I wasn't allowed to 'fix'

the art I did try to do some little things like fix the kerning (the space between the letters) in 'Oasis'. Essentially the art came in two versions – either a large photo of Liam or Noel that were alternated in publications. I think Liam got more placement obviously as his photo was more iconic. The posters were huge – two A0 sized sheets pieced together to form one giant poster. Back then, due to cost, we were mostly restricted to one or two colours for poster printing. Costs mattered even for Oasis, and more importantly the local promoters had to front the costs, so any savings were taken advantage of. Then sometime in September 1996, the wheels fell off the Oasis bandwagon during the USA leg of the tour and all remaining dates (including Australia and New Zealand) were cancelled. It was a major bummer to me as I was looking forward to that show, being hot on the heels from seeing them at Knebworth, not to mention it always sucks when you've been working on a show that is suddenly cancelled.

Fast forward to 1997 and the release of Oasis' third album *Be Here Now*. I found this album rather disappointing given the hype and embargo placed on it right up to its release day. The first single 'D'You Know What I Mean?' was decent enough, but the album was no *Definitely Maybe* or *(What's the Story) Morning Glory?* I tried hard with it but came to the conclusion it was no longer midnight at the oasis – more like 5:30 a.m. on Monday morning and time to go home. I did get given a nice promo box set of *Be Here Now* from the record company which made up for a little of the sonic disappointment.

In early 1998 we were informed Oasis was coming back down under for a new tour to promote *Be Here Now*. Again, we'd be handling the artwork, also through The Sequel but for this new run the Australian promoter had changed over to Michael Coppel Presents. Again, the artwork was supplied to us ('don't fuck with it!') but of course I did to try and tidy it up a bit, even if it was subtle. This time the band would also hit Wellington as well as Auckland, but no Supertop. Instead, the Auckland venue was the indoor basketball arena known as the North Shore Events Centre which had hosted Alanis Morrisette, Tool and Garbage in the past. Wellington's venue was the equally cavernous Queens Wharf Events Centre. The names of these two venues always caused havoc with art layouts; excessively long names that made fitting all that text onto a poster or ad a real pain! The supplied tour art was simple – back to the regular lowercase Oasis 'type in a box' logo and photo of the band (looking far more jovial than what was the reality). The Auckland venue changed to NZ Expo Centre (or to be exact 'The Carter Holt Pavilion at the NZ Expo Centre'), next to the Logan Campbell Centre. What a mouthful that was to shoehorn into the artwork. Damn those corporations and their vanity naming rights! The artwork needed to be updated. Arguably the Logan Campbell Centre (affectionately known locally as the 'Logan Concrete Centre') was on a par with the North Shore Events Centre with its reputation for awful sound. I'd seen a bunch of acts there including R.E.M. and the Beastie Boys and the sound was never great. These were the pre–Vector Arena days when Auckland lacked a large dedicated live venue. Like a charm I did receive my free tickets to the show and allocated my 'plus one' to my then flatmate Dave Bishop who at the time was playing with The Peter Stuyvesant Hitlist. We planned to drive to the show, to avoid relying on a taxi and then hopefully get some beers at the venue which wouldn't be knocked out of our hands by overzealous Oasis fans (1998 being the height of 'Lad' culture).

Paul 'Bonehead' Arthurs, performing at the Carter Holt Pavilion. Image by Niels Schipper

On the afternoon of the Auckland show I was walking up Queen Street by

Whitcoulls when I saw a guy across the road that looked very much like Noel Gallagher. I decided to cross over for a closer look and indeed it was very much 'our Noel.' Unmistakable with his haircut, black attire and striped T-shirt, I went up to him while he was waiting at the pedestrian crossing and said, 'Hello Noel, I'm a fan of yours and I'm coming to your show tonight!'. To bring my stalker level down a bit I also mentioned I had worked on the art for the tour, figuring that may give me some more cred with him. Noel was very polite, gave me a wee handshake and said something in Manchesterian like, 'thanks man, nice one' and off he went. Who would have thought? I'd once seen former New Zealand Prime Minister Jenny Shipley on Queen Street, but Noel Gallagher was the more exciting experience of the two.

And so, Dave and I headed to the show that night. I don't think there was an opening act, which is just as well for whoever that band may have been. Abuse from the crowd and/or Liam would have no doubt been on the cards. I seem to remember the show taking a while to start which didn't help the vibe. People were edgy and getting impatient. The tour in other countries had featured a lavish stage set including a Rolls Royce and a telephone box as props. Judging from the drab stage set in front of us that was not something deemed worthy for a shitty venue down in New Zealand. It felt like something was up and the rumours around the band's internal fisticuffs gave off the feeling that anything could happen tonight. Looking now at the setlist that's posted up on setlist.fm I can recall the wet blanket of opening songs 'Be Here Now' and 'Stand by Me'. Both songs are hardly the kind of rockers that would get a crowd hungry for Oasis gold going, but I guess they had to play them – new album to promote and all.

Liam was suitably twatty as soon as he hit the stage, the sound was pretty awful and the band was obviously aware that Liam was more than bollocked and their playing seemed to suffer because of it. This was not the Oasis I had seen firing on all cylinders back in 1996. Things finally picked up with the opening chords of 'Roll with It', then dipped again with 'D'You Know What I Mean?' only to go back up with 'Cigarettes & Alcohol'. That was the stuff fans had come to see but just when you thought it was 'getting better, man!!', Liam and the band buggered off stage leaving Noel to play an acoustic set. Talk about a comedown. Now, there's nothing wrong with watching Noel play a few songs on an acoustic guitar since he's actually pretty darn good at it, but this was part way into an Oasis gig where one is expecting maximum rock 'n' roll. This interlude was surely inserted to appease Liam so he could go backstage and not have to sing to the shitty crowd more than he had to. I guess having some of Liam is better than having none of Liam, but it seemed like they were taking the piss.

This was the first time a New Zealand crowd was getting an Oasis show and they were not getting much of one. After Noel's trio of tunes, the rest of the band minus Liam resurfaced to join him on 'Don't Look Back in Anger', again likely strategically placed in the setlist to prolong Liam's absence. Noel knows he can do Oasis without Liam if he wants to and he's gonna fucking show you. Nice one Noel. Liam's back for 'Wonderwall', 'Live Forever' (both of which come across as Liam performing Oasis karaoke) with Noel holding it all together with Bonehead, Guigsy and Alan White all under strict orders just to do their shit. 'It's Gettin' Better (Man!!)' also from the new album, gets a look in with Noel again carrying Liam along with a lot of backing vocals. 'Champagne Supernova' is a bit more convincing but then the show is all over until a brief encore. 'Acquiesce' (one of the best Oasis songs in my opinion) means both Liam and Noel have to deliver convincingly and the band choose to close with their cover of the Beatles' 'I Am the Walrus', which is fine, but you'd rather hear another Oasis banger surely?

Verdict? The show was patchy, a bit of a train wreck in all honesty and the band was plainly over this long tour that had started midway through the previous year. Liam's antics were overshadowing the enjoyment of being in the band and playing music. For me, having been spoilt seeing Oasis live at their peak at that now legendary Knebworth show, the Auckland show was a let-down and from that point onwards I greeted each new Oasis album release with only curiosity and a fleeting listen. Neither have I kept up with the Gallagher brothers' respective solo efforts (although I'm told they are fairly good). I'm still fond of the first two Oasis albums and was pleased to see the recent release of the Knebworth concert as a complete document. I was there after all!

Somewhere in my storage locker are some of those giant Oasis posters from 1996 along with the Knebworth ticket stub. Ironically, I now play in a band with someone who once opened up for Oasis on their USA *Definitely Maybe* tour. Yes, they said 'Liam was definitely, not maybe, a complete asshole, but it wouldn't be Oasis without that!'

Andrew Clifford

'My initial interest comes from having been quite a fan of The Smiths and the Manchester scene, including the 1990s era with The Stone Roses, Happy Mondays etc. Oasis came a little later but I had read of some connection with Johnny Marr so that would have also suggested an endorsement. I did a one-off show on bFM about the Creation record label, and the NME had just issued a free cassette of some key bands and it included a demo recording from a new band - Oasis. I probably still have the cassette. Anyway, that came out just in time for my show, so I played this rough recording of a group that was largely unknown and hadn't released anything - perhaps the first time they were ever played on radio, at least in New Zealand. I think I'd also been sent some promo photographs from a friend at Sony Music New Zealand, who were then distributing Creation. The first album didn't excite me as much as I hoped but it was different to what was going on at the time. Of course, the second album was huge with all the singalongs that everyone knows and Britpop was big by then too. As always, bands tended to eventually get to New Zealand a little after their peak, and that was true of Oasis too.

I don't think I was ever a big Oasis fan but had friends who were and I had a general interest in the Britpop and indie scene. I went with a couple of acquaintances I was hanging out with at the time, some of whom had a general interest but at least one might have been more of a fan. I had a free ticket because I was involved with bFM at the time - I was a poor student then so I don't think I would have paid for it. I think they were already on when we went and it was so loud and harsh sounding that I hung back by the doors and didn't go much further. I don't remember much more about the show itself - the band weren't especially charismatic and they just bashed through a shortish set that I didn't find particularly exciting or memorable. After that, their albums didn't exactly meet the standard of their first few so, like most people, I lost interest in the years following. I might've reviewed an album or two for *Rip It Up* or bFM but, aside from glimmers of potential in the occasional track, they were definitely fading at that point.'

Barney McDonald, Founding Editor/Co-publisher, *Pavement* magazine, NZ, 1993-2007

'Certain gigs arrive with a lot of baggage. By baggage, I mean expectation. The band has a turbulent history, or is cresting the wave of an international hit single or album, or is simply an act you never thought would grace these shores of ours with their illustrious presence. In a way, all of these things summed up Oasis when they played a one-off show in Auckland.

Pavement, the magazine I founded and co-published in Auckland, had recently photographed and interviewed the band in London, and now here they were – playing our fair southern city. The heading for our story – Bigmouth Strikes Again – alluded both to Oasis's roots in Manchester (the title derives from a single by fellow Mancunian legends The Smiths, who sadly never played New Zealand) and to the Gallagher brothers' propensity for outrageous, off-the-cuff statements in interviews. The press loves a good quote; I loved a great pull-quote. And sometimes headings or titles for stories easily suggest themselves.

Like Nirvana a few years before them, Oasis was the cool band everyone wanted a piece of. *Definitely Maybe* and *(What's the Story) Morning Glory?* were fantastic rock albums full of stellar songs and copious singles. To add spice, Noel and Liam Gallagher had such a devil-may-care attitude, doubtless bred of their Mancunian upbringing, that made them such engaging rock stars. Who didn't love Oasis at the time? And who didn't want to see the brothers strut their swagger live on stage?

As gigs go, the show was excellent, if not particularly histrionic. Oasis delivered the songs everyone wanted to sing tunelessly along to. In fact, the gig was so heavily anticipated that the crowd was lapping at the band's feet from the moment they took the stage. This isn't necessarily a good thing. You want bands to work hard at winning you over. Oasis didn't seem to have much to prove, but they were also the kind of band that didn't care for such showmanship. That's what I liked about them – that tempered punk insouciance.

In many ways, the uninspiring acoustics of the venue left the band to their devices. Even though I'd seen many acts at the adjacent Logan 'Concrete' Centre over the years – The Cure, New Order, OMD, Berlin, INXS, Beastie

Boys, Massive Attack, Beck, Sonic Youth, Helmet – the convention centre was definitely a step down venue-wise. Whereas Nirvana eventually played the LCC after outselling the capacity of the Powerstation then the Auckland Town Hall, Oasis wound up in the convention centre, which probably held a few hundred more people. As venues go, it was entirely devoid of any architectural personality or acoustic charm. It felt like a car park and we all just mucked in together. Our collective bodies probably soaked up the worst of the sound issues and I remember at the time feeling like Oasis sounded rather good live.

Was I seduced by the moment rather than the spectacle? Probably a little. It felt like this was an opportunity to make up for missing out on seeing Nirvana at their only Auckland show in the early 1990s. This time I could say I was there, that I participated in a historical event, and hopefully saw a great band play a great show. From my point of view, it wasn't exactly that. The sense of occasion did outshine the performance a few rays. But sometimes that just doesn't matter. It made an impact and left its mark. I still remember the show fondly, enthusiastically, along with a show by Radiohead in the same venue around the same time. And I put that down to the quality of the music and the undeniable presence of elder brother Noel and 'our kid'.'

Brendan McCarthy

'I was not a fan till 'Roll with It' came out in New Zealand and then I quickly backtracked and obtained everything I could. It's fair to say that given my musical career and obsession with songwriting and guitar, that I was a fan of just Noel really. I didn't understand Liam back then and pretty much thought he was a total knobhead. I learned every song that Noel had to offer and his songwriting style influenced mine heavily and motivated me to write as much as I could. I went to the gig with my best mate at the time. We were both into Oasis so the gig was a must-see. I think we bought tickets from Real Groovy records shop.

My overall experience was that I was star-struck and I guess you could say it was a lesson in rock 'n' roll at its peak in the late 1990s. Oasis could do whatever they wanted and they most definitely did. The gig itself was a hot sweaty experience. About two minutes before the band came on stage some idiot blacked out the lights. Everyone panicked and rushed forward. Hundreds

Liam Gallagher at the Carter Holt Pavilion, Auckland. Image by Niels Schipper

fell over including me. First time in my life I have ever had to stand on other humans to get up and then help others to their feet. I remember the band not playing that well, but I didn't care. They delivered their sound and their songs to the fans and that is what mattered to me. I am really glad that I got to see them here as it was the one and only time it will happen. I have since seen Noel live and he is excellent. I followed the band till the mid-2000s but lost interest due to life commitments and my lack of musical motivation. Luckily for me, music is for life and my musical motivation would return years later and indeed my love for Noel's songwriting would return. I now believe completely in Liam's talents as a solo artist and follow his progress.'

Clive Weston

'We weren't fanatical Oasis fans or groupies but were drawn to their sound and music by Liam's distinctive and unique vocals and their melodies – it doesn't work for me if you can't walk out of a concert humming a tune you've just heard. The Oasis sound and many of the band's melodies are memorable and as it has been proved, their best work stands the test of time. I went with my then-wife and imagine I booked the tickets over the phone and picked them up at the venue before going through the turnstiles.

I don't recall too much of the detail of the Auckland concert, as it must have been over twenty years ago, in the late nineties, I think. What I do remember is a packed house, the audience on their feet, Liam singing up a storm in the pose we came to know, hand behind his back & singing skywards up to the mike. The crowd loved it all with new material mixed in with the classic Oasis anthems.'

Clyde Leggett

'I had bought their first two albums and quite liked them so when I had the opportunity to see them in Auckland, I thought it was quite a good opportunity to see one of the bigger bands of the 1990s. What I couldn't believe was that a band as big as they were at the time was to play in the Carter Holt Pavilion, which I had never been in and didn't even know bands played there. It turned out to be a shocking venue on all accounts, especially the acoustics and then to top it off the band were very disappointing as Liam appeared drunk and disinterested. Not sure if that was his act or not but it didn't go down well with me, so a combination of that and the sound, I left about halfway through. I had gone on my own and didn't buy any more of their albums after that.'

Liam Gallagher at the Carter Holt Pavilion, Auckland. Image by Niels Schipper

Liam Gallagher at the Carter Holt Pavilion, Auckland. Image by Niels Schipper

Craig Holt

'I was a huge fan, had all the CDs at the time and played them constantly. A group of us from an English pub hired a van and went to the concert. We were in a very jolly mood, with plenty of drinks flowing. I still rate that concert as, one of my all-time favourite concerts and I have been to a lot of concerts, trust me. I enjoyed it immensely, as did all my mates. Hell, it was Oasis! Yes, they were loud, and yes Liam had attitude, but they were here and I was having a blast listening to them. No regrets from me. Maybe it was just the merry mood me and my mates were in that night and we were just over the moon seeing Oasis live, we didn't care about the imperfections of the evening, it just rocked.'

Daniel Phillips

'By the time Oasis announced they were finally coming to New Zealand in March 1998 after unceremoniously cancelling their Mt Smart Supertop gig at the very peak of Britpop in November 1996, it felt like a few lifetimes had passed for this 16-year-old. I had tickets to the Supertop show which was taking place right off the back of Knebworth when Oasis was arguably the biggest band in the world. As I was to find out a lot can change in 18 months ...

Of course, after the unprecedented heights of Knebworth, it all seemingly fell very quickly to pieces. There was the much-anticipated *MTV Unplugged* where the band were forced to perform without Liam and on the American tour Liam missed a flight, some shows were cancelled and in what was to become an all too familiar story the brothers grim had another fallout. The whole tour was abruptly cancelled and the one-off New Zealand gig was of course a casualty. It was the first concert I'd ever have cancelled - and to a 16-year-old that lived for music it was incredibly rough. We had to return our tickets to get our money back - $50 (a lot of money in those days) but I made a photocopy of my ticket to the gig that never was. To console myself I bought a massive unused concert wall poster from the *Rip It Up* classified section. It was two huge pieces; I never had the heart (or wall space) to put it up!

Being off the road seemed to help things in the band though and the brothers patched up their differences and retreated to make *Be Here Now*. It's hard to describe the hype and anticipation now but it was massive in the British music press and on MTV UK which had recently started screening here. The timing was perfect and Oasis seemed to be all everybody was talking about on MTV! I counted down the days and bought *Be Here Now* on its August release date and absolutely thrashed it. I still love it to this day, while it may be a bit bloated in places and never lived up to the impossible hype, I do think it remains their most underrated effort. For me, it was the perfect end to the incredible Oasis trilogy that started with (one of the greatest debut albums of all time) *Definitely Maybe* and exploded into the stratosphere with *(What's the Story) Morning Glory?* It ended with *Be Here Now* - and although it's never discussed with the same reverence as its predecessors, I think track by track it stands up pretty bloody well thank you very much.

Paul 'Guigsy' McGuigan at the Carter Holt Pavilion, Auckland.
Image by Niels Schipper

So, after all this hype and the 24/7 brainwashing by *Q* and MTV and *Be Here Now* on heavy rotation, imagine my excitement when it was quietly announced after what seemed like an age that following the disappointment of The Supertop, they were finally coming! Redemption! In a split second all was forgiven, but there was also some trepidation, was it for real? Would they make it this time? Would they have another bust-up just before they were supposed to get here and pull out again? For a school kid this was the really important stuff in life.

I had forgotten but the gig was originally scheduled for the North Shore Events Centre and moved to the Carter Holt Pavilion. It was a concrete warehouse behind the Logan Campbell Centre in Auckland Showgrounds, and aside from the Radiohead concert a month or so before Oasis, it had never really been used for concerts. In its brief concert lifespan, it didn't exactly receive much acclaim for its acoustics (and people say the Logan 'concrete' Centre is bad). This was pre-internet and presale days so I'm pretty sure I ordered tickets over the phone (or got my mum too, Ha!) on the first day they went on sale as I would have been at school. Even then I was terrified of gigs selling out. After securing the all too precious concert tickets there was still some anxiety and doubt as to whether the gig would actually go ahead. Would Liam and Noel have another bust-up? Would the band split before they finally made it down here? And after the change of venue would the gig even go ahead at all? Little did I know all these worries were much closer to reality than I could have imagined at the time. As the shows ticked down one by one it looked like finally our dreams of seeing Oasis on our shores would come true.

It was a school day and anticipation was sky high - I have no idea how I got through that day but as soon as school finished my friend Scott and I walked to his house and mucked around before the gig. His mum dropped us off, I forget exactly what time, but it was reasonably early, around 6 pm. I was shocked at just how many people were already there - the line snaked around the venue - and I remember being amazed by all the Oasis shirts people were wearing - I don't think I'd even seen an Oasis shirt before. There seemed to be a lot of British expats too - most people around us were Brits, I could tell by the accents. Anticipation was at fever pitch.

When doors finally opened and we got inside the venue we got a really good spot up front - maybe five or six from the front, centre stage. I don't recall a support act, but I'm pretty sure there was none which would have broken the law at the time but would have been fitting with the Gallagher ethos. As we inched towards showtime and the anticipation built even further, the squeeze started. The lights went down and the intro music started and finally Oasis ambled onto a New Zealand stage for the very first time.

Liam asked if we were 'mad for it' and the crowd went apeshit. The crowd surged forward and as the band launched into 'Be Here Now', jumped in perfect collective unison with the music like a giant pogo stick. Even if you didn't want to jump, you jumped, you had no say in the matter. I somehow managed to snap a couple of blurry shots of Liam on the disposable camera I'd smuggled in – how, I will never know. But once developed they were total rubbish unsurprisingly. Even at my young age, I'd been to a few concerts before - McCartney, The Rolling Stones, AC/DC, The Sex Pistols, Kiss - but I'd never experienced a mosh pit like this. Scott and I quickly became separated, within the first song or two, I was completely exhausted already.

One of my shoes had also come off in the mosh - and I remember being really freaked out about losing it and being at a concert with only one shoe on! I ducked down in the crowd looking for it (about the most dangerous thing I could have done) I remember people checking I was ok, on about the second attempt I somehow found it and put it back on. A little shell shocked and completely sweat soaked I retreated a few metres to escape the worst of the mosh - and it turned out to be the best decision I made all night. I was probably 20 or so back but there was plenty of space (and air) and I could see everything and enjoy and appreciate the music. The highlights for me were probably 'Acquiesce' and the similarly anthemic 'It's Gettin' Better (Man!!)' from *Be Here Now*. I also really enjoyed Noel's acoustic set maybe because it gave me an extra breather, but I remember being impressed he sang 'Setting Sun', The Chemical Brothers track he did the vocal on, definitely the biggest surprise of the night.

And just like that it was all over - it flew by. I found Scott after the show and we were both drenched in sweat - I looked and felt like I'd just jumped in a swimming pool, without feeling refreshed. As I got older, I'd later develop into somewhat of a mosh pit veteran - up the very front for countless concerts -

Noel Gallagher at the Carter Holt Pavilion, Auckland. Image by Niels Schipper

this gig was in effect invaluable training - a steep learning curve and a baptism by fire for the many years of gig going ahead.

My dad picked us up and I remember being so thirsty we stopped to get something to drink but all I wanted was a six-pack of beer - I was craving it - unfortunately my dad didn't play ball. I remember being a bit miffed about it, but nothing could dampen the adrenaline racing through my veins. And then it was off to school again the next morning and back to reality - it seemed like a dream already. When I think back now, I realise how lucky we were to get those shows.

I won a copy of *Standing on the Shoulder of Giants* and there were some great tracks on it but it just wasn't the same band, it was clear they had lost something. In 2002 I made my first trip to Australia to see and meet the Beatles producer Sir George Martin. Oasis was playing at the Enmore Theatre in Sydney the same night. I did walk by the venue and did want to see them - but I was also perfectly comfortable knowing I'd seen them close to their peak with the classic lineup plus I was seeing George Martin instead.

My biggest Oasis pilgrimage of all was finally going to Manchester in 2019 just before the pandemic. I paid a visit to Burnage and saw Liam and Noel's childhood home, Sifters Record Store and met Mr Sifter. I also went to Bonehead's old house and peered through the window into the front room where they shot the cover of *Definitely Maybe* and walked thru the garden where they filmed 'Shakermaker'. In London, I recreated the *(What's the Story) Morning Glory?* album cover and in Sheffield hung out backstage with Alan McGee (diamond geezer). It was the perfect end to my Oasis journey, but I still wonder if there are a few more chapters to follow before it's all over. Some 25 years on (and just like 'Wonderwall' so lovingly nicked from George Harrison) one must remember to always BE HERE NOW. Wherever that may be.'

Glenn Jeffrey – former *The New Zealand Herald* photographer

'While working as a photojournalist for *The New Zealand Herald* I was assigned to photograph the concert of Oasis at the NZ Expo Centre, as I was the late duty photographer that evening. We had recently received a new Canon digital camera, the DCS 520, so I decided to use it to photograph and transmit the photograph from the venue, something that was pretty new at that time.

I arrived early, to make sure I could get a connection to the *Herald* server and then, when Oasis came on stage, I shot the usual three songs that are allowed by bands, from the mosh pit. After the third song, all with Liam face upwards to the microphone, I went out to the foyer, selected one image, did a little work on it to reduce the 'noise' that the early cameras suffered from, compressed the image to about 400kb, and used the dial modem to send the picture back to the *Herald*.

As I was the only photographer on duty, I packed up my gear, and headed back to the *Herald* to await the next assignment. The picture made the front page the next day.'

James Pinker

'I wasn't a huge fan but did like the first album - liked the Beatle-esqe flavour and slightly punk nature. I went with Neil Finn as I was on his guest list. The gig itself, I loved it to be honest - VERY fucking loud - I do recall them playing 'Rock and Roll' by Led Zeppelin before they came on which I thought was pretty brave - very hard song to come on to. I didn't keep up with them afterwards - they got a bit wanky - so full of themselves - and I think the brothers hating on each other was bad news - they needed each other.'

Liam Gallagher at the Carter Holt Pavilion, Auckland. Image by Niels Schipper

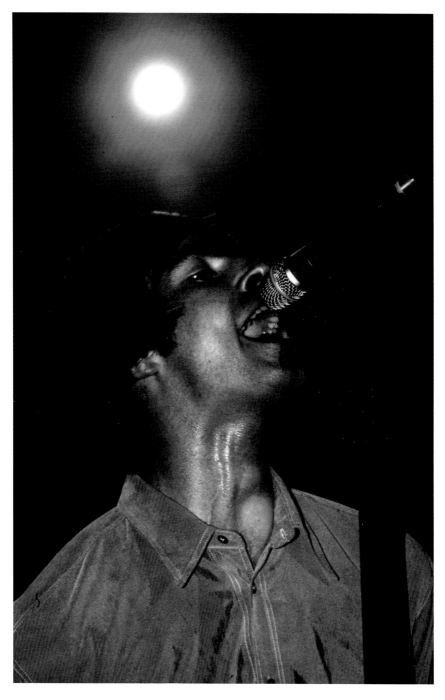

Liam Gallagher at the Carter Holt Pavilion, Auckland. Image by Niels Schipper

Janet MacDonald

'I was a huge fan of them before the gig. Loved them. I went with another girl from London who was travelling in New Zealand. The gig for me was very disappointing. We went early and were right at the front – right-hand side of the stage. Right in from of Liam. He was really stoned, looked bored and disengaged. The sound was average and the gig was seriously lacking in atmosphere.'

Jaye Cooper (attended both the Auckland and Wellington gigs)

'I was pretty much obsessed with Oasis at the time of the gig and went with a big group of mates and girlfriends to the Auckland show. It was such a buzz to finally see them live after they had cancelled 18 months prior. I enjoyed the show although I will say the sound mix was way too loud, my ears were ringing for days and to this day I haven't been to a gig that loud. I still follow the band and have seen both brothers live since Oasis split. At the time I had a mate who worked for Showtravel and he would organise all aspects of touring bands. I always said to him when he would offer me tickets and passes, 'If Oasis ever come, I've got to meet them.' He called me three months before the gig and said, 'Mate...Christmas is coming early I just booked the Oasis *Be Here Now* tour.'

I met him at the hotel when Oasis arrived in Auckland. I was pretty star-struck but have to say they were pretty decent lads. I got to spend an hour at the bar with them, Noel was really cool, drank a couple of Heinekens and chatted about music and trainers. Bonehead was quite possibly the funniest guy I've ever met, constantly taking the piss and telling stories from the tour. Liam was cool, had a quick chat and then he headed off to his room. I was absolutely buzzing for months after that night. Funnily enough, the night I met them Joe Cocker was in town for a show, he was also at the hotel bar, Bonehead was doing impersonations of him and was funny as fuck.

Different times back then alright, I didn't have a camera. These days you have them on your phone. One thing that took me back that night was they were just a bunch of working-class lads, no different to my mates back then, which made them so relatable. During that period from 1994-1998 Noel was untouchable as a songwriter, songs like 'The Masterplan' and 'Acquiesce' were B-sides...that's insane in today's world.'

John Campbell

'I was never a major fan, but they were as big as anything during those years of my life. Had a couple of their albums/CDs but couldn't claim to be a close fan. I bought a couple of tickets with some cash from a part-time university job. Took a girl along that I was trying to impress at the time - that didn't work out. It was memorable but terrible! It was the worst concert I've ever been to. Noel and Liam were at each other the whole time and lots of people left when one of them told the crowd to fuck off.'

Jonathan Gedye

'I had followed them since *Definitely Maybe*, when I first heard, 'Live Forever' and 'Supersonic' they had me hooked. I knew from then on out they were 'my band' and I would follow them anywhere. I went with my older cousin Andre; I was 14 at the time and he was 20. It was a good thing to have another fan in the family otherwise I don't think my mother would have let me go alone. We bought tickets at the box office in Aotea Square when they went on sale months before.

It was my first proper gig. I had seen the GMEX Manchester gig on MTV [Oasis performed at the Greater Manchester Exhibition Centre in December 1997, broadcast globally on MTV] a few months earlier and was desperate to see them. I rode the post-grunge wave having been a bit too young to be into the earliest Nirvana and Pearl Jam albums but loved anything early 1990s once my musical tastes started developing, when Oasis hit, I knew they were the one for me.

I think the gig was supposed to be at the North Shore Events Centre but got moved to the Auckland Showgrounds for some reason. The setlist mirrored the GMEX gig, my favourite part being the acoustic set by Noel in the middle of the set, he sounded absolutely on form, but Liam's vocals were a bit off (drunk). It seemed 'The Chief' was barely holding the band together after the

Australian shenanigans, Liam was belligerent but not as bad as what I heard from the Wellington show a day or two later. It's still a highlight of my teen years, and I relived it for years afterwards.

It was Oasis at peak popularity, the beginning of the end of the dominant years, fuelled on booze and cocaine. I wish they had conquered America and put a more lasting stamp on the musical landscape, but the infighting between the Gallaghers on those early tours doomed their chances. It was often a lonely road as an Oasis die hard in the early 2000s relating to my moronic friends riding the Nu Metal trends. I am very happy to see some new interest in the band as time has given them a chance to find their place in the musical landscape.

I've followed the band to this day and have loved all of Noel's solo work, and am glad to see Liam mellowing, though he's been such an arse I'm not sure they will ever reunite.'

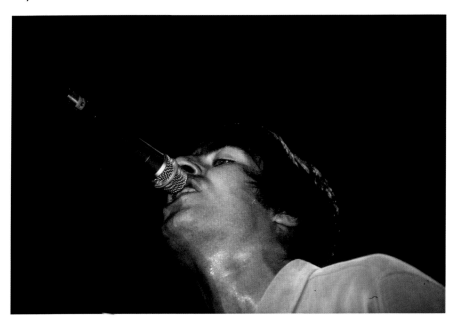

Liam Gallagher at the Carter Holt Pavilion, Auckland. Image by Niels Schipper

Karel Brooke

'My burgeoning love of music as a teen coincided with the Britpop boom. In my sphere, Oasis was akin to the Beatles, a hugely popular band who also had

Liam Gallagher at the Carter Holt Pavilion, Auckland. Image by Niels Schipper

the creative chops. Contrary to current opinion, I liked *Definitely Maybe* but adored *(What's the Story) Morning Glory?* I thought Noel did sad but uplifting better than anyone ('Talk Tonight', 'Cast No Shadow', 'Don't Look Back in Anger') and I hoped *Be Here Now* would follow the template of its predecessor. I remember mainstream radio playing the album in full on the day of its release. This was unprecedented, at least in my experience. Oasis had reached their zenith and there was saturation coverage. I remember loving the first few singles from *Be Here Now*. Listening now, they're more lumbering and generic than I recall but back then they sounded huge and exciting. The hype machine is a powerful beast and I was fully in its grasp.

I went with my girlfriend's younger brother. She didn't want a bar of Oasis, she preferred hard rock/metal, but his tastes aligned with mine and he joined me and a few of my friends for the ride.

My overriding memory of the gig was that it was extremely hot and extremely loud. One person in my group had to be taken out of the venue due to heat exhaustion. I'd been to rock gigs before, even intimate punk gigs, but nothing got close to how loud and brash Oasis was, almost unbearably so. You had to make a real effort to locate the melodies amidst the sonic squall. Liam and Noel were both pasty white and saturated in sweat, their Beatles haircuts stuck to their foreheads. Liam stalked the stage with a tambourine shouting out the odd indecipherable outburst. You couldn't take your eyes off either, both oozed charisma and self-assurance. The highlight was a mid-concert solo acoustic gig by Noel. It cut through all the rock 'n' roll trappings and got right to the heart of the music. It was also a relief to hear an acoustic after an hour of electric guitars turned up to ear-bleed levels.

I always return to their music and it grips me with a certain kind of wistful sentimentality. Their latter albums were patchy affairs. In the right place and in the right mood, I can still hear the same magic that made me fall in love with them in the first place. Watching old videos, it strikes me how gripping they were to watch for a band who did so little on stage.'

Ken Burns

'I wasn't an obsessive Oasis fan. My interest came from a work friend's recommendation. I just liked going to concerts. Oasis was loud and electric with great stage presence and at this time extremely popular. I hadn't been to the North Shore Events Centre so checked with some friends and three of us decided to go, though the gig did get moved to the Expo Centre. I went with two friends. One from work and the other a long-standing music fan. I got my tickets from Real Groovy record store in Queen Street across the counter.

The opening theme was 'Rock and Roll' by Led Zeppelin while Oasis walked on stage. It started electric and loud. Noel did a middle acoustic set including 'Setting Sun' from The Chemical Brothers. The band came back on and finished loud. There was a great vibe with the audience. I loved the whole night because it was one of a kind. I had never seen them before, and I'll never see them again. It sits in my top three concerts ever and I've seen a lot.

I bought the following albums which never had the impact of the first two. I was really happy to catch them while they were in good spirits.'

Mark Webster

'I guess I followed them as closely as one could from the other side of the world. I would have been aware of them from radio and Max TV I suppose but also because Sony Music New Zealand, as I recall, was one of our clients and we would have made the sound element of their TV commercials (TVC). I didn't buy the CD. I probably got it from Sony when I made the TVC. That said, I only have *(What's the Story) Morning Glory?* *Be Here Now* and *Standing on the Shoulder of Giants* on CD, so I didn't get given them all.

Went with Paul Stent and we got the tickets via Sony Music New Zealand. I think I felt underwhelmed as Noel and Liam weren't getting on. They were quite a different band live. I mean they didn't really put on a show. They just played the songs. I don't think I found it particularly engaging. I think I preferred to listen to the records.

I'm not sure it would be right to say I ever followed them. Not in the way I followed Weller for example. I would lap up any morsel of an article or interview on TV or whatever of him. I think with Oasis I had the CDs and enjoyed them.'

Paul Stent

'I went to the one at the Expo Centre. I went with a friend of mine, Mark Webster. We were both sound engineers who did commercials for TV. We did work for Sony Music New Zealand, and we got complimentary tickets. I wasn't much of a fan but worked on their commercials. Mike Bradshaw (Marketing and Promotions Manager at Sony Music New Zealand) gave us the tickets, so we went along and picked them up at the door. We stood at the front on the right and watched the whole thing. On the top left there was some seating and those were the VIP seats. Mark and I were looking up and thinking what a waste of spare seats and it turned out later...they were our seats. Mike never told us to go up to the seats; we just turned up and went into the crowd. The first thing Mike asked was 'Did you enjoy the view?' And we were like 'What view?' We didn't know we had VIP seats. The acoustics were good, concert sounded great. It was loud but in a good way. They were miserable buggers though; I don't think any of them smiled at all that night. Mike would come to my studio in Ponsonby Road, and we did all the Sony commercials, Oasis, Michael Jackson, whoever, all the Sony Music New Zealand stuff. We'd plug new albums and tours and add a 30 second montage and they'd leave me an album. I still listen to them on my commute. Not really a fan of the solo stuff.'

Noel Gallagher at the Carter Holt Pavilion, Auckland. Image by Niels Schipper

Noel Gallagher at the Carter Holt Pavilion, Auckland. Image by Niels Schipper

Matthew Walker

'My ticket was a gift from my dad as he had known about my love for Oasis (I was only 15ish in 1998). Dad actually got me into Oasis by accident after finding an old *Definitely Maybe* cassette tape somewhere and seeing if I'd like it. I remember thinking 'I hope this venue holds enough people.' Dad drove me and my mate there and picked us up afterwards.

My main memories of the gig were being so excited with it being my first ever gig. When I arrived with my best mate Ryan, Liam was leaning over the barricade near the front of stage with a can of Jack and Coke and a ciggy hanging out the side of his mouth. He had this sort of leering presence and looked like he could very easily explode if given the wrong look.

I remember the gig itself going on for quite a while longer than I expected, after seeing reviews of them leaving the stage early on the same tour. Highlights for me were Noel playing a few acoustic songs mid-set, including 'Setting Sun' and just the absolute batshit crazy atmosphere when they kicked into songs from *Definitely Maybe* and *(What's the Story) Morning Glory?* I also remember they played an encore. I can't remember all of the songs they played but 'Champagne Supernova' stands out in my memory as an absolute belter.

I just remember being blown away by the sound of the guitars and drums. It was unreal to me. It was pretty loud, but I LOVED it.'

Michael Glading, Managing Director, Sony Music Entertainment New Zealand (1986-2004)

'I worked for Sony Music for many years - first saw Oasis at a Sony Music conference at Gleneagles, Scotland, before they were widely known. The show they did that night (exclusively for Sony people) was mind-blowing - brilliant, loud rock! I was hooked from that moment onwards!

That Auckland show was the worst I had seen them. I saw them live two or three times, but that night was very poor by their extremely high standards. I have no idea when the bad blood between Liam and Noel started, but it was very much alive and kicking that night.

I did meet the band before and after the show - had a nice post-gig catch up with Noel back at the hotel they were staying. He was very hospitable and keen to chat. Liam on the other hand retreated to the bar, where he and Joe Cocker (coincidentally also staying there) drank into the small hours. Noel went to bed relatively early!

I do have a great story from that night; Noel and I were sitting together chatting for a while; he decided to go to bed but asked me to introduce him to our local Sony team (approx. 4 or 5 were sitting on couches nearby). So, I went around and introduced them one by one, explaining who they were and what they did. He had a nice quick comment and handshake for them all. The last person for him to meet was actually an EMI employee - so when I said, 'And this is XXX, but he works for EMI' he put his hand out as if to shake, and then, instead gave him the bird – and said, 'If you're from EMI you can fuck off'!'. It was hilarious - he turned to take off for bed and gave me a quick wink and a large smile. Top man that Noel Gallagher.'

Nick Capener

'I didn't follow them too closely before the gig, it was a colleague at work who had recently moved to New Zealand from the UK who introduced me to the music, he had a CD Walkman which was pretty cool back then, for me to listen to it on. I went with two guys from work, Robin and John, and John's wife Fiona (John and Fi named their first-born Liam so they were fans for sure). Can't recall how we got the tickets.

We had to queue up outside the venue and one lad with a few beers under his belt just kept singing the same song over and over. He wasn't terrible but the repetition got a bit much. Upon finally getting in myself and Robin made our way to about 10 metres from the stage (I was in my mid-twenties so seemed the right thing to do and Robin was very keen to get close). Eventually the lads swaggered out onto the stage and it was like a switch had been flicked that made the floor electric, bodies twitching everywhere and the noise…that was loud! My enthusiasm to be at the front disappeared pretty quickly as I spent all my time for that first song trying not to fall or get whacked in the mosh. Spent the next couple of songs pushing my way backwards until I was about 3/4 of the way back still on the floor. Liam didn't seem at all interested to be

Noel Gallagher at the Carter Holt Pavilion, Auckland. Image by Niels Schipper

there and came across as bored. My mate said that was part of his image, but I wasn't impressed. Caught up with the others after the show (prearranged as no mobile phones). Was a good talking point at work for the next few days.

Their music was good and the offstage entertainment they provided was fun too. I have found that Liam solo is a brilliant gig. Pre-COVID I'd go to around 20 concerts a year and his recent one at Spark [in 2019] is in my all-time top five. I saw Noel open for U2 at Mt Smart, he was good but doesn't have the same stage presence as Liam.'

Nilesh Vaidya

'My best mate and I were big fans. I can recall many summers BBQs with *Definitely Maybe* and *(What's the Story) Morning Glory?* blaring away on tape. And then many more when *Be Here Now* came out. From memory, there were about eight of us. We met at a mate's place beforehand and had a BBQ and beers while listening to Oasis.

It was loud. Extremely loud. And amazing. A great atmosphere. Difficult to recall now but I'm sure Noel and Liam got on fine. Until I saw Springsteen in 2016, the Oasis gig remained the best concert I had ever been to. No special effects, just rock 'n' roll. The rush and energy of the crowd were something else. I reckon I got my hearing back on the Thursday.'

Rachel Rose

'I was aware of Oasis' stellar rise, as I was back living in Manchester in the early 1990s, but I didn't follow them closely to be honest, although I did buy *Definitely Maybe*. I then went travelling for a couple of years in 1995 and 1996 and when I landed in New Zealand, they were massive. I bought *(What's the Story) Morning Glory?* and listened to it incessantly and I think it helped me with a bit of homesickness. I went with a really good friend (like a brother) Neil Lawton. We had worked together in Manchester and both supported Manchester City, going to games together. Two expats living in Auckland.

I enjoyed it, though I never had high expectations of the sound at the Expo Centre. There was a lot of energy and Liam was a very charismatic frontman. We got a shout-out from him and Noel as Neil and I were both wearing our

Manchester City shirts and we were near the front. I didn't follow them after the tour. I bought the next album but was disappointed with it. I haven't seen them since.'

Liam Gallagher at the Carter Holt Pavilion, Auckland. Image by Niels Schipper

Richard de Leun

'I worked at Sounds Music store at the time so was well aware of the band and looking forward to the show. I took a good mate along with me as I had complimentary tickets via Sony Music New Zealand. I enjoyed the show, even though the venue was rubbish. It was like an old air hanger out the back of the Logan Campbell Centre before it got rebuilt into the complex it is now. I recall the volume seemed to go up with every track and when they played the final song, 'I Am the Walrus', people were leaving with their hands over their ears as they couldn't handle the volume. I did see them again at the Livid Festival in Melbourne. I walked past Noel Gallagher in the VIP Bar, and was in awe to say hello.'

Richard Morris

'I loved the Britpop phenomenon! Blur was my favourite, then Pulp, Supergrass and Oasis. I didn't like all of Oasis' songs, but they certainly had a few classics.

I was keen to see them live. Blur toured the year before and they blew me away. I went by myself. My ex-wife's best friend was married to one of Oasis's accountants and he got me a free ticket.

VIP Pass for Auckland concert, courtesy of Richard Morris

I was bitterly disappointed. The band appeared tired and lacking any sort of excitement. Liam was in a truly awful mood. Belligerent beyond belief. I thought the bass player was decidedly average, as was the rhythm guitarist. GREAT drummer, and Noel steered the ship as well as he could. The gig was so loud it was painful. I stuck tissues in my ears and I could hear the speakers distorting. I'm a musician and sound engineer so I think I'm qualified to say the sound was absolute shit. A terrible venue too. I left after Noel did his acoustic set. I could've met the band that night, but I didn't hang around. I still have my official VIP pass.'

Robert Groothuis

'I was doing my OE in London from 1994-1996 which was the height of the Britpop Oasis vs. Blur wars. I remember Oasis being played on repeat at many of the pubs we hung out at, but more memorable was the Walkabout/ Outback Inn in Covent Garden. You would get the whole place singing along to 'Wonderwall'. When they were playing in Auckland in 1998 there was no question if we would go to see them or not.

I went with a mate who was also living in Auckland, but whom I also flatted with in London a few years earlier. It was at the NZ Expo Centre, and I remember it being very full. The mosh pit was all on, though I don't remember us being in the thick of it. It was very loud, no earplugs, so I paid the price for 2-3 days afterwards with my hearing a bit screwed up. I vaguely recall Liam walking off stage or some abuse between him and Noel but given their previous history of that sort of thing, it was to be expected and everyone thought it was just part of the show.

I wasn't ever a massive fan anyway. When I was travelling in 2005, I went to see them at Staten Island, Across the Narrows festival. A friend I had met earlier on my trip that year, had managed to get tickets through a music industry contact. Oasis was a lot more subdued than back in the 1990s.'

Sam Shearer

'It was awesome man. For me it was the first big concert I went to with my dad and younger brother. I'd never heard anything so loud in my entire life, and I still haven't been to a concert that came anywhere near the level of ear ringing as that. I was only 12 going on 13, I remember these kids slightly older than I, sitting behind us smoking weed and drinking a lot. It was the first time being really close to teenagers doing that.'

Scott Hornell

'I was a branch manager for the music store chain Sounds, and after the early album *Definitely Maybe* did okay, we all went to the Sony Music New Zealand listening party where *(What's the Story') Morning Glory?* was in the line-up. But as soon as that drum roll belted out for 'Roll with It', I knew it was better than most. It sold really well, and I was aware of the band from *NME* and a little bit of coverage in *Rolling Stone*.

I went along by myself. Looking back, I could have pushed management to get a complimentary ticket, but I didn't think it would be a large gig. It was booked in a strange place. They wouldn't have sold out a stadium at that time, so the

Paul 'Guigsy' McGuigan at the Carter Holt Pavilion, Auckland.
Image by Niels Schipper

big barn (Expo Centre) wasn't a great venue. I didn't like the place. They had retractable dividing curtains to make the place longer or split it in half. A lot of people hung near that divider; the smell of weed hung in the air. Until Oasis began, I didn't pay much attention. The mix of people was university students, hipsters and your regular blue-collar guys. Being from West Auckland, I had jeans and a jumper but there were a few Oasis shirts but no real fans visible.

When they began, I recognized the drum sound although that drowned out the guitar. What I do know is that Liam stood silent for some time and played the tambourine, which I noticed as Noel was singing most tunes. They played 'Cigarettes & Alcohol' which was great, and Noel played acoustic for a couple of tracks. But the lights were crap and it wasn't intimate in the same way a lower ceiling changes the sound. They should have been booked elsewhere.

I never really followed them after *Be Here Now*. With the ups and downs, you'd hear the band name but even when they'd play a record crowd in the UK, down under here, the story always had negative tones. Shame, as they had some good years before the split (splits, returns, splits).'

Stephen Lyon

'I was into them, but by no means a super-fan. Interested enough to be keen to see them in concert though, I went with my girlfriend (now wife), sister and brother-in-law (I think).

I don't recall all that much other than it was super loud and a real let-down. I kept trying to tell myself it was awesome, but it really wasn't.

Weirdly, the only song I remember with any real clarity was The Chemical Brothers number Noel played in his acoustic set. Like most people, I'd imagine I liked the first couple of albums but lost a bit of interest after *Be Here Now*.'

Steve Dee

'My wife introduced me to 'Wonderwall' on cassingle when it was first re-leased. I liked the song, but it wasn't until I heard 'Don't Look Back in Anger' that I really got interested so I bought *(What's The Story) Morning Glory?* on CD and was hooked. After listening to *Be Here Now* for the first time there

Noel Gallagher at the Carter Holt Pavilion, Auckland. Image by Niels Schipper

was no way I wouldn't go to the concert. I went with my wife. I think we got tickets from a record shop in Manukau City Centre.

We got there earlyish to get a car park but others had the same idea so that took a while. Once we got inside it became noticeable that the venue was too small. It was incredible to me that such a big band would play in such a shithole. Anyway, as we worked our way to the front, we could see down the space between the wall and the side of the stage. Liam was sitting down having a cigarette and he waved to us all as we called out his name. We managed to move closer to centre stage. Led Zeppelin started playing as the lights went down then 'Be Here Now' was the first song and the crowd went nuts. My wife and I were getting crushed and pushed around. I feared for her safety so, as I held onto her, I punched our way out of there and we made our way towards the back to catch our breath. I asked if she wanted to leave but bless her, she said no. That experience dampened the atmosphere for me and unfortunately, I don't remember too much of it, except for 'Don't Look Back in Anger' and Noel singing 'Don't Go Away'. I was disappointed they didn't play 'All Around the World'. We left as they went into the last song 'I Am the Walrus'.

I have all their albums. I was sad that they broke up. I much prefer Noel's solo career to Liam's. I didn't like Liam's voice after *Be Here Now* but listening back now it's not as bad as I initially thought. I have tried listening to his solo stuff, but it doesn't grab me whereas Noel's does, well, most of it does.'

Steve Donovan

'They were far from my favourite band, although I liked the first two albums well enough. The late 1990s saw loads of indie-type bands touring New Zealand, and I'd seen (or would see) plenty of those – e.g., Blur, Pulp, Radiohead, Beck, Beastie Boys, Bjork, Placebo, Massive Attack, Portishead – so it seemed like a natural thing to catch Oasis too. I thought their music would suit a live setting, even though I agreed with most people that the *Be Here Now* album, despite having a cracking lead single, was overblown tosh.

I have no memory of getting tickets, but for some of the 1990s I worked in Auckland's CBD, and I do have a memory of sometimes buying gig tickets from the Sounds record store – sometimes from the lovely Fiona McDonald! – So perhaps that was the way?

Uniquely for me, I went to this gig alone. I've been to well over a hundred gigs in my life now, and I'm pretty certain this might be the only one where I've been unaccompanied. I was originally going with a mate, but he pulled out for some reason, but I decided to go anyway.

Very few memories of the actual gig. My two abiding images are what I took to be Liam storming off stage and the band playing the next few numbers with Noel on singing duties, and everyone in the venue holding their fingers to their ears during the final song 'I Am the Walrus'. The sound was bad during the whole gig, but by the encore it was a screeching cacophony of feedback and echo. Remember the general bad vibes from the stage too – it was obvious they weren't getting on.

Sometimes I wonder whether the gig seemed worse than it actually was because I'd recently seen Radiohead on their *OK Computer* tour, and they were magnificent. But no, regrettably, I think Oasis were wank in their own right.'

Steve Sykes

'I instantly fell in love with Oasis after seeing them perform 'Some Might Say' on *Top of the Pops*. The gig was apparently great. They started with 'Be Here Now'. We were standing up really close to the stage and the venue was pretty small for the amount of people. We started to get squashed and someone stood on my ex's foot and ripped her nail off, so she got pulled from the crowd to get cared for by St John's. The biggest mistake of my life was being so worried I pushed myself through the crowd to get out and find her. I missed most of the gig, and couldn't find her, think I made it back in for the last song. Can't remember what it was now. But the icing on the cake is, after the concert I found my ex, after St John's fixed her toe, she was put on a chair at the side of the stage and watched the whole gig. I was gutted. They all came off stage and walked past her!'

Tonz Atkins

'It was supposed to be near where I lived in a suburb called Glenfield, on the North Shore. We had an events centre that was actually cool and I had seen

Noel Gallagher at the Carter Holt Pavilion, Auckland. Image by Niels Schipper

Liam Gallagher at the Carter Holt Pavilion, Auckland. Image by Niels Schipper

other bands there and couldn't fucking believe it that my band was going to be playing down the road from my local. Then it got moved again to some shithole of a venue.

I nearly met them. I thought I was so close when I used to drink at a bar in Auckland opposite the hotel they were in. I researched and rang around trying to find that out making out I was important. I was at the fucking door and they were there. The guy on the door said, 'Who are you after? Noel is upstairs but Liam is in the bar and who are you?'

I came out with, 'I know Alan McGee' and he said, 'hang on and wait here' and went indoors and I thought I had cracked it, but he came back out and said, 'sorry mate.' Just would have been so cool to have a chat. I found out where they were going to be staying and considered booking a room so could have a drink in the bar, I really should have.

The gig itself, I don't think a lot of people were ready for it I feel. Some couldn't deal with the attitude factor and were put off. I thought it was great, but I don't think my friends who I went with shared the same opinion.'

Vicky Fairchild

'I didn't really follow Oasis; I just went to all the gigs I could back then. I went with school friends aged 16 or 17. I just remember it was packed, standing room only, very hot and claustrophobic, and the sound was horrendous as it wasn't a space designed for sound. It was all concrete floors and walls and metal sheeting on the roof. Why they didn't hold it in the Logan Campbell Centre or North Shore Events Centre like all the other overseas acts at the time did I have no idea? We all bailed during what I presume was the final encore 'I Am the Walrus' as the reverb just went on and on and was painful to hear.'

* * *

The press reviews were mostly positive, glancing over the sound issues many of the attendees remembered from that night. After a peak of 26.1 Celsius in the day, it was a hot and stuffy Auckland evening. Combined with thousands packed into a small venue, it made for an uncomfortable evening for many.

One gig down, one to go, the band moved on to Wellington.

Liam Gallagher at the Carter Holt Pavilion, Auckland. Image by Niels Schipper

Chapter 6 – Wellington, March 10, 1998

Parkroyal Hotel, Grey Street, Wellington[127]

Oasis arrived in Wellington on Tuesday, March 10. The band stayed at the Parkroyal Hotel (now the Intercontinental) on the corner of Grey and Featherston Streets. The crew was deliberately booked at a separate location - the James Cook Hotel on The Terrace. Where possible, this was done to ensure that if chaos ensued where the band was based, the crew could still set up the gig as scheduled without disruption. That Tuesday the temperature peaked at 25 degrees Celsius, not uncommon for March, but also an indication of the long, hot summer New Zealand had experienced that year. February 1998 was the hottest month since records began in 1855, with a national average temperature of 19.6 degrees Celsius.[128]

Hotel rooms were in short supply across the capital with the Auckland power crisis driving high-profile events to Wellington and demand for accommodation to unprecedented levels. New Zealand's national museum Te Papa Tongarewa had recently opened on February 14, drew crowds into the city and within weeks caused Gallagher level controversy with its Picturica Britannica Exhibition. An installation which included a piece by British artist Tania Kovats, titled 'Virgin in a Condom', a 7.5 cm statue of the Virgin Mary encased in a condom caused widespread moral outrage, with protesters facing arrest following attempts to dismantle the artwork. However, Te Papa stood its ground and the artwork remained on display.[131] Other stories making the news included Prime Minister Jenny Shipley's visit to Japan on March 9. Having flown commercially with Air New Zealand, passengers were unhappy with delays in Tokyo due to Japanese protocols and Shipley having to disembark first.[132]

The location for the closing New Zealand concert was the largest indoor venue in Wellington. Opening in 1995, the Queens Wharf Events Centre was

Advert for concert at Queens Wharf Events Centre in the *Evening Post* – Stuff
Limited[126]

one of a wave of waterfront developments constructed in the mid-1990s. The
Queens Wharf Retail Centre stood opposite the arena, with Ticketek NZ and
Chicago Sports Café in the Events Centre complex itself. The Bond Store

Oasis at the Parkroyal Hotel, Wellington[129]

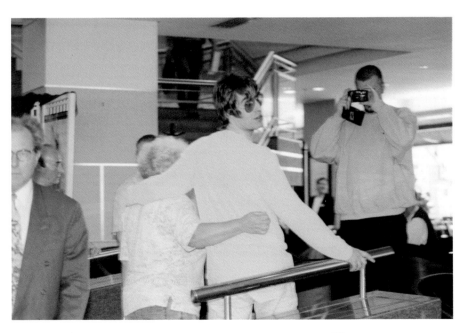

Oasis at the Parkroyal Hotel, Wellington[130]

building beside the Events Centre housed the Museum of Wellington City and Sea. Dockside Restaurant, Rock Pool (bar and eatery), Shed 5 Restaurant and Bar, and Photo Plus were some of the other businesses in the area.[133] While the retail centre was short-lived, the Queens Wharf Events Centre still stands today, now under the name TSB Bank Arena. Traditionally the home of netball, basketball, roller derby, book fairs and various exhibitions, the venue wasn't exactly known for its great acoustics with much debate amongst concertgoers as to who or what was to blame for a poor showing - the venue, or the performer.

Queens Wharf Events Centre, Wellington[134]

Nonetheless, 1998 was a stellar year for rock acts in Wellington, with Radio-head and Pearl Jam performing there ahead of the Oasis tour and Van Halen and Metallica after. With ticket sales strong in Wellington, a last-minute switch to an outdoor venue was discussed in the press, but always unlikely. Athletic Park in the Newtown area of the city hadn't hosted an outdoor concert since 1991 and Wellington Regional Stadium was still two years away from being open for business. Coincidentally, the same week Oasis were in town, Fran Wilde, the Stadium Trust Chairperson and Dr Ngatata Love, Tenths Trust Chairperson, turned the first sod of earth in the stadium's construction, on March 12, 1998.[135]

Queens Wharf, Wellington, with the Events Centre to the right[136]

The Wellington concert is often thought of as the defining moment in the tour. Based on the various accounts in the press, from attendees and by band biographer Paolo Hewitt in his brilliant book, *Forever the People, Six Months on the Road with Oasis*, a common theme shining through is that Liam Gallagher was drunk, the sound was terrible and a fight ensued between the brothers.[137] The relationship between the band and the New Zealand press was tense, as documented on the front page of the *Evening Post* on March 11, including an image of Liam at the Wellington concert.

Understanding exactly how this gig may have sounded to attendees is possible thanks to a bootleg audio recording uploaded to YouTube.[139] The setlist began with 'Be Here Now' - Noel in fine form on guitar. Liam decided to add something extra to the performance by playing the kazoo, much to Noel's outrage.

ALL MOUTH – "You stink like the rest of them," Oasis' Liam Gallagher told a Post journalist yesterday.   Picture: JO HEAD

Lout and about with Liam

By NEIL REID

Lager lout or angel? Will the real Liam Gallagher please step forward.

The Oasis frontman of television-throwing, groupie-scoring and alleged headbutting fame blazed into the Capital for last night's sell-out concert at Queens Wharf Events Centre.

So when the opportunity came to have a talk with the singer of the self-appointed biggest band in the world at the Parkroyal bar yesterday, I leapt at the chance.

Barely two minutes after the Oasis entourage and 10 hangers-on arrived at their Grey St hotel, Liam sidled up to the bar and ordered his staple bourbon and Coke.

Within seconds I too was heading to the bar. Then it was a matter of concealing a shorthand notepad so my cover wasn't blown.

By that stage Liam was making short work of his second drink. As the scrawny singer supped – clearly aggrieved that his precious drinking time was being invaded by media and fans peering through hotel windows – it was time to bond.

I blurted: "You must get pretty sick of the media, mate?"

Liam, who'd been discussing the merits of cigarettes with a "minder", looked at me and replied: "I get paid bloody well for this. But what f . . . me off is that cow who's taking 200 f . . . photos when only one will go in the bloody paper."

Flicking back his wayward strands of hair, eyes hidden behind glasses more commonly worn by 1970s B-grade actors, Liam went on to again call Evening Post photographer Jo Head a "cow". Then he poked out his tongue at her and gave her the fingers.

Four bourbons later and Liam was increasingly agitated at the attention from the media outside and about 20 fans trying to catch glimpses of their pop idol.

Liam asked his minders to tell the group to go away. However, the goatee-bearded bodyguard told him to settle down, and reminded him that any unflattering footage of the band was sure to appear on English television.

It was time to bring a smile to the grumpy one. "Why don't you go and play a bit of soccer? You like soccer, don't you?"

The reply: "My brother's the fit one. I played in Auckland and bleedin' got injured. I can hardly f . . . walk."

"Well, you should try New Zealand beer. What about Steinlager?"

"You can count on bourbon to taste like bourbon the world over. It doesn't change. Beer does."

Liam got up to leave. This was the 1990s pop icon's chance to thank thousands of Kiwi fans.

"Liam, I'm a reporter, how has the tour been?" Oops. Doctor Jekyll turned into Mr Hyde.

"You're a f . . journo. You stink like the rest of them. I knew from word one you were one. I could smell you."

"So there's nothing you want to say?" The reply was unprintable.

Later, we ran into the singer again, back at the bar. Tried another tack: "Good luck at the gig tonight, Liam."

That didn't work either. Liam pulled his trademark sneer and bid me farewell with a heartfelt "bollocks".

See **REVIEW** page 38

Evening Post, March 11, 1998 – Stuff Limited[138]

Unimpressed by the acoustics, Liam continued to act up, complaining loudly and unrepentantly. After 'Roll with It' he had the following to say:

'It's like nah, is everyone pulling us up - whoever's come in here I can't hear a fucking sound. And you's are great and God bless you all, fucking hell it costs a bit of money,

155

Fucking hell it's gonna rape our bank accounts'

'D'You Know What I Mean?' was performed, minus some verses and a chorus Liam failed to sing. 'Cigarettes & Alcohol', was announced, but Liam was now becoming obsessively focused on the sound, much to the frustration of the increasingly impatient crowd:

'It's not that fucking hard right, I'll pay myself to get some decent sound on this fucking stage right. I got fucking money here I'll pay for it. Not that fucking hard is it?'

The rest of the band clearly had enough, and after a failed attempt to start 'Cigarettes & Alcohol', Noel walked off, throwing his guitar to the ground. Backstage, a fight ensued between the brothers, not picked up in the bootleg audio. The crowd rallied a collective boo, unsure if the gig would go on. In the end, by some miracle the band did make a return, playing a total of 14 songs and holding it together, just, for the remainder of the show thanks to Noel's standout great acoustic set. A man with the weight of the world on his shoulders, trying to make up for his brother's performance with some excellent guitar work. Sadly, there is no recording of 'Champagne Supernova' which closed the gig. There was also no encore to the disappointment of many in the crowd. Based on information available in the media, and attendee recollections, this is the setlist for the concert:

Be Here Now

Stand by Me

Supersonic

Roll with It

D'You Know What I Mean?

Cigarettes & Alcohol

Don't Go Away – Noel Acoustic

Setting Sun – Noel Acoustic (The Chemical Brothers cover)

Fade In-Out – Noel acoustic

Don't Look Back in Anger

Wonderwall

Live Forever

It's Gettin' Better (Man!!)

Champagne Supernova

BE HERE NOW
STAND BY ME
SUPERSONIC
ROLL WITH IT
D'YER KNOW WHAT I MEAN
CIGARETTES & ALCOHOL

Acoustic Numbers:
3 Songs - T.B.A.

DON'T LOOK BACK IN ANGER
WONDERWALL
LIVE FOREVER
IT'S GETTIN' BETTER MAN
CHAMPAGNE SUPERNOVA

ACQUIESCE
I AM THE WALRUS

Setlist obtained from Wellington gig, courtesy of gig attendee Carter Nixon. The final 2 songs were not performed

In the dressing room after the show, the drama continued. A resigned Liam called for a band meeting, proclaiming this was the end of Oasis. Due to fly to Argentina the next day, Liam shared his intention to head to Mexico, claiming there was no love for him that night on stage in Wellington and that the magic had gone. With Noel already back at the hotel the meeting didn't actually occur until the next morning, when emotions weren't running quite as high, and the band were able to talk some sense into Liam. The meeting turned into an intervention of sorts and the band confronted Liam about his drinking before and during recent gigs.[140] The pressure of the pending court appearance in Brisbane was clearly taking its toll. Reviews for the gig in Wellington were less than favourable, with both Liam and the poor acoustics the target for reviewers.

IN YOUR FACE: Oasis singer Liam Gallagher in characteristic form during last night's concert at Wellington's Queens Wharf Events Centre. Later, fans were left baffled as brothers, Liam and Noel, left the stage for five minutes after an apparent argument about the sound system. They returned to complete the show. ❑ Review p16

MARTIN HUNTER

Image of Liam Gallagher on front cover of *Dominion*, March 11, 1998 – Stuff Limited[141]

Oasis could learn from Beatles

OASIS are sadly mistaken if they think they're bigger than the Beatles.

At least the Beatles knew what a professional show was and gave adoring fans something worth the ticket price.

Pity the same can't be said of Oasis.

Bad sound combined with a bad attitude made it one of the worst concerts I've seen.

The night started well for the fans, who were pumped up and ready to go — amped by the thought that they were going to see something big.

Poncing on stage came Liam Gallagher and the band. The first song was ear-drum splitting — and it got worse.

In the second song *Stand By Me*, from their latest album *Be Here Now*, Liam's voice got lost in a messy wall of noise.

Liam swaggered about the stage with his token tambourine.

Occasionally, he gave the fans a thrill by getting into the pit with them, but that was the only thrill

REVIEW ▮▮▮▮▮

Oasis in Concert
Queens Wharf Events Centre
March 10
Reviewed by Anna Fyfe

they received. In true Oasis-style, the expletives about the sound system started flying after *Roll With It*.

Yes, the sound quality was a shocker, but the fans had paid their money and deserved a professional show, even though conditions were less than perfect.

Like the true gentleman he is, and the one we've come to expect, Liam screamed about the "f***ing sound", claiming it would "rape his bank account".

His attitude dampened the crowd's spirit, and after *D'You Know What I Mean* he really let fly.

He walked out with wallet open, screaming that he would "pay for the f***ing sound" himself. An argument started on stage, and Noel led the band off

to shouts of "Boo" from the crowd. If the crowd hadn't paid good money for the concert, it would have been funny.

A gem of a solo set from Noel restored the faith slightly.

Accompanied by congo drums, he showed he was the real talent, with the wonderful sounding *Don't Go Away*.

This was followed by *Fade In-Out*, with unusual snippets from *Setting Sun* by the Chemical Brothers. I kept wishing he'd stay and Liam would lose his voice.

Expected hit of the evening, *Wonderwall*, was a pig's breakfast.

The beautiful melody was lost, and a now-returned Liam sang angrily, cutting off the extended notes well-known from the album.

After some more microphone throwing, the gig ended with a whimper on *Champagne Supernova*.

Liam Gallagher may have called Princess Diana a "lazy cow" — but at least she could deliver what the public wanted.

Dominion review by Anna Fyfe – Stuff Limited[142]

BELOW PAR – Looking gaunt and tired, Liam Gallagher whinged about the crowd, his microphone and the sound system.   Pictures: JO HEAD

Stage spat set the standard

What: Oasis
Where: Queens Wharf Events Centre, last night
Reviewed by: Mike Houlahan

Well, it went pretty much as expected. Oasis arrived, had a row, and left again.

In between though, this was the classic game of two halves. Searing, stunning moments of rock genius meets bog standard bar band desperately trying to keep time and tune. Oasis isn't a band to do things by half. When they're good, they're very, very good, but when they're bad, awful is a compliment.

With the mad circus surrounding Oasis in the last couple of weeks, they could, perhaps, be understood for having half a mind on the plane home. Understood but not forgiven for turning in an average show.

It's the hard-earned cash of the capacity crowd at the Events Centre, and thousands like them, that make Oasis what they want to be – the biggest band in the world. Their side of the bargain is to sound and act like they might also be the best.

On the evidence of last night,

REJUVENATED – After an unscheduled break, Liam was on form.

they were well off form. Having seen them before, this was a pale shadow of Oasis at their best. You know a rock concert has been a bit of a disappointment when the acoustic bracket is the highlight.

Things started off reasonably promisingly. Be Here Now and it's refrain of "Kickin' up a storm from the day that I was born" seemed likely to set the tone for the evening, and so it proved.

Stand By Me was a fairly drab affair, redeemed by a storming run through first single Supersonic. However, by Roll With It the cracks were starting to show in Liam's voice, which overseas reports had already hinted was under pressure.

By this stage, so was the man himself, whingeing to all and sundry about the crowd, the sound system and his microphone. The brothers Gallagher started yelling at each other, lots of fingerpointing went on, and their early exit was so predictable it

seemed as though they'd rehearsed it.

Five minutes later they were back, roaring through Cigarettes And Alcohol before Noel settled into his acoustic set. As stated already, this was probably the highlight of the show.

His voice was in much better nick, and it was good hearing it in such a stripped down format.

The band returned for Don't Look Back In Anger, then Liam trooped back and growled his way through Wonderwall, before falling apart on Live Forever, his voice so hoarse it sounded like he may have lost it completely.

To our lad's credit, he pulled through to rasp out It's Gettin' Better (Man!!) and final song, Champagne Supernova, which was dragged out to epic lengths by Noel.

Maybe he knew Oasis was well short of its promised two hours, and there was no way we'd be seeing any more of Liam that night.

The lights went up straight away, leaving the crowd knowing they could say they'd seen Oasis. But enjoyed them? Now, that's another question entirely.

Evening Post review by Mike Houlahan – Stuff Limited[143]

music

Oasis

Queens Wharf Events Centre
Tue 10/3/98
Reviewed by Simon Sweetman

Well here it is; the review of the band people either love or loathe (and it is likely the later in terms of *Salient* readership). My job then, is easy; I simply say the show sucked and sign off. Unfortunately that seems less than fair for a small group of fans and neutral music listeners.

The lights dropped around 8.30pm and the audience were treated to a blasting version of Led Zeppelin's classic 'Rock 'n' Roll' courtesy of the towering P.A. speakers. The song was played in its entirity before the infamous Gallagher brothers - and a rhythm section that could be anyone - loped out on to the stage. 'Rock 'n' Roll' was an apt intro, the packed Queens Wharf audience were there to see a "Rock 'n' Roll Show" - and that is precisely what was given.

Opening with the title track to their latest release *Be Here Now*, Oasis presented a veritable "Greatest Hits" package consisting of tracks from all three of their albums. In fact it seemed to me in the early stages of the show that we were about to be offered the ultimate Rock 'n' Roll show, until five songs into the night when Liam's incessant whining and cursing in regard to the sound levels annoyed Noel so much so that he left the stage, to be joined backstage almost immediately, by the whole band. Thirty minutes into this "Great Rock 'n' Roll Show" here was the Wellington audience quickly contemplating what constitutes value for money.

The relatively short time it took for the band to arrive back on stage, and launching straight into a searing version of 'Cigarettes and Alcohol' suggested to me that this sibling rivalry has now reached such expected proportions that at times the arguing is highly manufactured and even choreographed.

Noel delivered an acoustic set (with some percussion backing from drummer Whitey) consisting of *Be Here Now* tracks 'Don't Go Away' and 'Fade In-Out'. There was an ethereal sounding acoustic interlude which joined the songs. The more I listened however, I realised it had been lifted straight from the Beatles' ballad 'Across the Universe'. Now, I'm not one to jump to prosecution and I know what you're all thinking; Oasis. Steal? - From, the Beatles? (How peculiar!)

The band arrive back on stage (sans Liam) for Noel to run through a standard version of singalong fav 'Don't Look Back in Anger', then Liam gallops back out of his corner to lead a charged up, electric version of 'Wonderwall'. Great versions of 'Live Forever' and 'It's Getting Better' directly follow, before Liam insists there is only one song left.

'Champagne Supernova' (still a good song) is played out in penultimate glory. Liam climbs down into the pit and rests his ears against the wall of speakers. He is deliberately trying to detract from the frenzied jam on stage based around some excellent live guitar work from Noel.

'Champagne' ended after ten or so minutes - and that was it. The end. Oasis left the stage. The Rock 'n' Roll show was over.

To give Oasis bad press or a snide remark in a review is akin to transporting large quantities of coal to Newcastle - so I conclude by suggesting that whilst I was personally not disappointed, there were certainly no surprises. And not playing an encore does not confirm a New Zealand audience as being on your side.

Oasis, you'd look grumpy too if you were that ugly.

Salient review by Simon Sweetman[144]

Attendees interviewed for their recollections gave wide-ranging opinions on the concert and some fantastic insights into what went down in Wellington, on and off the stage. Twenty-five years on memories blur and there are differing accounts on who walked off stage and the reasons for doing so.

Adrian Szentivanyi

'I took my 10-year-old daughter who understandably doesn't remember much about it. We were towards the back, so the sound wasn't the best. Although some people say it was a great gig I remember differently. I think it was Liam who was drunk which pissed Noel off and if I remember rightly had an altercation with Liam but with the passing of time that's a bit hazy. I have been to over 200 international gigs and that ranks as one of the worst.'

Andrew Smith

'I'm an Oasis nut and went to Knebworth with my friends in 1996. The Wellington concert was amazing because we were so near the front. I went with my Debs and another friend of mine from the UK, Rob Burton. My best memory was having a beer in Chicago Bar prior to the gig, we were on the balcony looking over Queens Wharf. The next minute Liam wandered out of the pub across the square. As he walked across Queens Wharf (by himself) I was thinking what could I shout out? I yelled, 'Liam you wanker' at the top of my voice. He looked up and gave me the fingers then carried on into the venue. MENTAL! Everyone said the sound quality was bad, but I didn't care. Me and my friends saw them a few years later in Sydney which was another great gig, but the three days were a massive blur.'

Andrew Tait

'I followed them pretty darn closely. I was a huge fan as I was living in the UK at the time of their rapid rise and the whole Britpop thing. They just captured the times, a lot has been written about the New Britannia thing. Jackie and I managed to get tickets to Knebworth (still have the T-shirt and the ticket somewhere) in 1996. That was huge. A mega event. They were at the top of their game.

I remember we were standing in the general admission area towards the back and not in the mosh pit. The concert was ok (not a patch on the atmosphere

Rock band Oasis perform at the Events Centre. Photographer unidentified[145]

of Knebworth of course). The thing that stands out is the onstage tiff Noel and Liam had. They just saw their arses with each other, a song just collapsed, and Noel walked off stage. The band followed and sometime after that Noel came out alone with an acoustic guitar and a stool, sang 2-3 songs by himself, and blew me away. That was the best bit of the concert. He was (and still is) such a talented songwriter and confident performer. Eventually Liam returned and then finished the set as if nothing had happened. Classic Oasis.'

Angela Roestenburg

'I enjoyed the music of Oasis before I went to the gig, but I was not a big fan. My ex-husband was into music and wanted to go so we went together. I presume that we bought the tickets through normal channels. It was very loud. I lasted through the opening act. The sound mixing was totally off. Oasis was late coming on (I think the front guy was having one of his many tiffs). I think he was not into it and was quite negative, so I decided to leave. I told my husband he could stay as I'd wait in a nearby bar, however, he also decided to leave with me, and he was a fan. It was very disappointing.'

Asher Wilson-Goldman

'I had (What's the Story) Morning Glory? on CD which I listened to frequently. I can't remember if I had Definitely Maybe at the time as well, or if I bought it later. I would have been 12 when the gig happened so most of my music taste came via my (10 years older than me) brother - Nirvana, Primus et al. The ticket was a 12th birthday present from my (then-22-year-old) brother, who took me to the gig (along with his close friend Sam). It was my first proper gig! I'd seen a few outdoor concerts before (including ones my brother was playing in), but this was the first real gig, and certainly the first international band I'd ever seen.

The sound at Queens Wharf was terrible, so much feedback every time the guitars tried to do anything. I remember sitting next to a reporter for the Dominion newspaper, she asked us at one point which one was Noel and which one was Liam - I distinctly remember thinking it was strange to write a review of a gig where you clearly didn't know the band.

Anyway, Liam was a dick, as expected, and famously went off stage because the sound quality was so poor. I remember Noel coming back on and starting to play by himself which was fine and didn't overpower the system, but then Liam and the full band came back and it all went bad again. Despite that, it was my first gig. So, I still enjoyed it and have positive memories.'

Oasis fans at the Events Centre, Wellington. Photographer unidentified[146]

Oasis fans at the Events Centre, Wellington. Photographer unidentified[147]

Ben Gregg

'When it was announced there was absolutely no way I was missing this, as I had become a massive fan by this time. I would say I was obsessed and by now a collector, as I was buying whatever music shops in Wellington had to offer, as well as playing the Russian roulette of eBay at the time (most purchases turned up, but not all), and faxing record stores in UK & Europe for official releases and bootlegs. Regardless of this, to actually see the band live was an absolute non-negotiable. My family was very aware of my obsession, I would even say they were fans. My dad was a huge Beatles (amongst other British 1960s bands) fan so although he found them to be quite derivative, he also loved their sound, and northernness (his mother was from near Bolton); he just said they didn't know how to finish a song. In any case, lots of my friends also wanted to go so my parents gave me the money (cash) to buy all of my friends their standing tickets (10, I believe), obviously on the understanding they would all pay them back. I also bought four seated tickets for my family (Mum, Dad and two older sisters)

To the day itself, having passed 9 of the 10 tickets that I had purchased for friends (obviously keeping one for myself), I, along with a friend, arrived at the Events Centre around 9 a.m. before anybody else was there. But, within I'd say 20 minutes a couple of people turned up. Over the next few hours a few more, I would say there wasn't any more than fifty by midday. But, as the afternoon continued lots of people started turning up, slowly some of the other eight in my 'crew' turned up and enjoyed the advantage of having the obsessed me being there early and therefore were at the front of the queue despite being many hours after the dedicated.

In the many hours before the doors opened, I do remember chatting with the others around me and discussing favourite songs and information about the band. I sort of knew a few people around me. At some stage throughout the day, rumour was circulating that Liam was drinking at the bar across from the Events Centre (to be specific, directly opposite what was Chicago Bar). This area is (and was) paved, and therefore no cars are around, hence allowing people to wander in the area. I went across to try and meet him, but I did not see him, instead I used the opportunity to use the bathroom - bear in mind I was 17 at this point, and the legal age for drinking alcohol was 20 so I shouldn't have even entered the bar, but I couldn't turn down the opportunity to try and meet him. A person in the line for the gig near us said that he also went over and Liam was at the bar and he shook his hand. Many hours later, at a guess somewhere between 4 pm and 6 pm, Liam did walk across the paved area (with minders) towards the Events Centre and got swamped by people, I would say he was quite worse for wear at the time, admittedly so was I as I had had a smoke and a drink or two.

I do not remember exactly what time the doors opened but when they did, being at the front of the queue all day I was very keen to get to the front and directly in front of Liam, i.e. absolute centre stage. We were all told not to run, and although we were not running, we would've been disqualified in the Olympic walk. I managed to get against the barrier just left of Liam's mic so was extremely happy. I remember being desperately busting to go to the toilet but there was no way I was going anywhere. My friend whom I had turned up with at 9 a.m. didn't manage to get into the front row, but instead was essentially on my right shoulder behind a younger girl and was upset that he wasn't also against the barrier like me - I tried to calm him down, and luckily (for him, and probably for me) eventually he did get next to me up against the barrier. I retrospectively heard a few illegitimate tickets were floating about and that the gig was oversold. I was extremely squashed against the barrier, I had bruising on my ribs for quite a while following this gig so there may well be some truth to this; being squashed meant that it was very close, which also meant I sweated a bucket load, at some stage I realised I no longer needed to go to the toilet, which was an absolute win for me.

The gig itself was very messy but awesome. The crowd was loving it. Around that time in New Zealand, or at least Wellington, crowds were quite crazy, lots of moshing, lots of waves of movement, lots of craziness; this was no different, but crazier. In terms of my memory of the gig itself, I have a few lasting memories, one is Noel's acoustic songs, which I would say was the highlight musically, starting with 'Don't Go Away', I absolutely loved that song at the time and was so happy that we got that. But then he played 'Setting Sun', and lots of people were looking around not really knowing or recognising the song, but again I thought it was awesome, as I knew exactly what it was and shouted every word. He finished off with 'Fade In-Out', just brilliant. Once Liam came back, it was very obvious there was tension between the brothers, due to Liam being wasted. But another lasting memory for me, which was earlier in the gig, Liam leaned out into the crowd extending his arm holding his tambourine, I managed to jump up and forward and grab the tambourine and was tugging with him for it - I pulled hard and just about pulled him off the stage and he glowered at me, so I relented and he took it back and started singing again. 'It's Gettin' Better (Man!!)' was absolutely awesome (messy awesome, of course!) and I don't think Liam even finished his parts, but it was a great version. There was confusion following this, as people were expecting more but (I don't think) there was any more to be given/heard; and I think (and thought at the time) it is brilliant that Wellington got the full theatre of Oasis live.

We are now 27 years on from when I first discovered Oasis, and they have had such a massive impact, and influence, on me. They in some sense come into my mind every day, and I am still collecting as much as ever, some of these people on Instagram put me to shame, but there's always something to buy, so I just try to get reasonable deals on older stuff, but I do always buy anything new immediately - pretty costly shipping over to here though.'

Bill Allan

'There were a couple of things about Oasis at the time. The first thing I liked about them was the accent. Manchester, and not that generic accent most singers use. I was also dealing with life issues, so I gravitated to them more and more. So, I was excited to have tickets, but a bit disappointed it was in such a small venue. Queens Wharf, Wellington. I think when it became clear something wasn't right with the band on stage, I started to lose interest a bit. My brain was taken over trying to work out what was happening and what was to happen. After the meltdown and stage walk-off, I was plain disappointed and couldn't get back into the groove.'

Bruce Hay Chapman – Facilities Manager at Queens Wharf Events Centre in 1998

'I dealt mainly with the road crew. I recall sitting up on the catwalk looking down on the band thinking 'those two aren't getting on.' The Queens Wharf

Liam Gallagher at the Queens Wharf Events Centre, Wellington.
Photographer unidentified[148]

Events Centre despite all the grumbles about acoustics, always had one thing going for it… it was a small venue, so it was easy to get a good view. I remember thinking that Oasis fans almost anywhere else in the world would be looking at tiny little figures on stage or a jumbo screen but here we got to see them. Great light show too.'

Carter Nixon

'I followed the band very closely. I worked at a record store from 1992 to 1997 and can distinctly remember the day the Sony Music New Zealand records rep came in with a video to play us of an exciting new band that he said was going to be the next big thing and it was the video to 'Supersonic'. I was a fan instantly and was super excited when it was announced that they were coming to Wellington touring an album that I loved (and still love, *Be Here Now* is super underrated.)

I went with my girlfriend of the time and a bunch of band buddies. We were all in local bands and a big group of us went together. I was in a band called Crumb and my pals were from a band called Breathe. We all bought tickets from the local ticket place. Fairly sure they were from the Ticketek booth at the Opera House.

I remember the gig itself being insanely loud. One of the loudest gigs I have ever been to. Way too loud for the venue and the sound wasn't great. A couple of times having trouble deciphering what song they were playing; it wasn't great. The venue is famous for it. To see them on stage was so exciting though. I didn't care I just wanted to see Liam and there he was. He is my favourite.

Liam kept ranting between songs about how bad the sound was and that led to the infamous fight where Noel told him to shut up and sing and Liam said fuck you and Noel stormed off. The band then all left the stage to a chorus of boos from the very annoyed audience. They eventually came back to finish the show, but it was very half-hearted and the crowd were never back on their side and it was a turning point in how people felt about them in general here. Everyone I knew who was there pretty much hated it and never got into them again. I loved that we got an onstage fight and a clearly drunk Liam. For me, a great gig and I stuck by them right till the end. I got every album the morning they were released, every DVD, the live Pay Per View shows that were on Sky TV and love them to this day. Top five all-time band for me.

My friend worked in the bar of the hotel they were staying in and had been asked to stay open for the band when they came back after the gig. When they arrived after what had clearly been a pretty disastrous show on what had been a bad leg of the tour, a pretty angry Liam came into the bar and at one point grabbed my friend by the collar and angrily slurred 'You know who I am? You know who is the greatest rock 'n' roll star in the world? Me' and was just generally unpleasant to be around.

I would've loved to have seen them again and I hope one day they get back together. If they do, I'll go wherever they go see and them again.'

Chris Morrison

'I got into Oasis in the summer of 1995, when I first heard the track 'Morning Glory' at a backpackers in Auckland and it sounded so much louder than every

Liam Gallagher meets the crowd at the Events Centre. Photographer unidentified[149]

Liam Gallagher up close with fans at the Events Centre. Security personnel Rob Rankine close behind. Photographer unidentified[150]

other song on the jukebox (remember them?). A month or so later it was hearing 'Champagne Supernova' and away you go. Great band and one a 20-year-old me could really get into. I loved Blur as well and never did understand the beef those two bands had. Worse, I couldn't understand punters that liked one and hated the other. They were both phenomenal bands. I was an *NME* reader and had just started buying *Q* magazine etc. and loved all things Oasis, loved their B Sides. I'd bought some bootlegs and was blown away by how different and rowdy they sounded compared to their records. To my ears, they sounded better live. I had tickets to a show in Nov 1996 that got cancelled. Oasis - there was always something happening. When *Be Here Now* came out - it was cool. We just had the MTV channel so 'D'You Know What I Mean?' was in high rotation. When the gigs in New Zealand were announced I queued up to get tickets with a whole bunch of other punters. That even made the front page of the *Evening Post* in Wellington. By the time Oasis hit New Zealand - they were massive news.

My experience of the gig was pretty crazy. I'd got both brothers to sign an autograph for me. That said - it was before the gig and apart from the brothers taking separate cars to the soundcheck - there was nothing too untoward there. I met Liam first - a mate of mine worked at IBM and rang me at work saying I had to get down there as Liam was playing noughts and crosses with all comers in The Rockpool. He said he's pretty trashed. I got out of my suit, made my excuses and raced down there. I saw him leaving and got him to sign a picture. He looked like a 1960s George Best - just super cool. I told him he was a 'fucking great singer.' Can't remember what he said back but I didn't want to bother him any more than that. Pay your respects and move on. I managed to get Noel to sign a CD of *Be Here Now* too and asked him about his guitar (he said he was playing an Epiphone Sheraton) but he seemed pretty short on chat, but that's all cool.

The gig was a bit of a calamity, it's got to be said. Liam came out with a (what sounded like) duck caller and used it instead of signing a line or two of the first song 'Be Here Now' - but considering this was the arse end of the grunge era when singers would say the inanest crap between songs, I didn't bat an eyelid at that. When he had a go about the sound and eventually had a row with his brother and stormed off it was like a nightmare unfolding. 'Roll with

Noel Gallagher at the Queens Wharf Events Centre, Wellington.
Photograph by Lee Pritchard

It' sounded amazing (it's the only time I ever 'got' that song). Noel came back and did an acoustic set for three or four songs then called 'Liam?'. To which Liam walked back on stage and they played 'Live Forever', 'It's Gettin' Better

(Man!!)' and then a mega long version of 'Champagne Supernova'. What was interesting about that last song was seeing Noel gesture during his guitar solo to someone offstage to 'Get the car.' And that was it. I had heard previously that if a band can play 70 minutes, then they don't have to refund tickets. The gig stopped right around the 70-minute mark. So, I left the gig thinking that Oasis had split up at the gig I was at. I was pretty crestfallen that night.

One bad gig doesn't make a band bad. And to be honest, the gig wasn't terrible. When they fired up, you could tell how great they actually were (which was a line I used whenever someone would start on about how bad it was) and here's the thing, it was memorable. I've seen hundreds of gigs and none were as rock 'n' roll as that one. Professionalism in rock 'n' roll is highly overrated. The truth is – it was a great one to have gone to. The brothers fighting onstage with Noel walking off first. The fact they didn't split up after that gig was a massive relief. I followed them ever since too. I still love both brothers' music and am happy they aren't working together. Liam's stuff is really good, and Noel's stuff is properly great and more diverse sounding than Oasis sounded latterly. Both are underrated as solo acts. The fact is if Oasis was still a thing - the world wouldn't get as much Gallagher music.'

Craig Owen

'I was more of a concert follower than really an Oasis fan. At the time I preferred Blur, but I'd go to any concerts I could. I assume I brought the tickets from Ticketek. We had seats at the back of the Events Centre – although if I recall, it was mostly General Admission. I took my son who would have been about 10 at the time. My wife (at the time) probably came as well although I don't remember. The gig was chaos – my joke about it was that it was the best and the worst gig ever. We spent a lot of time waiting and I remember that it was very short.'

Dan Herbison

'A good mate of mine Gane was a die-hard Oasis fan. He introduced me to Oasis only a couple of months before the concert and I'd have to say, I was going in there with not much more than a handful of 'Wonderwall' and 'Supersonic' lyrics tucked away in my 17-year-old brain. There was a group of about six of us. We all managed to get our hands on fake tickets through a friend Karl. Karl was a wheeler and dealer. Back in the day there were no barcode scanners, just a door person ripping off the ticket stubs and letting concertgoers in one by one. The ink on one of the fake tickets had run so badly, it was a fight for the five better quality tickets when Karl was giving them out. Surely enough, the smallest in our group, our mate nicknamed Ratboy due to his physical appearance, lucked out and got the ticket that may see him get thrown out, as opposed to letting in. Ratboy did get in, but it took him a skinful of booze to build up the courage to even present the ticket.

The gig was all over the show. Somehow, we wrangled our way up to the front. I wasn't the tallest of concertgoers and found myself hard up against the steel barriers with the top of the barriers pushing on my bottom few ribs. With constant pressure from behind I had to raise my hand to get pulled out, and in the process, I lost one of my shoes, not to be seen again. This would've been about halfway through the concert. While I don't remember too much of the music performance, my memory of the gig is primarily centred on the chaos and disorganisation of what I understood to be a world-class band.

Oasis was off-stage at the time I was pulled out from the front, and as I recall, they remained off-stage for some time. I waited near the back, off to the side of the main group of concertgoers. I saw a friend of mine who gave me a bit of a rundown on what was going on backstage.'

Anonymous recollection of the catering crew, via Dan Herbsion

'Hey. Shit! That feels like a lifetime ago … I guess it was! They were so good but yeah, they were at each other's throats all day. Including the sound check. We had to stop selling alcohol at one point in the concert because the crowd was so angry that they went off stage multiple times to argue. Noel was a prick, but Liam was so lovely, totally opposite to what we expected because of the way the media portrayed them. Liam was saying thanks etc. for all the food we provided in the green room, but nothing from Noel.

During the time the band walked off they were just going for each other, when they came angrily off stage, we shut down the catering/drinks for the green room at their manager's request and we were asked to stay outside.'

Oasis perform at the Events Centre. Photograph by Lee Prichard

Dan Trolley

'I became a fan of Oasis in 1996 when they were at their peak. There was a lot of anticipation for *Be Here Now*, I remember the first single 'D'You Know What I Mean?' video making its New Zealand TV debut - it was a great time to be a 16-year-old Oasis fan. I went with about four or five of my friends. There was a huge line to get in. A few of our other school friends were in line already so we jumped the queue. I remember an older guy in line saw us cutting in and he said, 'Oi what does the sign say?' It read no crowd surfing. We laughed at him.

I remember the Oasis gig well. There was a string of shows from international bands during the summer in Wellington (Foo Fighters, Beck etc). The show was not good. The sound was terrible, it was a wall of noise, Noel's guitar was overbearing, way too loud and high in the mix. Liam wasn't singing the songs properly (later found out it was sound issues). After their argument on stage (which we all thought would turn physical as it looked heated) we thought the show would end. After which Noel played an acoustic set, which was particularly good - especially as he played The Chemical Brothers song he sang on and a great version of 'Don't Go Away'. Liam was drinking on stage and appeared drunk throughout the show and did not perform well at all, unlike his brother. I remember the gig was on the news, (Channel One) Noel was briefly interviewed, it was outside the hotel as he was getting into a taxi, asked about the show he just said, 'The singer was drunk.' There was footage of the song 'Be Here Now' in the news feature too. Also, in my music room at high school there was an article/review from the *Evening Post* newspaper with a photo of Liam stuck on the wall the next day - not sure why it was there. It stayed up for the remainder of the year as a reminder. I remember the gig well as I was a massive Oasis fan, quite a contrast from the Blur gig in Auckland six months previous.'

Darren Jobson

'Well, yes, I'm a huge fan of Oasis. Right from the start. My family are from UK, Newcastle. And I've lived there. I went with a mate Mike, he's a fan too. We had a drink in the pub opposite, The Rockpool I think it was. Me and Mike having a drink and Liam walks in, Mike is an Arsenal fan wearing his top and I'm

Oasis at the Events Centre, Wellington. Photograph by Lee Pritchard

Oasis at the Events Centre, Wellington. Photograph by Lee Pritchard

a Newcastle fan wearing my top. We asked for a pic, and Liam said, 'Yeah but not with that Geordie,' meaning me. He's a Man City fan, fair enough. They had a pic. He took off. We went outside and saw Noel too.

Liam Gallagher, Mike and unnamed fan. Images courtesy of Darren Jobson and Mike

Queuing up for the gig was a bit of a wait. Got in, can't remember any warm up band if there was one. Oasis came on, they were brilliant. Could see the tension on stage. Maybe a third of way through a bust-up happening between Noel and Liam. Lots of booing. To be honest we thought it was great. Pure rock 'n' roll. I Love Oasis, Liam and Noel. Greatest Britpop band ever.'

David Yardley

'I had been a fan of Oasis since I heard 'Supersonic' sometime in 1994. Then *(What's the Story) Morning Glory?* came out, with the huge song that was 'Wonderwall', and I became a big fan of their music. Not such a fan of them being drunken yobbos, but definitely a fan of their sound. On March 10, my friend Cory Smith and I went and saw Oasis at the same venue that had hosted The Corrs. I have so many vivid memories of the Oasis gig with Cory. Prior to the gig, we had seen Liam in the bar of the Parkroyal Hotel which was right across the road from the venue. We head over and line up outside listening to the soundcheck. But Liam was still at the hotel bar, drinking with his entourage.

Cory and I settled into the concert. 'Stand by Me', 'Supersonic' and 'Roll with It' all pass before there's the first hint of trouble. Then Liam, clearly pissed, addresses the crowd in his thick Mancunian accent – 'I could buy a better sound system with me fookin' pocket money.' Clearly, he's unimpressed, as Noel yells out 'D'You Know What I Mean?' They're about to play my favourite Oasis song, the mother of 'Wonderwall'. Starts ok, then into the 3rd verse, the guy whose job it was up there on stage to do the singing, stops singing. 'Sing you wanker,' I yelled out, I wasn't impressed. Anyway, they played 'Cigarettes & Alcohol', and then brothers Gallagher had a tiff on stage. They were having some verbal unpleasantries only ten metres from where Cory and I were standing. Then, they leave the stage. It's so ridiculous, it looks like it's planned. But five minutes pass, maybe a third of the way through the gig and they remain off stage. Noel returns to the stage, armed with an acoustic guitar. Sings three songs, including 'Don't Go Away', and then the rest of the band minus Liam, return for 'Don't Look Back in Anger', before we finally see Liam back for 'Wonderwall' and two more songs, Liam's voice practically gone. At the end the crowd slowly drift out and the roadcrew starts disconnecting amps and microphone stands. It was quite unbelievable really, and that concert has grown in infamy in numerous worst-ever concerts in New Zealand lists. Yes, I continued being a fan after the tour, but my experience of them was soured somewhat. I got all of their next four albums before they disbanded. I was pleased I saw them, but it was a very low-quality gig from a band I expected so much more from.'

Deborah Ruru

'My fandom for Oasis developed when I started expanding my musical interests after I went through an intense Beatles obsession (around the release of Beatles *Anthology* documentary in 1995). Knowing that the Gallagher brothers had a slight obsession with them, I was drawn to their music as well as my musical interests expanded at the time into Pop/rock (I also liked The Verve's rock sound around the same period). I owned *(What's The Story) Morning Glory?* on CD so definitely liked a lot of their songs before their tour, and because of that, I seized the opportunity to attend their *Be Here Now* concert when I found out they were coming to Wellington. This was my first concert experience as an 18-year-old, just having started university.

My experience of the gig was one of excitement, purely due to it being my first gig. The let-down came from the negative buzz of the Gallagher siblings arguing /whinging/unprofessional behaviour plus the shortened set time but overall, I enjoyed it for the opportunity to listen to my favourite hits being played and sung live - nothing beats that experience.

I don't believe I followed the band hugely after their tour as the songs on their later albums didn't really attract my interest. I'm more about songs rather than artists i.e. I might like 0 songs, 1 song or multiple songs from a band, depending on the songs and my musical taste. My musical interest morphed away from rock into pop/r&b after that so that changed what I listened to going forward.'

Diane Richardson

'I went to the Wellington Oasis concert in the late 1990s. I gather Liam was uptight about the sound. He felt the sound check hadn't been done properly. I remember him commenting on it saying he felt like his bank account had been raped. It was pretty loud for that space.

It looked as though Noel was trying to rein him in a little. Noel pointed at Liam at one point and said something with a stern face. Liam stormed off. Noel came out and played on his acoustic for quite some time and did an absolutely superb job.

Liam came back out, they played on. Liam came down the front by the mosh pit and mucked about for a bit, even putting his ear in towards the speaker. He didn't appear fazed by people leaning over the fence and touching him. When he threw the microphone down, we knew he wasn't coming back out. They flicked the lights on pretty quickly.

Shortly before the concert, Liam came out down the side of the stage very quietly and spoke with a few people that noticed him there. He was in a good mood it seemed, until the music started.'

Graham Henderson

'At the time I was a massive Oasis fan and the Britpop indie scene in general. I went with a bunch of mates. One of my mates pre-purchased the ticket for me. I do have a tale of how my friend and I hitched from Dunedin, got kicked off an Ansett plane in Christchurch (due to being a bit dodgy with our student IDs) continued our hitch to Picton, and then caught a small plane from Picton to get to Wellington for the gig that night. Then proceeded to get ready for the gig if you get my meaning. I remember the PA and the sound being awful. Liam slagged it off all night. Highlight was Noel's acoustic solo set.'

Oasis at the Events Centre, Wellington. Photograph by Lee Prichard

Noel Gallagher at the Events Centre, Wellington. Photograph by Lee Prichard

Ian Tucker

'I was in Wellington at Chicago's bar having dinner before the concert when we saw a figure stumble out of a bar on the other side of the waterfront. I thought that person looks familiar. Sure enough it was Liam pissed as. Security raced out and got him; they came right under where we were yelling down at him, he looked up with a toothy grin and gave us the fingers. Priceless.

I was a massive fan before the concert in fact I was a bit obsessed. I remember the reviews in the *Dominion* the next day absolutely slated them, but I loved it. It wasn't their best work but that's rock 'n' roll, every night's different. I went with my wife's sister and her husband. We wanted to stay at the Parkroyal Hotel as I knew they would be there, but my wife's sister was too stingy and sure enough we were sitting at the pub next to the hotel and the band turned up. Big regret. I still follow the boys. They are hilarious. Would love to see them back together. The kids tell everyone my funeral song will be 'Wonderwall'.'

James Quilter

'A mate and I used to go down and sit outside concerts (we would have been about 16) the sound outside was usually good. Before the show, we were walking around the waterfront and saw Noel standing out the back of the venue having a durry, so we went and talked to him. He let us in the back and had a security guard take us backstage and let us into the show. This was in Wellington. It was a long time ago, so my memory is hazy. I feel like at one point Noel threw his guitar down and left the stage. I am not certain if he came back but I think he did.'

Jared Vincent

'I got in the back door. Back of stage at the Wellington gig at Queens Wharf Events Centre. Noel was chatting to someone else just outside the side of stage door that opens to the harbour side, the very corner of the building and I was walking by and mumbled a sob story about how I'd 'lost my ticket' and they let me in. It was all just on the spot magic, a huge bluff under random and unlikely circumstances, but it really happened.

I didn't get to stay backstage, obviously. I was ushered into the crowd pretty quickly after I was let in, but still an amazing concert. The concert itself, apart from the poor sound quality was actually pretty cool to hear and see them live. I'm still a huge fan of the early stuff, 'Champagne Supernova' is a song that my 18-year-old daughter and I sing out loud when she plays it in the car, which she does often. And I love 'Wonderwall' and 'Don't Look Back in Anger'. To be honest they're still one of my favourite bands to add to a playlist.

That experience at the then Queens Wharf Events Centre was incredibly random and an absolute fluke for a young lad like me who was simply walking to the train station at the time via the waterfront. But music was life in those days.'

Jaye Cooper

'I flew down to Wellington by myself as I was the only one out of my mates that got tickets for both gigs. I met my mate Rob for a couple of beers before the gig and he told me he had seen Liam in the afternoon and that he was gone, apparently been drinking whiskey since 10 a.m. The gig itself was a shambles, Liam was plastered. The only words Noel said all night were at the end 'thank you, goodnight.' My mate Rob was backstage and told me Liam and Noel had gone into it backstage before Noel's acoustic set. They had a massive fight in the dressing room. On the way home I wondered why I had bothered even going to the Wellington gig, but hey that's rock 'n' roll right.'

Jax Sanders – Queens Wharf Events Centre Event Manager in 1998

'I was the Event Manager for the venue but knew a few of the touring crew as I am from the UK and had only just settled here, they were all over it and sick of the drama by the time they got down here. I went to meet them when they arrived out the back, some familiar faces from 'back home' and well-known local crew. We were chatting and the van with the band arrived, someone slid the side door open, and Liam Gallagher just fell out on the ground. Quite a few eye rolls and 'here we go again' comments.

We also had this ridiculous situation with Wilson Parking that they wouldn't let anyone through the barrier to the loading dock, so we went and saw the dude in the underground cubicle and said the band would be arriving at this time and to ensure their quick passage (lots of fans around). I would go out

186

and press the buzzer and say, 'Hi it's Jackie and please let the band through' very simple. We went through it with him. I say it's me, I have the band, put the barrier up. So, they arrive, I press the buzzer and he's like, 'What!?' And I said, 'It's Jackie, please let the band through as they are here' and he was like, 'Who?' And I said, 'The band' and he says, 'Which band?' And I'm like 'For fuck's sake, Oasis' and he says, 'Who?' And the band can hear all this and start screaming at the speaker, 'Two Big Macs and fries please' and it just descended into chaos. It was just hilarious as at the time not so many large acts came to New Zealand, so coming from the UK where these guys would be treated like gods, to New Zealand where they weren't, was quite funny and frustrating at the time as I felt we were in Hicksville.

I had walked out front when the fight happened and heard the boos and went back in, backstage was a mess. The M&M machine (with only blue M&Ms in it) was flung across the dressing room. It was a mess back there! I had made the staff sort out the blue M&Ms. After the gig and pack down, we headed over to the Parkroyal Hotel as the crew invited us. We had the right passes so no issues getting in, but after a couple of trips to the bar, we realised that the staff had mistaken my mate for a member of the band. We drank till after 3 a.m. on Liam's tab. Thought we better head out while the going was good and as we left the head of security stopped us (eeek!). 'Have they shut the bar on you?' he said. My mate in his best Manchester accent was, 'Yes but no worries, we will go check out town.' Well, this security chap was having none of that and took us back to the bar and insisted they open it again for their special guests, so they did and we drank a few more on Liam's tab and then did a runner.

We were getting all these requests for a refund after and we asked for an official reply, Bridget Darby of The Sequel sent us, 'They bought a ticket to the Oasis experience, that's what they got.'

Liam Gallagher at the Events Centre, Wellington. Photograph by Lee Pritchard

Jezza Smith

'I followed them reasonably closely since *(What's the Story) Morning Glory?* I can't remember how I got the ticket, but I think I went with Ben Christie, Adam Criscillo and my brother Mark Smith.

Had a blast - I was too drunk though. Everyone was clearly pretty jazzed to have such a big-name band down under. I was in the mosh pit during the very first number but was clearly being too active as the bouncers reached over the front gate, dragged me out and promptly threw me out a backstage door. I thought my gig was over as there was a no re-entry policy. I went round to one of the front entrance gates and tried to get back in, but they said no chance. I went and sat on a gutter nearby. Then, some young fella came up to me and asked me if I wanted to buy a ticket. I didn't have any money. He started to walk away but then suddenly turned back and handed me the ticket with a smile. I went to a different gate and they let me in! Epic! After the gig, I pulled the ticket stub out of my pocket and all the ink was smeared - it was clearly a fake.

I remember Liam was wearing some kind of necklace during the gig. He and Noel got into a spat mid-show and Liam walked off.

Years later [2020] I had the opportunity to work with Liam filming him for a promotion for Clarks shoes in the UK. We got chatting and he actually remembered that exact gig because of the necklace that I remember him having. He said that Noel had yanked it off his neck and snapped it mid-show which pissed him off and that's what caused the fight and why he bailed.

Funny huh?!'

Jonny Potts

'Wagged school to buy *Be Here Now* on release day, of course. That's what being a fan does to you at that age. In regional New Zealand in the nineties, Cool Britannia was half the world away. *Select, Q, NME* and the rest carried breathless reports of an impossibly cool and vital movement, shimmering with youth and tunes. Oasis were the titans, the proper rockstars at the top of the

Liam Gallagher at the Events Centre, Wellington. Photograph by Lee Pritchard

heap. Even if some of us had reservations about the look or the spirit of the group, their hits couldn't be denied.

It was easy to be a fan. Easy to blast 'Supersonic' or 'Don't Look Back in Anger' or 'Columbia' and feel some of the esprit de corps that had made Knebworth a peak that felt not only right, but necessary for the band. Oasis needed something big, an explosion, a catharsis. All that energy needed to go somewhere. The desire to see them in concert, to be around other people who wanted to share in that collective excitement, was easy to feel too. I'd just left school when Oasis played Wellington in March 1998. The two guys I'd gone to the record store with on release day had gone off to university in the South Island, and I went down to Wellington to stay with friends who weren't on the same buzz. I'd go to the concert by myself. But first I'd try to meet them.

I found some obvious Oasis fans at the airport, and I remember a group of us standing on the side of the road, planning to stop their van by staging an *Abbey Road*-style crossing. That's what being a fan does to you. You think your corny, annoying stunt will be lapped up by your heroes. At any rate, all we succeeded in doing was annoying some considerate drivers, who slowed down to wave us across the road. We weren't going over the road though.

A group reconvened outside the Parkroyal Hotel along with some other fans. We were told to keep out by the doorman. I got talking to a couple of guys from Dunedin with Beatle haircuts, and a girl from Palmerston North. We all kept our distance and didn't interfere when Liam was delivered to his hotel. At one point he was walking across the lobby, I think on the way to the lifts. I called out 'Liam!' He stopped and gave one of his open-mouthed shrugs. I had a pair of green John Lennon-style granny glasses on me that I'd bought from the $2 shop the day before. The door was open, the lobby was clear, and Liam Gallagher was looking at me in mock expectation. I wound up and sent the glasses scuttling across the floor. He tried to stop them with his foot, but they sped past and hit the concierge desk. He picked them up, gave me a wave, and pissed off.

I don't know how long it was before he emerged, inevitably, in the hotel bar. We were told, again, by the doorman, to keep away. We could see him in there though. And the doorman wasn't watching us the whole time. He was opening car doors. So, I went in. The doorman was opening a car door, so I went in to meet Liam Gallagher. He was sitting with two guys. The one to his right was obviously a bodyguard. I approached them and stopped. They stopped talking. The bodyguard said 'No.' It was clear and strong and he was looking directly at me. But I wasn't there to talk to him. I looked at Liam and said, 'I just want to shake your hand, man.' Liam stood up, put his hand out, and said, 'You can shake it, but it's not my hand.' I shook it anyway.

The doorman grabbed me hard by wrist and led me out. I'd embarrassed him. He shouted at me, giving me a lifetime ban from the premises (I have since violated this ban multiple times). It didn't matter I'd just met Liam Gallagher. That's what being a fan had done to me.

I needn't have bothered risking it. In the line outside the gig that night, Liam showed up again. The Dunedin guys followed him to a nearby bar and offered him a cigarette. Liam responded that he had his own fucking cigarettes. He did, however, sign a Benson and Hedges packet for them. I visited those guys a few months later, showing up unannounced to their huge, cold flat. The B&H pack was framed and hanging on the wall, along with a photo from the Dominion of the Wellington gig they'd come up for.

When the doors opened, I ran towards the stage and secured a spot in the front looking right down Noel Gallagher's microphone. There was no support act. The Dunedin guys were in the front as well, closer to Liam, on the Bonehead side. Be here now.

My main memory after the lights came up was that it was over fast. Yes, we'd had 'Live Forever', see a fight and Noel had done 'Setting Sun' on his acoustic. We'd had everything that we could really have hoped to see in an Oasis show. Noel had even laughed at me when I sang along to a backing vocal from the record that he'd changed for performance. Both Gallagher brothers acknowledged me on the tenth of March 1998. That felt significant. I was a fan, that stuff meant something.

The Dunedin guys were buzzing. They'd just seen Oasis. But it felt a bit off to me. It was like they were trying to convince themselves they'd seen a better show than the one I had. We went to the Malthouse, with the girl from Palmerston North. The four of us had met each other that day and we were a gang for that day. It wasn't my first-time drinking underage in a bar, but it was the first time I had been out of school, smoking cigarettes at a bar with strangers, my ears ringing from a rock concert. It should have been more exciting.

It should have felt like the start of something. But seeing Oasis at that point in time – after Knebworth, after *Be Here Now*, and maybe even after my own school years – made the night feel more like a closing of something, rather than an opening out. The scene that had been stoked by those UK music magazines fell apart so quickly that the documentary *Live Forever* would consign it to the past just five short years later. I kept listening to the band, but I never felt the same buzz again. It was one thing to see the fights on the news, to see the crowds at Maine Road, to read about the coke binges and the bad behaviour … but after I'd seen these short, human guys struggling with themselves in a Wellington basketball arena, I couldn't ever be that young fan again. I couldn't kid myself.

The next day I got the bus back home. I sat with the girl from Palmerston North, and we took an earphone each and listened to a mixtape on my Walkman. She thought the piano on the Stooges' 'I Wanna Be Your Dog' sounded like the last song we'd heard at the concert: 'It's Gettin' Better (Man!!)'. I could see what she meant, but to me the Stooges were on a whole other level. A few years later, the Stooges got back together, but I never managed to see them live. I'm still a fan.'

Joy Wadham

'I had heard Oasis on the radio and enjoyed their music but at that stage didn't own any of their albums. I remember them advertising it as the smallest venue they had ever played so it sounded like it would be a special experience to go to. I went along with my cousin Amy; we were both 17-year-olds and it was the first concert our parents let us go to by ourselves. Little did they know that we got separated from the start and didn't find each other till the end. Amy had come over from Blenheim, especially for the concert. I felt so bad that I'd lost her from the start. She was at McDonalds opposite the entrance to the venue - probably in a long queue and everyone was rushing in, so I thought I better rush in before I missed my chance... not my wisest move! Especially with no cell phones in those days.

I loved every second of it. I was up the front and right in the middle of all the action. I swear Liam blew me a kiss at one point, Noel must've been singing and he was taking a break sitting on the platform where the drum kit was and he looked over and blew me a kiss - but it was to all of us - just I was at the front. I remember at one point Liam got frustrated with the microphone and threw it over - I heard later that they thought the sound at the venue was bad. They didn't play for that long - maybe 1 1/2 hrs, apparently because they weren't happy with the sound. But once it was over, we rushed out and ran around the back of the venue (opposite the Frank Kitts Park playground) to get a final glimpse of them driving away.

I became a big fan, I bought all of their albums and loved even the B-sides. I bought the Oasis guitar book and taught myself to play the guitar by playing their songs. When I met my husband nine years later, he was a fan too and so we often play the songs and sing along together - especially ones like 'Talk Tonight'.'

Julie Strong

'I was at the Wellington gig, we flew from Invercargill and stayed at the Parkroyal Hotel. Happened to stay on the same floor as the band. Our tickets and travel were all arranged via a travel agent. We were big fans of the band and followed everything they did. We loved everything as it was our first big concert.'

Kezna Cameron

'I followed them quite closely at the time. I went with my partner. Can't remember which outlet I got my tickets from. It wasn't a great experience. I was disappointed Liam stormed off the stage leaving his brother Noel to do the concert alone. Was quite early on in the Wellington show he stormed off, complaining of shit sound.'

Kylie and Shaun Blake

Oasis at the Events Centre, Wellington. Photograph by Lee Pritchard

'I was not a massive fan but loved their raw and melodic sound. Man, those guys could write and perform a tune that was equally rock anthem and timeless pop classic. Probably got the tickets from Ticketek in those days. The gig was great and it was amazing to see the fellas perform. I was hugely disappointed when it was cut short because of one of Liam's trademark tantrums. When I reflected on this a little while later, I decided that it was an authentic experience. I had seen one of his legendary tantrums in the flesh. Not really the thing to do when thousands of people paid decent cash to see you perform though. I am glad that I saw them though. Shameful behaviour at best from a man in that position, but part of what the band was. I even wondered if it was part of the show.'

Laurie Morton

'I followed Oasis fairly closely before the gig. I had their albums; I think the first song I heard from them was 'Whatever'. It was on a compilation album my sister had. Then *(What's the Story) Morning Glory?* came out. I can always remember thinking about how unbelievably catchy their songs were. Had no idea at the time that Noel had nicked most of them!

Liam Gallagher at the Events Centre, Wellington. Photograph by Lee Pritchard

I can remember getting the train with my mate Rowan from the Hutt Valley to Wellington, then walking to the Opera House where Ticketek was. Can't remember how long we queued up for, an hour or two. Anyway, we got tickets.

The day of the gig arrived. Rowan and I got the train again. I got on at Silverstream, Rowan at Manor Park. We arrive at Wellington train station and walk a short distance to Queens Wharf Events Centre. We join the queue. At this stage it's not a big queue at all. We are just around the corner of the venue, talking shit and smoking durries as we didn't have smartphones to keep us occupied while waiting. At some point word spreads along the queue that Liam is in the bar opposite the venue. Quite rudely I tell Rowan to save our spot while I bugger off to see if the rumours are true. To my utter surprise they were. Liam is propped up at the bar, pint in hand (a handle) and making small talk with anyone brave enough to talk to him. It's a bit of a blur, I can't remember what he said to people or what they said to him. He was pissed but pleasant. After a while he gets up to head back to the venue. A line of people had formed in the bar. Most people are just staring at him, star-struck, including me. I was quite close to him where he sat and as he walked off, he playfully punched a few of us in the stomach (including me) and simultaneously said 'Hhheeeeeeyyyyy!' Then he was gone. I will never forget that moment. Seems ridiculous now. We all then took off back to our spots in the queue.

When they opened the doors and let us in, Rowan and I boosted it to the front and managed to be right behind the first lot of people at the very front if that makes sense. We were close to centre, closer to Bonehead than Noel. I can remember 'Bittersweet Symphony' playing over the PA system and wishing The Verve might be the support band as I loved them but knew it wasn't a reality. As it turned out there was no support band (not that I remember anyway).

The show starts and I'm blown away by the sound. Fucking loud and clear. The venue isn't known for its acoustics but when you are at the very front it doesn't matter. Other than the obvious well-known moments I can't offer up much that's new. I can remember watching Bonehead strumming away and making eye contact a couple of times. Not hard when I could nearly reach out and grab him. Between the front barrier and the stage was a very small gap where photographers were positioned. I can remember at some point Liam spitting at a woman photographer. She wasn't looking so had no idea. It wasn't a big dirty loogie or anything like that and I'm not sure it was intended to be aimed at her. Anyway, not a great moment for Liam. For what seemed like the whole show I really struggled to hear Liam's vocals. I could hear the instrumentation clear as a bell, maybe they were drowning him out? Maybe the set-up wasn't right? Maybe it was my position in the venue? Maybe it WAS the venue, I don't know. I know he was pissed off with the sound, getting his wallet out and offering to pay for a decent set-up. I thought that's what his road crew were for! Noel on the other hand I could hear OK. I'm stoked I could, as he sang and performed well, obviously annoyed at his brother and feeling like someone had to be professional. But Liam's Liam. You wouldn't want it any other way. I recall being worried they wouldn't come back when Noel stormed off. But they did and then launched into a mega 'ciggies and piss' which was one of (and still is) my faves. 'Champagne Supernova' was at the time my absolute favourite song, so I was thrilled when they played that at the end. I remember Rowan being crowd-surfed to the side of the venue near the end. It may have been during the penultimate song which I believe was 'It's Gettin' Better (Man!!)'. I'm not sure if something was between that song and 'Champagne Supernova'.

And that was that. An exhilarating experience for an 18-year-old lad. I can remember getting out into the cool evening air dripping with sweat and feeling like the night shouldn't end there. We bumped into Ms Ducker, a teacher from our college that we had both finished at the previous year. She had been to the gig. I can't recall the conversation. After that we got the train home, in those days you had to be 20 to get into pubs.

It's cool to know that this gig is a fairly prominent one in Oasis history and to have been there is awesome.'

Oasis at the Events Centre, Wellington. Photograph by Lee Pritchard

Lee Moores

'I was an early follower of Oasis as I am originally from Manchester and was, and still am keen on the Manchester music scene. I had heard their first album when it first came out and liked what I heard. Obviously *(What's the Story) Morning Glory?* had been a massive hit and when I heard they were coming I was keen to see them in the flesh. Got tickets through Ticketek I think from memory. I went on my own straight from work.

My experience of the gig was quite strange. Before the concert I walked down to the venue in the hope that I might catch a sound check. I had on a Manchester City football shirt and a guy approached me asking if I wanted tickets. We got chatting and he told me he was from Manchester, I asked whereabout and he knew a good friend of mine who coincidentally had just visited me from the UK. He mentioned that he had been following the band on their tour to Australasia and was trying to make a few quid by buying and selling tickets. Anyway, after chatting with him, I decided to get some dinner before the gig. Upon returning to the gig, I bumped into the same guy and he said I should have stayed because he had been drinking with Liam in the pub opposite the venue. He mentioned that he was pretty wasted and not to get my hopes up on a good show. Needless to say, he was right. The gig was pretty average to be honest, Liam was obviously pissed out of his head and Noel was well and truly pissed off with his brother's behaviour. Anyway, Liam walked off and Noel completed the set. I don't think the crowd was that happy on the overall show and felt a little ripped off. The next day in the Dominion someone had written a review slagging the band and in a later interview Noel actually thought that the review was fair.

I felt ripped off to be truthful I had really been looking forward to the gig. Nevertheless, I have seen many bands and artists since and sometimes you get good gigs and other times you do not.'

Lee Pritchard

'I became a big Oasis fan while I was living and working in the UK, about 1994. I saw R.E.M., Radiohead, Cranberries concerts, and closely followed Oasis around the release date of their sophomore album, absolutely loved

'Wonderwall'. I also was in UK, when they appeared on the Brit Awards, and had their big stoush with Blur. I was hoping to see Oasis in the UK, but never managed to. When the New Zealand concerts were announced in far smaller venues than the UK, I jumped at the chance to grab tickets and travelled from Napier with friends to the Wellington show.

I cannot remember much other than stuffing my camera down my pants, as was the case with most concerts I attended pre-cell phone. I took a roll of black and white and also colour and somehow must've changed the film in the concert darkness! I followed Liam when he stormed off stage and got pretty close to the sweating drunken mess as he blew his tweeter, staked his tambourine and his punching fists to the giant speakers, so very loud! He was absolutely dripping in sweat, while his brother Noel continued to play, what to me was actually an alrighty show.'

Lucy Atkins

'I loved them. To start with years before the gig, I'd heard of them in passing - the name Oasis and some of their songs since my brother was a fan - but hadn't really become a fan until *(What's The Story) Morning Glory?* came out, or at least that was when I first became aware of them. My brother had the album and I remember seeing the cover of it. Then my friend Jo got it and I clearly remember her saying to me, 'There's this really good song on it called 'Wonderwall'. Quickly became very involved and listened to them all the time and followed their lives via music magazines - not so much the internet back then. Side note - years and years later when I was living in London, I was a Beatles tour guide and on the way to a location, my walk would pass over Berwick St, where I would stop and indicate to my group that that was the location of the cover photo of the Oasis album. Always a popular part of the tour!

I got tickets in person from the box office at the Wellington Opera House. Jo and I showed up in the middle of the night to camp out. There were about three people already there. Jo and I went to the gig together, but we met our friends there, waiting outside who were also big fans. My brother and his friends were also there - anyone who liked music went because it was a big deal for Wellington.

Oasis at the Events Centre, Wellington. Photograph by Lee Pritchard

When they arrived in Wellington for the concert, Jo and I went out to the airport to see them and hopefully meet. We met another fan out there that we had met lining up on the day we got tickets. Unfortunately, they had got in earlier or managed to swerve us and we found out that they were already en route to their hotel. We knew where they'd be staying - there was only one decent hotel here then - so we went there and saw them just arriving and checking in. We were very happy and called out and they turned and waved and pulled the fingers at us.

Then the real highlight was hours later when we were lined up outside the venue waiting to go in. I heard someone say, 'Is that Liam?' and point. Several metres away was Liam and maybe two or three other people, walking towards the doors of the venue coming from The Rock Pool bar. Everyone seemed frozen but I was like 'RIGHT here we go' and grabbed Jo and went running over fast. Our friend Mike that based his entire style on Liam's look followed. I went right up to Liam, took his hand and shook it and said, 'Hi Liam my name is Lucy, it's great to meet you.' He looked me dead in the eye, with something of an acknowledgement but more with a look of surprise that someone had actually approached him. I think Jo then did the same and I snapped a photo and then also Mike too. By this time, when others lined up saw that a few of us had been brave and gone over, so more people went over too but he was whisked away as it got too crowded. We were so excited! He looked incredible up close like that and his hand was soft as anything.

It was so exciting. We got in early after lining up at the door for so long and rushed to the front. Jo and I spotted Liam backstage, just over on the right-hand side off-stage and we screamed out 'Liam!' to which he turned to us with a double set of fingers, we were honoured! It was a great gig, but the crowd was rough. I was experienced at holding my own and managing mosh pits, but this was really extreme and a bit violent. I actually had to get carried out of the crowd at one point when I fainted but found my way back to the front. The music was great. I remember there being some discussion about the sound quality being poor, but I liked it. For me the big highlight was being right up the front and so close to them. I also remember Noel doing an acoustic set, alone on the stage right up close to the crowd. It was absolutely beautiful. Liam and Noel fought - I seem to remember it was on stage or to the side of the stage

The *Be Here Now* Tour programme. A Microdot/Brian Cannon publication

- and the show finished earlier than expected. I was disappointed about this because we had been expecting to hear them cover 'I Am the Walrus' which I wanted to hear (as a Beatles fan) but that didn't happen. I seem to think one of them apologised the next day that it ended early.

I never saw them perform again but I always got their albums and continued to be a fan. My brother also remained a fan and when he moved to the UK, he would often get to exclusive gigs that they did last minute. I was always excited to hear about these. Much later when they came out with *Don't Believe the Truth*, I was really excited and impressed and felt that it was a return to form because not all of the albums were as good as I'd hoped they would be. Although I lived in the UK for many years, I never saw any of them out and about anywhere. A few years back when Liam came to Auckland, although I LOVED the album, I didn't make the journey to see him (but my friend did and had a cool encounter with him!)'

Luke Peacocke

'Time flies, 25 years since Oasis in Welly. I don't have any of the receipts or paperwork. Not sure where that all went. From what I recall the day went like this: It was a quiet morning at Lifestyle Sports. Liam and his bodyguard were one of the first customers. He had obviously been drinking but was in a friendly mood. I broke the ice by talking about football. I got a ball down from the stand and we kicked it around for a while. Bodyguard was in the background not getting involved. Liam gave me his Amex. Black and heavy Centurion card. Never seen one before. I held it as he started looking at shoes. He picked out some olive Reebok walking shoes. I measured his feet. Around size 7. Too small for a man. I went upstairs to the storeroom to find something that would work. Luckily, I had a women's pair that looked identical to what he was after. I felt I had to disclose and said I need to let you know that these are women's shoes. He laughed and said, 'Sometimes I feel like a woman.' Deal done. He invited me to the concert. I already had a ticket. Liam wore the shoes, fought with Noel and the concert was a shit show.'

Lifestyle Sports store on the corner of Willis Street and Mercer Street, Wellington. Photograph by Wayne Shepherd, c.1980s-1990s[151]

Marc Cramer

'I followed them enough to buy their albums (rather than steal them in the early days of digital). A really good friend, whose flat I spent a lot of time at (and met my wife) was massively into them. I think it was his idea that we go. We went with my friend and his flatmates from memory but no idea how we got the tickets. They lived just over the road from the Michael Fowler Centre, so we probably lined up at the Ticketek office.

The gig itself, hot, with shitty, tinny sound. Started off okay but then Liam got stroppy about the sound and stormed off – everyone was saying what an arse he was and how unprofessional it was. The best bit for me was the solo, acoustic songs that Noel then did while Liam cooled down. Then Liam came back and the crowd went wild. I looked around and thought, 'Really? No wonder he storms off if he gets a reaction like this when he returns.' They got back into it though and we just enjoyed the rest of the night.'

Mark Edwards

'I was a huge Oasis fan prior to the gig in Wellington. I bought their first CD single, 'Supersonic', while in university at Waikato in 1995 or so and became a fan from there. They filled the gap The Stone Roses had left and their sound and attitude connect. I went with a bunch of mates, all from Waikato and from jobs at the time. I don't recall exactly who was there but two of my closest friends from university were there. I recall there being some interruption due to Liam and Noel having a disagreement but that was minor to me. I partly had expected this and felt at the time it was part of the Oasis experience. It didn't detract from my experience of the gig. I recall little detail other than that I enjoyed the night immensely. Seeing them at the Enmore Theatre in Sydney a few years later however, was more memorable and I'm glad I went to that concert as I remember it all.'

Matthew Pender

'It's hard to explain to kids today why Oasis was so huge. Putting their music on alone isn't enough. It was Liam. The patron saint of day-drinking gallivanters. He made everything he did seem like the coolest thing ever. Adidas Tracksuits.

Oasis at the Events Centre, Wellington. Liam Gallagher wearing his recently purchased olive-coloured Reebok shoes. Photographer unidentified[152]

Crochet hats. Cans of Stella Artois. He was the last real rock star, and he and his brother were the kings of the boorish narcotic 1990s. They ruled the world in the mid-1990s. By the time of their greatly anticipated royal visit to New Zealand in 1998, their decline had started, though nobody, much less them, knew that at the time.

I was 21 when I went to their show in Wellington. The perfect age for Oasis at their world-straddling peak. They seemed like they were drunk all the time, doing drugs, stumbling in and out of bars. And writing songs about it. Best of all, they - Liam and Noel - were brilliantly funny. That was the key to it all. Their interviews were just as good as the music. This was before everyone had the internet, so you kept up with bands by reading the music magazines - Q, Mojo, NME, The Face. There was a mad, unhinged unpredictability to it all. The way rock 'n' roll should be.

And at their Wellington show, they - or at least Liam - delivered on that 100%. I was there with my brother Scott. I had a great night. Liam had one of those cardboard party hats on and those paper whistles that go in and out and he was blowing it into the mic when he wasn't singing.

They opened with 'Be Here Now'. Liam started shouting abuse in between songs - I learned later that he was complaining about the sound, but at the time it was just a stream of gruff Mancunian that no one could understand and the whole crowd replied with 'WHAT?' and laughed.

After a few songs you could see Noel pointing at him and telling him off and the crowd were going 'OOOOHHH' like it was school. We were enjoying it. It was the Gallaghers, and when Noel stormed off stage, followed by the band, I felt we were getting our money's worth!

Liam stood alone for a second, tossed his tambourine over his head and walked off too. We, the crowd, started a slow clap and foot stomp until they finally came back out and when they ripped into the next song we roared. I was convinced they must do it every night as part of their act.

When they left the stage at the end, we all started to clap and stomp for an encore, but the house lights came on immediately like a sober slap in the face and it was over.'

Mikaela Gerraty

'I was into Oasis since about 1995 - bought every CD and single they released. I went to the gig with my older brother Chris. He was a radio DJ, so got tickets through his work. Oasis was supposed to come in 1996 - only going to Auckland. I was going to go up on the radio tour bus with my brother, but Oasis cancelled the concert. When they came to Wellington we had seated tickets at the very back. My brother didn't want to stand. I loved the gig, I come from a small town - so it was my second-ever concert. I still remember when Noel came onstage after he and Liam had a fight - and Liam didn't want to come back onstage. Noel then did an acoustic set, determined to not let Liam ruin the concert. Liam did come back on eventually. I continued to follow for a while after, but once the band split up I kind of moved onto new groups.'

Miles Coverdale

'Was there any band bigger in the world at the end of the last century than Oasis? If there was you wouldn't know it, everywhere you turned, there they were. The radio, music TV, the magazines and thanks to their almost constant drama, the news. It was a wonder wall of media overload and love them or hate them you certainly couldn't ignore them. So, when it was announced they would be bringing their *Be Here Now* tour to New Zealand in 1998, it was a no brainer that this was the hottest ticket in town. A ticket that back then required you to actually travel into town and buy in person from a ticket outlet, a slow but enriching experience. You could buy over the phone or online but it was almost impossible to get through to anyone and the internet back then seemed to crash more times than it ran, and that would require you to have a computer which I didn't have and wouldn't have until well into the next century. Better to take time off work, queue and get those tickets yourself. Which I duly did.

Thus, there I was, in another queue, a few months later clutching those precious tickets as I waited outside the Queens Wharf Events Centre with a mixed bag of Britpop devotees, indie hipsters and middle-aged rockers shuffling expectantly waiting for the doors to open. I wasn't the biggest Oasis fan, not actually owning a single sliver of their music, I was more a Blur or Pulp fan, with several of their albums happily nestled in my vinyl collection, but you didn't need to be. Ever since their debut *Definitely Maybe* hit the ground in 1994, they seemingly owned the airwaves, you could hear 'Roll with It' blasting out of cars, worksites and beaches all through that summer and when *(What's the Story) Morning Glory?*' dropped in 1995 it was a total FM takeover. There was no way you couldn't absorb the Oasis effect, as whether quietly in the background or blasting in your face, their music surrounded you almost constantly. I knew enough of their music to be more than a fair-weather fan, but I was by no means a convert, yet.

The doors opened relatively early and through good luck, and uncharacteristic, for me, early arrival and some fast legs, I took up a front-row position against the crash barriers. Being taller than most, standing over six feet, I always feel for those that have to endure watching what might be their favourite band from behind my large frame, so I usually hang around the mixing desk to give everyone a fair go. I'm not sure why I went up so close this time but feeling a little guilty I slid off to the left-hand side of the stage and slumped over against the rail to at least make myself less of a sight screen. My best friend who was a total Oasis disciple at the time and also not vertically challenged squeezed in

Liam Gallagher at the Events Centre, Wellington. Photograph by Lee Pritchard

next to me and together we waited and hunkered down for the show to begin. The wait seemed eternal and we spent our time fending off latecomers who kept trying to slip in between us for a better position and endless conversations over whether *Parklife* or *Different Class* was the better Cool Britannia album. I can't remember if there was a warmup band, I'm thinking not, but at some point, the house lights went down the crowd surged forward and we knew it was time for the main act.

They sauntered onstage, took up their positions and without further ado launched into their night's work. Liam was centre stage of course, leaning forward slightly, hands behind his back, snarling into the microphone. Noel, feet planted, took up the right-hand side of the stage. I found myself directly in front of Paul 'Bonehead' Arthurs whose prematurely balding scalp was more prominent than his face as he kept his head down staring at his guitar pedals either in concentration or constraint not wanting to take away from the music or Liam's spotlight. Lurking in the background the bass player and drummer rarely caught the eye; you knew they were there, but they never did anything that would cause you to take your eyes off the three-up front.

Not that they did much. The first thing I noticed about Oasis live is they don't move, at least not worth mentioning. The second thing is they don't need to, the sheer power of the music hits you like a wall of bricks. 'Supersonic' is one of the few numbers I remember distinctly from the evening, it was played early in the night and just pinned me like a butterfly in a case. It felt like the room was literally pounding you through the soles of your feet and just like the band onstage you didn't need to move much you just absorbed the song into your body. So far, so very good. 'Roll with It' arrived and with it the crowd made its presence known almost drowning out the band with its sing-along lyrics erupting out of several thousand throats in unison. I found myself shouting along almost without realising it until it suddenly dawned on me that the off-key voice that had suddenly appeared in my ears was my own. For the sake of those around me I mouthed the rest of the song. I'm not sure how many songs they played but it can't have been more than five before they launched into 'D'You Know What I Mean?' off their latest album and it was met with a happy roar of familiarity from those around me.

I can't remember much about the performance of the song, but I remember that having not said virtually anything since the show started it was with surprise that as it ended Liam suddenly launched into an expletive-laden rant which caught us all by surprise. I can only remember something about the sound on stage, an almost unintelligible stream of invectives and then the bemused look on the faces of the band as he turned and walked off stage left. Noel for his part took off his guitar and strode off backstage in the direction of the departing Liam and the rhythm section fell in behind. Bonehead who had stood stock still for the whole show, had raised his head at the commotion and seeing his bandmates slinking offstage behind him managed a 'fucks sake' as he unslung his instrument which, as I was only a metre away from him, rang rather loudly in my ears as he stomped off in disgust.

The crowd despite some jeering seemed to stay in good spirits and before too long were chanting football style for a return. We were mollified by the seeming unconcern of the roadies who moved about in a business-as-usual manner, making slight adjustments of the onstage gear and lights, and the knowledge that walk-offs had been reported before at Oasis shows with regular frequency. Perhaps it was all part of the show, those around me clearly thought so as everyone looked relaxed if a little impatient. The return onstage of the band with a rather sheepish-looking Liam after only a short break seemed to confirm that this was nothing to worry about. The band launched into 'Cigarettes & Alcohol' another crowd favourite, Liam now with tambourine in hand took up his position front and centre and literally dared you to not watch him. For someone who has the stage presence of a wax statue it's amazing how he can make the spotlight look like it's only bright when it's on him. He eats up the attention and it's very hard to look away when he's singing, it's a trick very few can pull off and despite a constant diet of touring acts since I've not seen it done better. As the song moved into its long outro he straightened and standing stock still surveyed the masses out before him and then for no apparent reason, hopped off the stage and down into the security pit between the stage and the crash barriers. There with all the punters reaching out to touch Britpop royalty he slowly moved along the front holding his tambourine out in front of him, just out of reach of the grabbing hands that stretched out to him, nodding and taunting as he went, 'Yeh' he mouthed repeatedly as he walked along towards my section.

Noel Gallagher at the Events Centre, Wellington. Photograph by Lee Pritchard

Seeing his game in advance I took my hand back as he came along and at this, he stopped right in front of me and looked me in the eye, slowly chewing what was either a real or imaginary piece of gum, he held out the tambourine towards me and yelled, 'Do you want it?' I blinked and slowly reached out to receive this unexpected trophy when in a flash he quickly threw it over my head to the crowd behind, I never took my eyes off his and he just stood there looking at me, as I slowly straightened to my full height. The sudden surge from behind as obviously a few eager fans jostled for this gift from the gods made it hard to hunch down anyway. At this, Liam cocked his head and in slow motion turned and walked off, neither looking at the fans nor back at his band as he sauntered off with as much arrogance and disdain as I've ever seen a human being convey through the simple act of walking. Having seen a bit more of Liam through the wonders of the internet it turns out that this is not unusual, it's just the way he actually walks.

As he disappeared into the darkness I turned to look back at the stage and straight into the eyes of Bonehead who was watching me intently. He gave me a look that was either, 'Now you see what I have to deal with,' or 'Great! look what you've gone and done now.' Anyway, he quickly turned away to look at Noel and I realised that while Liam had been in the pit the song had morphed somehow into Led Zeppelin's 'Whole Lotta Love'. This meandered along until it came to a rather clunky end and Noel and the team walked off again backstage. I looked back at Bonehead but this time there were no expletives from the beleaguered Oasis guitarist, just a resigned look as he scuttled off stage.

This time the wait was much longer and the crowd were a little less happy, if this was all part of the show then perhaps, they should have brought a better show. When they did reappear, there was no Liam. It was into the acoustic numbers now and Noel did the singing duties seated front of stage. This was no surprise because we'd heard this was an integral part of this tour and most of us were looking forward to the big electric ending with the whole band to finish. After the acoustic numbers, things seemed a little flat after such a good start to the night. Liam's antics taking some of the steam out of the performance. Noel is a good singer and obviously the main songwriter but when he's fronting things the lights just don't shine as bright. The band again scuttled offstage, and the roadies set the guitars up and ran the seats off for hopefully the big finish.

Back again they came and again no Liam, it dawned on us that maybe this wasn't part of the act. Liam returned eventually and 'Wonderwall' got a massive cheer and some of the excitement returned, briefly anyway. A few more songs came and went, I really can't remember them all that well and then they were gone. When the house lights came on, we knew it was over, no encore? Perhaps everything after the acoustic set was the encore? There was much confusion and a lot of standing around as everyone seemed to be wondering what had just happened. It became apparent as the gear was quickly getting dismantled, perhaps a little too fast, that they weren't coming back. What to make of it all? Most people were OK with things, it wasn't like that infamous Deep Purple concert where Ritchie Blackmore had walked off after 15 minutes and never returned or the Lou Reed show where he never showed up at all. We had seen the band, they had played most of their big songs, it had been good until it wasn't.

I can't say he looked that inebriated to me, but he has such an expressionless face mostly all Beatle hair and rock star glasses that perhaps it would be hard to tell, certainly, it didn't affect his speech or singing voice greatly. It was hard at the time to not feel like it was all somehow stage-managed, it just all seemed so arranged. Was it disappointing? Yes, a little, you saw at the start how big they could be and if they really went for it, I'm sure they would blow most bands off the stage, the problem was it was taking too much effort to project that much, so often. Maybe they were running out of steam? Was it just an off night? One thing, I was really glad to have been there. Despite more world tours they never made it back to Wellington, that one night was all we ever got. Another thing, by the end of the week, I had everything they ever made on vinyl added to my collection, so they made me a believer with one of their most lacklustre shows, maybe it's a good thing they didn't play a great one. My biggest regret? They didn't play 'Acquiesce', which is by far my favourite song. Hopefully one day one of the Gallagher brothers will return and put that right. I'll be waiting.'

Morgan Bennet

'It was a long time ago. I was a big fan before the gig. I remember *Definitely Maybe* being advertised on the telly and loved 'Live Forever'. Got the two albums and the 'Whatever' 12" and the two singles box sets too. I went to the Wellington gig by myself as my mates weren't fans. It was massively loud (should have had earplugs). Was deaf for two days. Liam seemed pissed off the whole time (about the sound). Noel gave him a telling-off at the back of the stage. Liam walked off, the crowd chanting 'Liam's a wanker' wasn't going to help. Noel's acoustic 'Fade In-Out' was my favourite. 'Setting Sun' was brilliant. His acoustic set was incredible. 'Don't Look Back in Anger' too! Then Liam did come back for 'Wonderwall' and 'Live Forever'. I do remember Guigsy was wearing a pink shirt.'

Ollie Labone

'I became an Oasis fan, like many, in 1995 around the time of the *(What's the Story) Morning Glory?* release. I was 13 going on 14 at the time. They soon became my favourite band and were the reason I started playing guitar. I went with one of my school friends, Jason. I bought the ticket from Ticketek. Looking at it, it was $65, which was an expensive show in 1998. I went to see Radiohead a couple of months earlier at the same venue, and that was only $39.

It was the second gig I saw at Queens Wharf Events Centre, after Radiohead in January. The venue was packed, and there was definitely an air of anticipation, as the fans had been waiting for Oasis to come to New Zealand for several years. We had all heard the stories about Liam getting in trouble on the Cathay Pacific flight from Hong Kong to Australia, being charged, so didn't know what mood he would be in. We were seated in Block 5 upstairs, facing the stage. Don't remember there being any support act but may have forgotten it. I remember being disappointed that they hadn't brought the *Be Here Now* stage set with them. It was just a plain stage with the backline set up. Don't even remember them having a banner at the rear. They walked out to the opening 'Be Here Now' loop, then launched into that song. It was loud, as you'd expect. Liam was wearing shorts, which was not very rock 'n' roll, in my opinion!

Liam started complaining fairly early in the set about the on-stage monitor sound. Lots of gesturing, and at one point he got his wallet out and said he would pay for better sound himself. At one point a fan down the front managed to steal his star-shaped tambourine, which he also complained about until he got it back. He was clearly drunk, and Noel was getting grumpier with him as the set went on. Lots of words are spoken and gestured. Eventually, it came to a head, and the band walked off stage, only about 6 songs into the set. It was pretty much a clichéd Gallagher bust-up. After a little bit, Noel came on and did a short acoustic set, sitting on a stool in the middle of the stage. The 'Setting Sun' (The Chemical Brothers) cover was particularly good. The rest of the band came on after the acoustic spot, but Liam still wasn't happy. They finished with 'Champagne Supernova'. I particularly remember this, as Liam walked off after his verses, and Noel dragged it out for ages, soloing. I think he realised they were quite short on time from what was expected. Also remember thinking it was strange that they didn't play 'All Around the World', which was the current single at the time.'

Patsy Knight

'All I can really remember is waiting for them to arrive on stage, when they finally did, they didn't disappoint in their arrogance. Then later on when they had their argument on stage and Noel walked off with the rest of the band, I remember people standing around me complaining about the lack of professionalism. I turned and said to them, 'I don't know why you're surprised, it's not the first time and certainly wouldn't be the last.' I also heard people outside saying we should get a refund, but it's Oasis, it's what they do and if they expected a lovely friendly show well they came to the wrong one. I enjoyed the show or part of it, they were exactly what I thought they would be, and I wouldn't have hesitated to go and see them again.'

Paul Frawley

'Was a fan of the band but not full on – thought it was great we were hearing English rock 'n' roll again – was awesome to see Oasis, Blur, Pulp, Supergrass and other Britpop bands high in the charts instead of the usual dross. Went with my brother and a mate. Lots of other friends went - there was a real

Liam Gallagher at the Events Centre, Wellington. Photograph by Lee Pritchard

buzz, but fans also knew Oasis could be erratic live. Think we got the tickets from a retail outlet Ticketek.

It wasn't the greatest Oasis performance to be honest – and I have seen some cracker shows from them online. The band seemed more annoyed with the shit acoustics of the Events Centre. They were really bad back then and most bands hated playing there. We still followed the band, but I think the *Be Here Now* period was the decline for Oasis. I recall a singles B-sides album was later issued – they still had their loyal fans.'

Peter Henneveld

'I suppose I don't really remember much of it, that's quite telling, isn't it? I just remember Liam storming off and saying something about the sound company raping their bank account, and not feeling like he had much to give, end-of-the-road sort of gig. And then there was the feeling of having been had and we have so many more interesting bands in New Zealand alone. I find Oasis more like a mirage, you think there is something there and when you get there you realise you were fooled. And then again 'Cigarettes & Alcohol', what a tune!'

Ross Murray

'People were leaving with their hands over their ears halfway through the gig saying the sound was terrible. The last song was 'Champagne Supernova', and that version was amazing, worth the price of admission alone, if I had paid of course. We saw Liam at the Crazy Lounge in Cuba Mall and my friend Sima Urale, the film director was having lunch. Liam was at the table with her and he said to her that he was in the biggest band in the world, and she said in all honesty that she had never heard of Oasis. That threw him a bit, so he invited her to the show. She said, 'I have a lot of friends' and he said, 'I don't care' and called this guy over and he put us all on the VIP guest list. Great, as I wouldn't have liked to have paid for the fiasco that unfolded that night.'

Ryan Holmes

'I discovered Oasis when I was watching Juice TV and 'Morning Glory' came on. It just grabbed me straight away and I had to know who this band was.

Then a few weeks later everyone I knew was listening to this song called 'Wonderwall'. I quickly had *(What's the Story) Morning Glory?* on cassette, followed by *There and Then* on VHS and *Definitely Maybe* on CD. I then waited with anticipation for *Be Here Now* and its release. So, at that stage of my life Oasis was everything.

I was 15 and in high school at the time and when it was announced they were coming to Wellington I had to go. Before the days of the internet, I would have to line up at the local Ticketek office in Palmerston North and purchase my ticket. I went with a couple of mates from school.

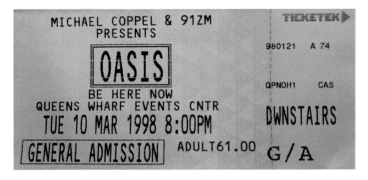

Ticket for Oasis concert in Wellington. Image courtesy of Ryan Holmes

This was our first ever concert so it was super exciting. We spent the day at school with people talking about us going and our minds on the trip. After school finished my mum drove us down to Wellington and dropped us at Queens Wharf. I remember there being a huge line to get in and waiting in anticipation. I bought a T-shirt and a tour booklet and remember waiting in the mosh pit. Then I remember the screech of 'Be Here Now' starting and the crowd surging. I remember the awesome energy and myself trying desperately to hold onto my purchases. Then came Liam mumbling into the microphone and something about the sound which resulted in him walking off stage. In a while, they came back on and you couldn't wipe the smile off my face for the next few hours. Then it was the ride back to Palmerston North talking nonstop about the experience we just had.

I've followed them forever and have all the albums on CD and Vinyl. The box sets, the best of, the live DVDs and documentaries. Had to travel to Australia to see them live again in 2005 as I couldn't trust they would come back to New Zealand and luckily I did. I moved to Queensland 10 years ago and have seen Liam solo live now twice, once in Brisbane in 2019 and Sydney in 2022.'

Sam Wicks

'It was an article in *The New Zealand Herald* that put Oasis on my radar. On the back of the hype surrounding the band in the UK, it talked them up as the second coming of The Stone Roses, primed to follow through on what the Roses promised.

The dirgy sound of grunge won over New Zealand audiences as it had everywhere else, and a bunch of mouthy lads who wanted it all felt like a reset. Having not heard a note, I bought *Definitely Maybe* on vinyl at Real Groovy the day it came out. It was the same copy I asked Noel to sign 18 years later.

I was in Manchester when the 'Battle of Britpop' went down, 'Roll with It' and 'Country House' fighting for the number one spot. When I went to the Reading Festival a couple of weeks later, there were posters for Oasis' upcoming tour across the site. Two months out from its release, the buzz behind *(What's the Story) Morning Glory?* was everywhere.

New Zealand didn't get a look in till the tail end of the *Be Here Now* tour. When a Wellington show was announced, I made plans to see them with my mate Arron Goldman and his little brother Asher – Asher's first concert – and joined the queue snaking down Manners Street to nab tickets.

I'd seen enough shows at Queens Wharf to know the sound was going to be subpar. Liam worked that out soon enough, waving his wallet in the air and telling the crowd he had enough money to sort it out. Then Noel walks off stage, then Liam, followed by the rest of the band. While everyone around me is booing or just bewildered, I'm thinking, is this amazing that we're witnessing a *Wibbling Rivalry* incident or are we being cheated?

I talked to Noel [interviewed on Radio New Zealand] when he played Big Day Out in 2012 and he had no memories of the visit – or the bust-up. Given that Oasis was nearing the end of the *Be Here Now* era, scraps like that were

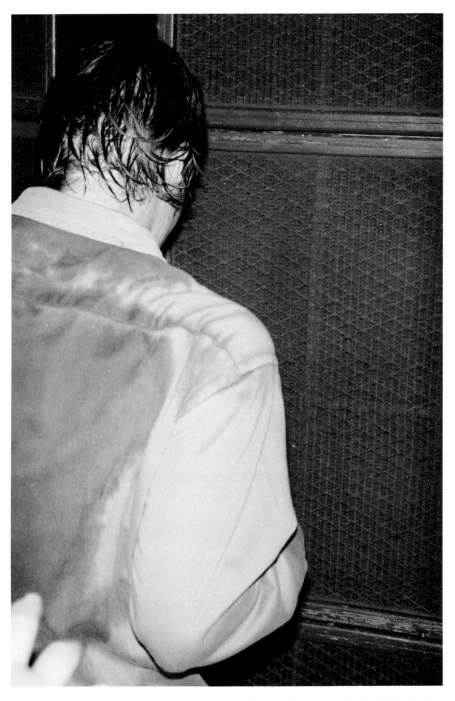

Liam Gallagher at the Events Centre, Wellington. Photograph by Lee Pritchard

probably par for the course. He did clear something up though, with a wink and a smile – we *had* indeed been cheated.'

Sarah Stratton

'My friends and I had a very teenage experience of the concert - we would have been 16 and lived in Nelson, and it was a big deal that we were allowed to travel to Wellington and go to a big concert without an adult escort. I wrote a diary at the time with photos and other newspaper clippings etc. from our trip (as we did before social media).

We enjoyed the show. We were three 16-year-old girls from a small town who had a bit of a crush on Noel and Liam, and it was our first big gig so the whole spectacle and singing along with the crowd etc. was an awesome experience for us and we were buzzing. We did realise that it had its issues (Liam was obviously drunk and stormed off a few times) but I think we just figured that was part of the deal with Oasis. As a singer/guitarist myself I also really loved Noel's solo set.

Oasis concert ticket for show at Queens Wharf Events Centre.
Image courtesy of Sarah Stratton

We were also pretty excited to have a close encounter in town on the afternoon of the 10th when we were in Cuba Mall just down from the bucket fountain. There were a lot of Oasis lookalikes in Wellington that weekend, so we didn't realise it was them until we were passing them coming towards us - Liam was in his brown jacket and Noel was wearing a yellow jacket. We came to a stop and obviously all had a sudden look of realisation on our faces as a woman sitting at a table outside a cafe nearby piped up, 'Yeah girls, it was them'!'

Serra Clarke

'I'd been keen on Oasis for a while, just since *(What's the Story) Morning Glory?* really. I was a huge concert junkie though and was 17 that year and went to every rock show that came and chased after the bands trying to meet them. I went with school friends. We got tickets from the ticket place, it was I think on Manners Street, somewhere in town. We had to queue for tickets back then.

Before the show everyone had to queue for hours outside. The queue used to spiral around the square between it and the building opposite which had a couple of bars. I went after school I think, hours before the show.

We heard that the band were drinking in the pub opposite, so we headed over there and tried to walk in, but as schoolgirls back when the drinking age here was still 20, there was no hope. Went back to the queue and when near the door everyone started cheering. Liam and others, not Noel, were walking across from the pub so I trotted over to him and asked him to shake my hand and he did, then being the dummy I was, I said, 'Shake my other hand' and he said, 'Fuck off'. Went back to my friends in the queue.

The show was not great. Liam was very drunk and as always there was the nonsense between the brothers. He left Noel to sing some of his songs and went off halfway through. To be honest I don't even remember the music it was all about the drama with the brothers.'

Shannon Thomas

'It was the late 1990s in Blenheim and my friends, and I were all around 17 years old. We lived for three things - football, girls and music. We would play and talk football all through school and the weekend and listen to Britpop whenever we could. While we loved Blur, The Stone Roses, The Verve and U2, none of them came close to our favourite band - Oasis. I had been listening to *(What's the Story), Morning Glory?* on repeat for a few years and knew the words to every song - *Be Here Now* had just been released and I could not get enough of 'Stand by Me' - although critics have since felt this was an average album, to me it's still a favourite.

The boys and I felt we were English, we thought we were David Beckham, and our girlfriends were Posh Spice. It was a magical time for us. Then, one day we heard that Oasis was going to play in Wellington - we knew we had to go. Being small-town boys who had barely left Blenheim, our parents wouldn't let us head over by ourselves, so our football coach agreed to take us over. We would stay at the flat of the older brother of one the boys, get up and ferry over on the day of the concert and back the next. So, we got our tickets and started prepping for the greatest time of our young lives.

Heading across on the ferry, the excitement of going on an adventure by ourselves and seeing the Gallagher brothers was almost uncontainable. We arrived and headed straight for Queens Wharf Events Centre to see the location and check out the scene - it was packed. The band was doing a sound check and we could hear them practising and the excitement factor ramped up.

We strolled through town, dropped our gear off and headed back to make sure we arrived in plenty of time for the gig. We entered and took our seats; I recall being on the upper level and quite close to the left of the stage. Before the show started, we remember seeing Liam backstage and talking to the crew, I still remember that clearly to this day.

Then it was time, the lights turned off and the band came on and opened with 'Be Here Now'. We would sing along at the top of our voices for the opening half of the set, totally in the moment and now it's just a blur, but I clearly remember that Liam and Noel had an argument, Liam was unhappy about something and stormed off - we didn't know what was going to happen. We hoped that they would come back on and if not, we would have been devastated. Noel came back on and saved the day with the brilliant acoustic set - I was blown away when he sang 'Setting Sun' by The Chemical Brothers (also loved their albums and knew the words). Liam came back and they finished the set and although we would have been happy for it to go for another six hours it was a good mix of songs. Of course, they did have to sing 'Wonderwall' which blew the roof off.

After the gig and heading back to our place, we could barely talk with our voices almost gone. I don't think we slept much that night, with music and adrenaline still running through our veins. On the ferry home, I feel like we all felt a bit different, it was like a rite of passage for us, our first adventure out of home, seeing our idols and realising what the world outside of little old Blenheim could bring. I still think very fondly of the gig and those first few Oasis albums, but after *Be Here Now* I felt they were never able to recreate the magic, a few songs here and there were great but as a whole, that was certainly their peak. I feel privileged to have seen them at the top of their game.'

Shelley Turnbull

'I really liked their music, had a CD, and followed them as much as I could in those days without the internet as we have now. I went with my sister and a friend. I lived in Levin and drove down and back that night. I was disappointed, the acoustics were not good, the band was disappointing and Liam stormed off stage too often and Noel improvised on the guitar for much too long. I had anticipated it so much that it was a huge let-down. Afterwards, I'd follow them to a point, but I'd never go see them live again. I didn't want to waste money buying their merchandise again.'

Slow Boat Records, Cuba Street, Wellington

'Noel came into the store and bought a bunch of records and signed some stuff. We did not, then, accept AMEX, so he had to go away and get cash.'

Spencer McAndrew

'I was always a massive Beatles fan and I never got into Oasis until *(What's the Story) Morning Glory?* when I heard that album I was blown away. To me there was nothing else like it previously. Being a keen guitarist the opening riff to the title track was a Hallelujah moment!

So, in September 1997 I took a year off work and went travelling around the world. I already had my flights booked and Oasis was playing Birmingham my hometown just after I left. I had to plot out where my round-the-world flight tickets were going to coincide with the Oasis world tour and to my luck I was in New Zealand at the same time. I phoned the box office for The Wharf in Wellington from a pay phone in Zimbabwe, armed with a stash of prepay cards I got through and booked the tickets. I think the phone call to get the tickets cost me as much as the tickets themselves.

Liam Gallagher at the Events Centre, Wellington. Photograph by Lee Pritchard

Was it my best-ever Oasis gig? No. I remember leaving feeling a tad disappointed as I'd looked forward to it for so long and it was gonna be the highlight of my round-the-world trip. I remember the crowd being really restless as the band left the stage there was lots of booing going on and Noel came out just with an acoustic and did a few numbers which the crowd loved. I've since read and I think it's well documented that the sound was particularly shit and Liam was moaning about it. I have this recollection of a guitar being thrown and then the band walking off stage. I'd love someone else to verify this as I could have sworn it was the Union Jack Epiphone but I've probably made this up in my head.

I never missed a tour in the UK after that. I think my best gig was at Finsbury Park where I met up with a London lad whom I'd met in New Zealand. We both travelled the country on a bus called the Kiwi Experience and we had a cassette of *Be Here Now* and we used to share a headphone each from a Walkman listening together – 'All Around the World' was apt and is the song that reminds me of my trip.

The other memorable gig was seeing Noel at the Teenage Cancer Trust show at the Royal Albert Hall, again going to that with my travelling mate Marcus. I have a T-shirt from the Wellington 1998 gig, surprisingly still fits me and I recently wore it to Noel's gig in The Forest at Cannock Chase, I wouldn't part with it for anything!'

Spencer modelling his Oasis t-shirt from the 1998 Wellington concert in 2022

Tim Baird

'I followed Oasis pretty closely. I was working in record stores at the time and they were pretty hard to escape. I went with my friends Fraser and Keiran. We travelled up from Christchurch to Wellington to see them play. We were late to the gig as we were too busy drinking our body weight in beer. By the time we got into the venue the band was already on the stage, and damn - they were loud. The venue isn't exactly noted for its acoustics, and Oasis sounded like a jet plane about to take off, and you're right next to the jet engine standing on the runway. And I've seen some loud bands in my time – I've seen Bailterspace (Flying Nun band from Christchurch), who was floor-movingly loud. Oasis was even louder than them, and that's quite an achievement.

The gig itself was a mess. Liam and Noel were at each other the whole time, and Liam eventually got pissed off to the point where he left the stage halfway through the gig, followed by the rest of the band. Noel flung his guitar to the ground. So, we ended up with around 3 songs of just Noel on guitar by himself leading the crowd in a sing-along when he returned. Then Liam saunters back on, followed by the rest of the band. He still looks pissed off but manages to do a few more songs. He throws what looks like his wallet (!) into the crowd. Then, that was it, they were off. Gig over. At least Noel remembered that people had paid to see a gig and held the thing together as best as he could. It felt like the others couldn't wait to get out of there to be honest. They were burnt out and looked like they needed a nice cup of tea and a lie-down. Not the worst gig I've ever seen though. When they hit it on the classics, they were great.

I didn't buy any of the albums though after *Standing on The Shoulder of Giants*; however, 'Shock of the Lightning' and 'Falling Down' are great tracks from later on in my opinion. But later stuff like 'Lyla' was just naff to me.'

Tommy Fogarty

'I followed them from the release of *(What's the Story) Morning Glory?* I had been in New Zealand for a couple of years and had missed their sudden tabloid explosion but was aware of the whole Britpop phenomenon. I'd heard their stuff on the radio in Wellington, mainly 91ZM and they reminded me of the old type of groupie-shagging, guitar-breaking, bar-brawling, drug-taking rock bands of the 1970s. I also liked the whole Plastic Paddy/Catholic Irish vibe about them. They had the same upbringing as me except that they were brought up in England.

Noel Gallagher performs at the Events Centre, Wellington. Photograph by Lee Pritchard

I went with my wife, one of our best friends Nic Richards, her then-partner and another friend of ours. I enjoyed the gig. I'm a United fan and was in the front and middle giving them stick about football. There were a few football chants going on that night. The crowd had a football crowd vibe which was unusual in New Zealand at that time, so there must have been a lot of other expats there. The band hadn't been absorbed into the Kiwi zeitgeist at that point. Liam spent the night whinging about the acoustics and the sound set up in the Queens Wharf in Wellington. He reckoned it was 'raping his bank balance.' He even took out his wallet to show to everyone. He eventually stormed off, followed by the rest of the gang. Noel and the others came back on after a slow hand clap and did a cool acoustic set. The crowd in the mosh pit were chanting 'United top of the league, United, United top of the league!' All the way through to which Liam replied, 'All right ya wankers, we fucking heard ya.' The Gallagher's are City fans and City were shite at the time. Liam had been drinking all day apparently.

I love the whole vibe around Oasis, they are working-class football fans from a council estate and they embrace their Irishness in a way that Jimmy Carr or The Smiths don't. One thing that does annoy me with them though is that they don't correct people on the pronunciation of their surname. Every Irish person knows that the second g is silent, the boys know this. Why don't they tell people? To Irish people hearing that second g pronounced is like nails on the chalkboard.

I did follow the band after that, to the extent of buying *Be Here Now* and *Standing on the Shoulder of Giants*. I like to watch any interviews with Noel, he is very interesting and has quite a different perspective on life.'

Tony Rarere

'Prior to the gig I was a huge Oasis fan – I still am now. I started listening to them in 1996, just after they released 'Don't Look Back in Anger' as a single. I knew 'Wonderwall' before that but didn't pay much attention to the band. When I discovered 'Don't Look Back in Anger', I started taping on my old tape deck any Oasis songs that came on the radio. We didn't get our first internet connection until 1997, so I could only hear them on the radio. Even when we got internet, the Oasis website back then only had short samples of their songs – no songs in full.

I managed to scrape together $20 in mid-1996 and bought *(What's the Story) Morning Glory?* on cassette tape – which I still have to this day. I was 16 years old when they announced they would be playing two gigs in New Zealand. Initially I was going by myself, so I went over to the Napier Municipal Theatre (I lived in Hastings) to buy one ticket at the ticket office. At some point they released 'All Around the World', and a cousin of mine (who also lived in Hastings) saw the video on TV and decided he liked Oasis (based on the one song he knew!). Somehow, he found out I was going to the gig and asked if he could come with me.

On the day of the gig, I borrowed my parents' car and drove myself and my cousin four hours from Hastings to Wellington. I was still just 16-years-old. I can't believe my parents (a) let me go all that way with just my 16-year-old cousin, and (b) let me borrow their 1995 Holden Berlina, it was a nice car back then.

For me, the gig was incredible, amazing, unbelievable – all those sorts of words. I know that people slated that gig, said it was rubbish, said it was a mess, and so on. But as a 16-year-old true Oasis fan, it was (and still is) the best gig I ever attended. I was smack-bang in the middle of the arena, about 20m from the stage. I'm just under 6-foot-1, but still struggled to see the stage clearly. But I still felt the bass hit me in the chest when the first song kicked in. I had never heard 'Don't Look Back in Anger' played like a heavy rock song before, up-tempo with massive distortion.

I remember we (everyone standing in my area) all sensed something was wrong when Noel stopped playing and was yelling at Liam. We weren't sure if he would storm off but knew he had done so in recent gigs. Then when Noel and the others left, it only felt like a few minutes before Noel returned by himself and did his solo acoustic set. That was my favourite part of the gig. It was my first time hearing an acoustic 'Setting Sun'.

I heard somewhere later that they were off-stage for 30 minutes. Not sure about that as it didn't feel like very long. I became an even bigger fan after the gig. I convinced myself I was going to be a world-famous rock star one day. I played in a band when I got to university where we did Oasis covers and my 'originals' – all of which sounded like re-writes of Live 'Forever' and 'Stand by Me'.

Even though they went quiet for a couple of years (I remember that wait between *Be Here Now* and *Standing on the Shoulder of Giants* feeling like an eternity), I remained a huge fan. Luckily we got *The Masterplan* during that time – which blew my mind. That album of B-sides was better than any album by any of the other bands I listened to at the time.

I was halfway between Hawkes Bay and Auckland in March 2016, on my way to Noel's gig when I got the email saying it was cancelled. And I saw Liam in Auckland in July 2022. They are the only two musicians I would go out of my way to see. I was lucky enough to get hold of a Noel Gallagher Supernova Epiphone in 2008. My brother worked at the Rock Shop in Auckland and bought it for my birthday that year.'

Wendy Black

'I was in high school when I discovered Oasis. I saw the music video for 'Supersonic' on a local backyard TV channel and was immediately intrigued. What followed would be described by most as an obsession! My best friend Charlotte was quickly recruited as a fellow obsessive. Between us we bought all the things. The CD singles, the albums, any magazine that featured anything remotely Oasis. To start with they were hard to find here in New Zealand as they didn't really get well known here until *(What's the Story) Morning Glory?* Anyway, in 1996 they announced a concert for which my parents let me stay home from school so I could devote all my time to being on the phone getting tickets. Honestly only took about 20 minutes, there clearly wasn't the rush that

Noel Gallagher at the Events Centre, Wellington.
Photograph by Lee Pritchard

I was expecting. Unfortunately, this concert was cancelled. I can't remember why.

Fast forward to March 1998. Charlotte and I travelled to Wellington from Christchurch to see them at the Queens Wharf Events Centre, on what I guess was the tour for *Be Here Now*. As we cruised around Wellington CBD on the morning of the concert, we came across the venue and saw that people had started lining up outside already. So obviously we joined them straight away. I remember it was fun chatting away to other fans. At some stage in the afternoon, we heard shouts of 'Liam' and realised he was walking across to a bar right opposite where we were standing. A few people at a time went over to the bar and eventually I decided I had to go to. Leaving Charlotte to keep our place in the line (I was going to be quick so then she could go after me), I went over to the bar.

Sure enough it was Liam! There was one girl there who was screaming and crying just being near him and I thought to myself, 'I bet that's what all my friends would have expected me to be like!' I waited for a bit then decided this was my only chance. I had come over in such a hurry I didn't have my camera or even a pen. Nothing to capture this moment. I went up to him and gently tugged his jacket. He turned around and I said, 'Can I please shake your hand?' He put his beer down, shook my hand and said something in his thick Manc accent and laughed. I said thank you and promptly left to go tell Charlotte the amazing news. As I walked back to the concert line it slowly dawned on me what he had said in response to my request to shake his hand he said, 'As long as you shake something else as well.'

Probably a good thing I didn't get what he meant at the time. He left the bar not long after.

Charlotte and I were in the front row, over Noel's side for the concert. I remember at the point where he and Liam had words and then Noel walked off stage. Followed by the rest of the band not long after. Not sure how long it was till they came back but the crowd was starting to get a bit restless. They came back out and finished the show. Being my first big gig and my favourite band in the world I obviously loved every minute of it so any problems were totally unbeknown to me.

The morning after the concert Charlotte and I were walking around Wellington CBD exploring before we caught our flight home that afternoon. We actually walked past a hotel that had a camera crew and some fans hanging around, so went over and started chatting. Yep, this was the hotel Oasis was staying at. A journalist started asking us questions, in particular, how did we find the sound quality at the concert? Being that we were super fans at our first big concert and right up the front, we didn't know any different and just said, 'Oh yeah it was great.' The journalist then filled us in on the fact that the sound was not good and they assumed this is what Noel got pissed off about and left the stage for. (We found out much later that Noel was pissed off with Liam being very very drunk).

We had nothing better to do so we hung around outside the hotel. I saw a familiar face walking into the hotel and went over to say hi. It was Paolo Hewitt who was writing a book on them at the time. We chatted for a bit and had a photo with him. Then we saw Alan White come down into the lobby. We went in and asked for a photo with him and then went back outside. Sometime later Noel came out to talk to the press. He signed autographs for fans as he was talking to the camera crews etc. Charlotte managed to get beside him and this footage was shown on TV3's *Nightline* that night. Was pretty exciting but Noel was NOT in a great mood. He left and we hung around a bit longer. Bonehead then came into the lobby so we raced in and got our photo with him then I think we were asked to leave the hotel which was just as well as we needed to get to the airport for our flight.

It was an amazing experience for us. I know I put all my photos and ticket stub etc. in a photo frame but I'm not sure where I've put it. Moved house a few million times since 1998.

It was interesting reading Paolo's book when it came out as it explained really what had gone on. Of course, we knew Liam must've been pretty drunk as he seemed well on the way earlier that day when I saw him.'

* * *

Despite the drama onstage, overall fans in Wellington were well behaved with only two arrests.[153] A few fans opted for some skinny dipping in Frank Kitts' Lagoon post-concert according to the *City Voice*. [154] The day after the gig, the band had some downtime in the morning before flying to Auckland. According to the press, they missed their 12 pm flight. Liam kept a low profile but Noel did stop to sign some autographs and briefly talk to the press. Asked about the poor performance in Wellington he blamed Liam for being drunk.

MARTIN HUNTER

Oasis lead singer Liam Gallagher leaves Wellington after his band's patchy performance on Tuesday night

Bad show? Liam was drunk, says Noel

By ANNA FYFE

LIAM GALLAGHER of the British band Oasis was blamed yesterday by his brother Noel for Tuesday night's concert which fans said was disappointing.

At the Parkroyal yesterday, Noel surfaced several times but Liam remained elusive till late afternoon when the Gallaghers and their entourage caught a flight to Auckland, bound for Argentina.

Asked if the sound system had caused the problems at the concert, Noel replied: "No, it was Liam, he was drunk."

He said The Dominion's less-than-favourable review of the concert was "probably right".

Gallagher said he didn't

Noel Gallagher

feel particularly happy with the concert. He denied that the band was in trouble. "What's it got to do with you mate? The band is always in trouble, but we manage."

He said he had seen little of New Zealand during his

WITH A NAME LIKE OASIS, YOU'D THINK THEY WOULD TAKE MORE WATER WITH THEIR GROG...

BROMHEAD

two-day visit.

"We've been keeping our heads down".

While signing autographs for about 15 fans waiting outside the Parkroyal, Gallagher said he didn't know how his brother was feeling after the

concert and a heavy night's drinking.

"Ask him that yourself".

It was reported that Oasis missed their first flight to Auckland at noon and the entourage left well before the band, who headed out to Wellington airport at 5pm.

They were due to fly to Argentina at 7pm yesterday.

Gallagher confirmed that they would make the flight.

Brother Liam did not appear till the band was ready to leave.

He left the hotel from the basement.

Frank Thorne, a reporter from The Sun of London said the night before the Auckland concert, Liam had been binge drinking quadruple vodka and orange, as well as Jack Daniels, and was hurling insults at people.

Dominion article 'Bad Show? Liam was Drunk' – Stuff Limited[155]

237

Noel Gallagher leaves the Parkroyal Hotel[156]

Noel signing autographs when leaving the Parkroyal Hotel[157]

Noel leaving for Wellington airport in the back of a van[158]

Chapter 7 - Crew Recollections

Just like the fans who muscled their way through the heaving crowds to see their idols on stage, and the press who reviewed every performance and documented every scandal, the crew responsible for making it all happen also came away with some lasting impressions from the tour. The unsung heroes of the tour, the crew ensured everything went to plan (as much as it could) each night and have some unique insights into what went on in the lead-up to, and the night of, the gigs. For this book five of the crew on the *Be Here Now* Tour who travelled to New Zealand shared their memories of life on the road with Oasis in Australasia.

Roger Nowell – Bass Guitar Technician- interviewed in March 2022

'I was the bass guitar technician on that tour, originally when the band got a crew, Jason Rhodes (my mate and ex-Skeletal Family tech) and Phil Smith, mate of the band were the crew. Phil shared a place with Mani (from The Stones Roses). So, when The Stone Roses got back together, he left to work with them. I took over from Phil halfway through an American tour. We had a lot of downtime, as Liam usually didn't do more than three gigs in a row. I don't remember Liam and Noel having a spat in Wellington, they did have a few in my time with them however! I got a tattoo in New Zealand I remember that.

When I joined the Oasis crew, Guigsy had two basses. A black Fender Jazz which was Noel's and his White Telecaster bass. Also, a Gibson Les Paul recording bass. By the time we got to New Zealand, Fender had given him a 62 Relic Jazz, a Standard Jazz and a 58 reissue precision bass. He bought himself a 62 Jazz. So that's what he took out. He normally only played the 62.

It was getting to the end of the tour. We partied pretty hard in those days. So maybe a little knackered by then.'

Steve Honest – Keyboard Technician – interviewed in March 2022

'On the *Be Here Now* tour I worked as the keyboard technician to Mikey Rowe. Back in album preproduction Spooner (Paul Heywood) had called me and asked me to bring Micky Simmonds along for an audition for Oasis, but I felt Micky was too old and a bit too middle-class for the guys and they would not get along. Though Micky is a stunning keyboard player, I took it upon myself to change out the guy I brought to the audition.

I brought Mikey Rowe instead. Mikey was playing with a band called Rachel Stamp, signed to Warner's who I was tour managing at the time and felt he would fit with Oasis like a glove. Plus, he had all those feels and licks the guys would like, he was a great player and understood the same music feel Oasis was into.

The day-to-day routine was luxury from a crew perspective, recording, rehearsals and touring. When we eventually got to it, it was always well-catered, with good hotels and transport and a relaxed work pace. The guys took their time and got very little done every day but they had fun and liked to get the crew involved in anything that was going on.

We had a lot of R and R time between shows and legs of tours and on tour there was always some sort of party going on, pints of vodka and orange being the tour drink abroad. The New Zealand leg was great fun. I'd been there before with Grant Lee Buffalo and R.E.M. and was very keen to go back to what I've always maintained is one of the most beautiful countries on earth. I know the mood in the camp was a little tense when we got to New Zealand. Bonehead and Liam had some friction and Noel and Liam were busy being Noel and Liam. This generated much more attention than we needed and often the tour was threatened with cancellations and people having to lose their jobs and go home. But we got to New Zealand and had some down time. By the time we had got to Auckland morale was a little tatty, drink and drugs had spun out of control but the band encouraged a party atmosphere, so you could not put a foot wrong. Roger (Nowell) got a tattoo on a drunken night out we had with the lady who played Xena Warrior Princess (Lucy Lawless), she recommended a tattoo shop and Roger dived in!

'The Country Club' as we 5 stage techs were known, stayed close. I did have a huge amount of memorabilia and tour swag but I had to sell it all in the early

2000s. I needed surgery and wanted it done in private health and so I sold all my tour stuff to raise the money for the operation.

Mikey used a Roland Mother keyboard which controlled a rack full of samplers and synths, which I switched using software midi routing on a laptop. We also had a Wurlitzer analogue keyboard which was lovely and growly. There was a 2nd keyboard player, after the first two shows we did in LA and then opening for U2 in San Francisco. It was felt Mikey was struggling to cover all the parts needed so I was offered the gig of 2nd keys player, I turned it down and Paul 'Strangeboy' Stacey was brought in and we went out with two keys players for the rest of the tour.'

Gareth Williams – Monitor Engineer at Knebworth and *Be Here Now* tour - interviewed in May 2022

'It's strange venturing down memory lane after 24 years (I was interviewed recently about Knebworth for the 25th anniversary and was surprised at some of the songs on the setlist. (We did those?) I have forgotten so much (it's called healing) but there are still one or two memories of that trip to New Zealand. So, if you'll allow me…

Firstly, I remember that before we headed off, and to save money, only the FOH [Front of House] and Mons control packages were flown out for the Hong Kong/Australia and New Zealand tour that year. However, the monitor speakers that were waiting for us in Hong Kong were such a shock for the band that they very quickly insisted on flying their Turbosound TMF350s (2 x 15" plus 1 x 2" bi-amped) and BSS 780/760-amp racks to Australia. I can't remember what they had in Hong Kong but it was nowhere near capable of delivering the levels the band were used to. Plus - one of the things companies couldn't get their head around was my strict 'No Limiting' demand. The last thing I needed was a processor telling me when a speaker/amp had had enough. I'd be the judge of that and I pride myself in saying that despite the punishment, I NEVER blew anything up. I probably came as close as you could mind…

On the flight from Hong Kong to Perth, Australia, Liam had a well-reported 'incident' where he threatened the pilot. Thankfully, I was asleep and missed it - not for the first or last time - but there were police waiting for us at Perth airport and all hell broke loose. The Pilots' Association threatened to boycott our flights indefinitely but in the end, a deal was done that we could fly - but there would be undercover security on the planes. We, the crew, were told to be on our best behaviour because the flights were absolutely rammed with press from the UK and beyond. In those days, everything Oasis did was a story and you literally couldn't go to the toilet without a member of the press following you in. I'm probably still black-listed on Cathay Pacific - who knows?

I don't remember anything unusual about Australia other than that we kept our heads down and got on with our jobs. I don't recall anything untoward regarding the shows - but every flight was still filled with press (we'd read about our flights the following day in the paper!) and huge guys in suits. Huw (Huw Richards, FOH Sound Engineer) though was showing signs that he'd had enough - I don't blame him!

When we got to New Zealand, it was my first time working with Oceania. I'd heard of Greg Peacock but never met him and we got on fine. Quite a few of his crew had come over to the UK and worked with Brit Row so we weren't complete strangers. I think he and Huw probably got off on the wrong foot though. To get the levels required both FOH and on stage with Oasis you had to rip up the rule book. Suppliers were understandably cautious about handing over the reins, given the reputation of the volume by then, but again, for all that level, Huw was a very responsible engineer. It was VERY loud - but that was his brief. That's what Noel wanted. Can't have been easy for the bloke who owned the boxes though…

I seem to recall power being a problem nationally which was a worry. Generators were being shipped in from all over to supplement the power grid. I think it was Greg that told me that Elton John had been in Auckland the previous week and though the rest of his gear had been shipped on to the next destination, his generators were commandeered. I'm sure there'll be a record of it somewhere.

I remember that after the penultimate show in Auckland, Huw spoke to Maggie (the Tour Manager) and said he didn't want to go to South America, our next leg. That was a shock to all of us. As we flew (closely guarded, as was the new norm…) to Chile, he flew to London. It felt very strange.

244

I don't recall these shows being louder than any of the previous ones. And as for Liam 'losing the plot a bit,' that was too regular an occurrence for me to single out Wellington in particular. We were already on a suspended sentence as far as the rest of us were concerned. I'm sure it is well documented somewhere - it always was! - But by then, we were used to the headlines. Wellington though was a very weird show for everyone, band and crew, as we knew it would be Huw's last.

So, there you go. I don't really have much to offer about New Zealand I'm afraid. We brought our own BRP control and monitor package and used the Oceania Flashlite system. It will have been very loud - because it always was - and then we went to Chile with a new engineer. Frankly, how any of us got through that year is a bloody miracle.

I remember the tour finished in Mexico City though and all the shows the band had ever done were listed in the tour programme. I did a quick count up that afternoon in catering and turned to Guigsy and said, 'Would you believe it - this is my 100th Oasis gig'. He calmly leaned across the table and said 'OK. You've got the job'.'

Michael O'Connor – Oasis Production Manager 1997 – 2009 – interviewed in May 2022

How you got involved with Oasis

'I started working with them in the first Earls Court show they did in 1995. I was the Lighting Crew Chief. I was asked to do their show at Earls Court, their first big arena show. I worked with Eric Clapton and other people like that previously and worked for a Birmingham-based company called LSD (Lighting Sound Design), they were the people who provided the lighting for Oasis and then they turned into a company called PRG. Anyways, I worked for them freelance, and I was contracted to come in and do that show at Earls Court and it went very well, they were huge, absolutely huge shows. The show they played before Earls Court had 900 people at it over in Belgium, and then Earls Court had 19,000 which was mad.

It was a horrible building to work in, awful. They used to steal, the people who worked there used to steal from the offices; phones, computers anything from the office, it was absolutely mad. They had to put security in the office which you don't normally do. So, then I did a few dates with them after Earls Court up in Scotland. I was asked to do Maine Road, but I wasn't available. So, then the next thing they asked me to do was Knebworth in 1996. I was actually out with another company at the time with Mark Knopfler from Dire Straits and I was with him for 17 weeks, so I wasn't available. I could do the Knebworth shows, but I couldn't do the rehearsals in Birmingham, I couldn't do the first gigs in Scotland [Loch Lomond], but I could join them in Knebworth. So that's where I came on board and after the two shows at Knebworth we went over to America.

That's when Liam got off the plane bound for Detroit. Noel did the first show without him, then Liam joined. And at that point, the press was hounding them, the tabloids. They had some row, some sort of disagreement on the tour in America and Noel flew back from where he was in New York on Concorde and flew home. We were loading-in in Charlotte, he was back in London. We didn't find out until lunchtime there wasn't much of a show, he wasn't even in America. But that's the way things happened with the band. It was just a band that things happened to and wasn't always their fault.

Taking on the Production Manager role

I was only working on lighting at that point on those tours in 1995 and 1996. A person had come on board to take on the production role from another Production Manager who had been there from the beginning. That Production Manager used to work with Pink Floyd, and big bands like that and he couldn't quite comprehend working with these guys, it just didn't equate. So, in the end, that's when Maggie (Tour Manager) asked me the following year to do Erasure, to see if I could do the Production role as I hadn't done it before. After doing that she asked if I would do the Production for Oasis.

Be Here Now tour

We went into rehearsals in August 1997, band rehearsals. When we came out of the rehearsals there'd be fans and the press outside as well. We'd moved from Bermondsey to the London Docklands Arena. The press was camped outside as we went into full production rehearsals. They wanted photos of anything literally, the set, the band and anyone who was tagging along. We had big curtains blocking off the entrance so they couldn't get any photos. They were always outside waiting, then Princess Diana died. The press disappeared, gone. In the space of one day, that was it, we didn't see them outside again, which obviously worked in our favour as we didn't have the pressure of them trying to get in.

Europe 1997

We headed off on a European tour which wound back into a UK tour. Oasis went off to the States to do a TV show then came back and did more European gigs. We did an arena tour in the UK and Ireland in December 1997. In the middle of that European tour there was a French truck strike, we were actually in France when it happened. We managed to get out of Lille, over the border to Belgium and we air freighted the backline down to Spain. And about a week later we used local trucks, we managed to get a show in Zaragoza, Madrid and I can't remember if we did one in Barcelona. And then we managed to re-join the trucks who managed to pick up all the gear. In Madrid we had no stage set, literally nothing, a local drum riser and that was it, and it was an absolutely brilliant gig. The Tour Manager (Maggie) saw that, and thought, 'Why are we lugging all this stuff around with us?' We were going to America, and we decided we were not going to take it all to America. So that time, September to December was the only time Oasis toured with a custom-built stage set. After the Wembley show in the UK the full set never left the country – no clock, phone etc.

Australia 1998

We went over to America in January 1998, then we went over to Japan and Hong Kong and then we flew that infamous Cathay Pacific flight to Perth. Oasis was the only band if you were crew, you didn't want to go in Business Class, you'd prefer to go in Economy to avoid the grief, I'm not joking! Prior to that, Oasis was offered a stadium tour of Australia and they pulled out. So, when they arrived in Perth it was really big news, because the band were finally in Australia, after all these years of waiting. There were loads of press, we arrived late at night. As we got off, some of the people who were in Business Class saw the press and went over and told them what a bunch of idiots they were and on about all the carry-on on the plane. So that all kicked off. They made the mistake of going to an island off the coast of Perth (Rottnest Island) and Liam said he'd stab the pilot, which wasn't a particularly good idea to mention that, considering we had to fly all around Australia. From that point on, Liam had to have a police escort down to the airport, to the gate and at the other end we'd be met by police and walked out of the airport. What other band would you work with that around?

Anyways we continued. I remember in Perth the following day on TV, the weatherman was discussing whether the band should be flown around Australia, on one of those early morning breakfast programmes. And I'm thinking what the hell. Everybody was talking about the band; you can't imagine the scale of the conversation that was going on at that time.

In Brisbane, Liam had an argument with a fan. The following day we were loading in and for some unknown reason, I don't know why, to this day I don't know why, they moved the stage position in the arena, and by doing that, they run the electric cables along the floor and into the back of the stage, but that created a buzz, on the amps. The guitars they used were old-fashioned guitars and they picked up the radio frequency coming off the electric cables. We spent ages trying to improve or reduce the buzz. We got it down to a level but there was still a buzz there, but there was nothing we do about it due to the position of the stage.

That morning we were loading in anyways, I was sitting where the catering was and there were televisions in the room, and the news came on and it mentioned Liam had been arrested. Now, I didn't know, I hadn't heard a word, that was the first I'd heard of it. It was about 10 a.m. I was just eating my breakfast, so I met Maggie and I said, 'What's going on? Have we got a show here or what?' And she said, 'Keep planning on the show.' We kept going, working on that buzz, and it was reduced, but it was still there. The band weren't happy with the noise, literally there was nothing we could do about it. That was the last show in Australia. On our arrival to Australia, we came in as heroes and when we left Australia it was like a dog with its tail between its legs getting out of the country. In the space of 10 or 12 days it was unbelievable. The coverage in Australia was completely nuts. Every live programme, Oasis would come up in conversation, everyone had an opinion on it.

New Zealand 1998

When we arrived in Auckland, I think to be honest, people were just glad to be out of Australia. But leading up to all of that the Front of House Engineer was having a change of heart. He'd gone a little bit off the wall. In Hanover, the volume was up so high, it was absolutely excruciating. Management had pulled him up, but it seemed to be getting worse and worse as we were progressing. In New Zealand, you're as far away as you could be from getting someone to come out and cover or replace, you couldn't be further away if you tried. A guy was on the tour, the promoter rep for Australia and New Zealand called David Hughes. He was brilliant at dealing with all the grief that was going on. He heard us talking about what are we going to do about this FOH [Front of House] engineer and he mentioned he knew someone in Australia who was very good. He mentioned him in Auckland. We did the show in Auckland and it was still loud and then we had a meeting in Wellington. And this is the funny part, I can remember a lot of things, but I can't remember how we got from Auckland to Wellington, obviously we flew, I can remember walking into the Queens Wharf Events Centre, I distinctly remember walking in, but no recollection whatsoever on how we got there. It's bizarre, no recollection of how we got there.

We had this meeting with the FOH Engineer and I think even Noel has mentioned this in an interview, we discussed what is the problem and you've been asked to turn the sound down to an acceptable level. Obviously, you're not enjoying yourself on the tour, there's an issue here, what's the problem? His issue was, 'There's too much choice in catering' ...that's what he said. There's too much choice in catering. We all looked at each other and thought, 'Did he really just say that?' And then he walked out of the room. So that shows you where he was at the time.

We did the show in Wellington, there's a little bit of argy-bargy in the middle between Noel and Liam. Liam goes off stage. Noel used to do an acoustic set about halfway through the show, which was always good, it gave everyone a break and a chance to get their breath back and then they'd come back on and pick it up again, so the crowd could go mad again. Everybody looked forward to that little acoustic session. So, Liam went off stage, he went into the dressing room and smashed up the mirrors, you could hear that on stage as the dressing rooms were right behind the stage, I think they might have been curtained-off partitioned rooms, something like that. Even the audience could hear the glass smashing. Then he came back. We knew it was going to be the last show with this FOH Engineer because he was going to be sent home. It was kicking off, a whole combination of things and it all came to a crescendo over the sound, it was something that they could all agree on, that they didn't like it.

The remainder of the tour

We were then flying to Chile, where the next show was. David Hughes got in touch with Bruce Johnston who was an Australian engineer. He had to fly from Melbourne to Sydney, Sydney to Los Angeles and Los Angeles to Chile. And he came in, having never seen the band, never heard the band and all local equipment, local PA, local desks, all we toured was the backline, the shows sounded incredible. When Bruce took over, we did five shows in South America and two in Mexico. All different PAs and equipment and they all sounded great. And then it was the end of the tour. Everyone thought, if he can do that, he's got to be great when he has his own desks. So, he stayed with us until early 2009. His assistant Dan then took over.

Setting up tour requirements

We would send a list of our audio and lighting requirements, and companies would come back to us. There weren't that many choices in New Zealand. But Britannia Row had a relationship with Oceania so there was a connection there and they passed our requirements on. Gareth Williams had a good head on his shoulders and would put a list together of what all the requirements were, he talked to the FOH Engineer and either he or I would send it on or Gareth would work with his connections.'

Paolo Hewitt – band biographer and tour DJ – interviewed in 2022

'That tour [*Be Here Now*] was extremely significant. Up until Knebworth, everything was in the balance, a bit chaotic a bit edgy. It was the first time they were regularly playing to 20, 30 thousand people and it kind of lost its edge. People say that tour was so chaotic, but not really when compared to what went on before.

The Australian tour

These things build. You have to take into account what had gone on in Australia. The Australian press was hostile from the start. They weren't particularly welcoming. The impression I got was that if a band travels that far to Australia or New Zealand, the press didn't like it if the band gives the impression that 'we've done you a massive favour coming this far,' Oasis didn't have that, but the press was against them anyways from the start.

Noel and Liam

Noel got the hump a bit with Liam for causing all that fuss. It speaks to how those two were operating. Noel was very much the professional, he wanted the band to be as big as possible and anything that got in the way of that, Liam kicking off and the press getting hostile, would have given him the hump. There was always that tension between them, you know, Liam saying without me doing what I do and looking as I do, talking as I do, no one would be interested in what we do. And Noel saying without me, writing the songs, no one would be interested. There weren't many shows in Australia, but the tension got worse.

The Wellington gig

Liam had too much to drink and came on with that kazoo and thought it was funny, but it really really angered Noel and he finally snapped and threw his guitar down. The rest of the band had to walk off; it was a bit chaotic. Noel must have gone straight back to the hotel afterwards. I remember going into the dressing room afterwards and Liam was lying on the couch saying, 'That was a good ride wasn't it? We had a good laugh?' That's the end of that.'

Be Here Now tour in general

To be honest with you the tour was so big, it was un-Oasis like. Noel wanted them to be huge, the biggest band in the world. I don't think they were the kind of band who could do that as they always had Liam there, he was always the wildcard element. People loved that about them, but he also prevented them. On that tour, you couldn't mess around. It was a big thing, professional, with 54 people on the road. Whereas before they're playing to 2,000 people and it could all go off and things could happen. But now it was huge. Liam was talking a lot on the tour about forming a new band or having a break. They wanted to play the 100 Club, they wanted to make it fun again. That tour wasn't fun in any sense, it was a drain. It just went on and on.

They had been touring for four years. In the USA they toured hard. They went to every little town from New York to LA to try and crack it and be as big as possible. They really put the graft in. But on *Be Here Now* they were travelling in separate cars and it wasn't them. It was too big. As I mention in the book (*Forever the People, Six Months on the Road with Oasis*), there's a lot of talk of the old days on the road. Do you remember this gig and that? I never heard them talk like that. It was always about the old days. Before it was always fun. It had become a different beast.

The Wellington show was a culmination of that and what had gone on in Australia. They never changed the setlist. Most bands mess around with it, they have their standards and add a few others. But Oasis had the same set every night. After six months of this, it was hard for me to know when a good gig was a good gig.'

Chapter 8 - Aftermath

'Yeah those years were pretty wild. I can't even remember a lot of it. I'd read some things and think, 'Did that really happen? I can't remember' and then I'd see the pictures. It was like our trip to Australia and New Zealand. I really don't remember much about that whole fucking tour because I was very, very drunk most of the time.'
Liam Gallagher, 2006[159]

On the evening of March 11, 1998, Oasis left New Zealand on Aerolinias Argentinas flight AR1881 from Auckland to Buenos Aires.[160] All up, the band was in New Zealand for approximately 67 hours. They never returned. In South America, the band performed some of their better gigs in the entire *Be Here Now* Tour, inspired by the larger crowds and adoration from South and Central American fans. At the time of their visit to New Zealand in 1998, the Britpop movement spearheaded by the band was falling out of fashion and Oasis' claim to the musical throne was under severe threat from The Verve, Radiohead, and The Spice Girls. While *Be Here Now* sold eight million copies worldwide, the Spice Girls were fast becoming British music's newest global icon with their 1997 album *Spiceworld* shifting over 14 million copies. Pop music made a strong return in the UK in 1998, with the top five biggest-selling albums of the year coming from The Spice Girls, The Corrs, George Michael, Boyzone and Robbie Williams.[161]

Phil Smith (Tour DJ), Pete Bell (Stage Manager) and Alan White at Auckland Airport, March 11, 1998, prior to departure to Argentina. Photograph by Robert Rankine

Oasis tour group at Auckland Airport, March 11, 1998.
Photograph by Robert Rankine

Oasis tour group at Auckland Airport, March 11, 1998. Robert Rankine hugged by Alan White. Photographer unknown but the image belongs to Robert Rankine

Oasis tour group at Kiwis' Cafe, Auckland Airport, March 11, 1998.
Photograph by Robert Rankine

Paul 'Bonehead' Arthurs and Alan White, Auckland Airport, March 11, 1998.
Photograph by Robert Rankine

Oasis' moment to capture Kiwi audiences had been and gone, with the band well past its 1996 peak in popularity by the time they made it to New Zealand. With two cancelled tours, patience had worn thin and the Gallaghers themselves admitted this in interviews prior to the tour. Musically, few Kiwi artists were likely to get a record deal in the late 1990s by proclaiming to be the next Oasis. Instead, New Zealand witnessed a resurgence in homegrown talent and a focus on local songs on local airwaves. The Feelers debut album *Supersystem* went on to become the 2nd biggest-selling album in 1998. The following year, Shihad would score their first #1 album with *The General Electric*.

It would be easy to end the recollections of the tour here but seeing the rise in Kiwi rock music in the mid to late 1990s, I was keen to understand how Oasis may have influenced the New Zealand music scene, and New Zealand musicians. A number of Kiwi artists were approached for this book to talk about the influence of Oasis on their careers. Unsurprisingly, many said there wasn't any. Three artists agreed to share their stories of how Oasis influenced them and the musical legacy they left.

Tom Larkin – Shihad – interviewed in 2023

Tom Larkin is a founding member of Shihad, New Zealand's greatest rock band of the last 30 years. Formed in 1988 they've topped the New Zealand Album chart on six occasions to date. Tom is also a band manager and music producer, sharing the Producer of the Year award at the New Zealand Music Awards in 2018.

'In 1995 we were on tour in Europe and Oasis mania was everywhere. You'd be going through London and see all the posters up on the tube and all that. They were a huge buzz band at that point, with only one album out. Phil [Knight, Shihad guitarist] bought a couple of things while in London.

We ended up at Roskilde Festival in Denmark and Phil and I were like, 'Are we gonna go check this band out or what?' They were playing the Green Tent. It was absolutely packed. Overflowing every angle. We had the advantage of having access as we were performing at the festival so we utilised that. But the first thing we loved was that they came on and it was fucking blisteringly loud. I've always loved that in Shihad and we have a saying when we're doing our own mixes, 'Are the guitars loud enough?' We've always had a thing about the volumes and wide pan guitars, left and right, getting them to the maximum scale they can perceivably get to before everything blurs into incoherence, always trying to find that line to see the furthest the guitars can go. Anyways, we walked in.

What came across on their recordings was this great voice, this new kind of tone and fashion. The way they carried themselves was very influential. The songs were songwriter driven, had their apparent influences which were obvious. Sex Pistols meets the Beatles, that's loosely it. That's very appealing. You can't really go wrong mixing those two. But the recordings didn't really, I suppose present what they were really like live at that point.

It was an absolute skyscraper of guitars. It was similar in terms of its bandwidth like watching AC/DC for the first time in 1991. That same amount of height and reverence to the guitar impact was just fucking colossal. It was fucking awesome. Anything like that we fucking love. All those tunes but in that jet engine taking off context which hadn't been communicated in the recordings at that point so it was ultra impressive. Fuck that was incredible, what a moment.

You're at the moment watching the band break, the fast growth the buzz is all around them. Whoever booked them took a gamble and had no idea what they would turn into. It was way bigger than what they hoped for. The tent was at capacity.

We thought we're not really seeing much here, let's go on the front barrier and watch it under Liam. So we did, we went to the front barrier and sat right under Liam and lasted about three songs until we got moved out by security. We walked out of there with complete confidence, it was astonishing, amazing songs, sonic as fuck, they sounded brilliant, they looked brilliant. It was the real thing, legit. Not many bands had all of it, but they did. It was rare to see the whole thing.

The impact they had definitely influenced the writing of the fish album [Shihad's third album was called Shihad, with fish on the cover, colloquially known as the 'fish album,' released in September 1996] in so far some of the approaches, the chord choices and it linked the Beatles back into Shihad which is obviously an influence for everyone. It linked it back into a conscious influence I think and certain aspects of the fish album would reflect that, wouldn't necessarily sound like Oasis, but it would echo some of that approach we picked up on. Oasis wasn't a blinding influence, but part of the mix. Part of the mix to explore other things, not part of the DNA, but referencing those older influences and opening up to their approach.

[Upon the suggestion that 'Pacifier' has a certain Oasis vibe]…

I hadn't joined the dots on that one, but I see the point the in vocal cadence. It's funny how influences are strange. A lot of stuff you can consciously take on but it's also in your subconscious. I had not joined the dots on Oasis and 'Pacifier' as it was an album cycle later. And Oasis was definitely not a conscious influence at that point. By the time we got to The General Electric it would be more subconscious. A great call on the chorus being Oasis-like, it's a Liam Gallagher phrasing and tempo for sure. Its' also got this Celtic scale which I think is important for any anthemic song, especially in European music, a Celtic tonality which Oasis would have as well.

258

I was at the Wellington show in 1998. Liam was having a go at the Sound Monitors Engineer and Noel wasn't having it. Noel and Liam were chest-to-chest on the stage. You talk to people who've worked with Oasis as crew and the one thing they say is what a great gig it is. It stems from Noel's time as a guitar tech and so he made sure the crew are well looked after and respected.

I've always loved Oasis. I count myself very strongly as a fan. I think they were a phenomenon. They had a certain type of personality make-up you don't see. They were funny, a form of tongue and cheek. Absolutely brilliant. It was a privilege to see them at that age and stage in Roskilde. Rock and roll history in the making.'

Lawrence Arabia – interviewed in March 2022

Lawrence Arabia is the musical guise of New Zealand artist and composer James Milne. Winner of Best Male Artist at the 2013 New Zealand Music Awards and winner of Best Alternative Album at the 2016 NZMA ceremony with 4th album Absolute Truth.

'I was a huge Oasis fan at the time. I saw Oasis at the Wellington show on that tour.

Bonehead and Noel signed my copy of the 'D'You Know What I Mean?' single outside their hotel. There was a piece on TV3 *Nightline* at the time in which I appear in the background waiting for autographs.

At this time (1995-1999) Oasis was a big influence on my songwriting, world-view and fashion sense! Their influence definitely waned for me over the ensuing few years, but as a teenager they were a huge touchstone for what I wanted to do with my life. I remember the show being way too loud and pretty horrible really. A bit of a drunken sludge. It was my first proper big rock show experience and I ended up missing a few songs because I needed to faint and go and spend a few minutes in the first aid room.'

Sven Pettersen lead guitarist for The Checks and current project Racing – interviewed in 2022

The Checks were a New Zealand rock band formed in Takapuna in 2002. They supported Oasis on the Australian leg of the Don't Believe the Truth tour. In 2005 they won the Breakthrough Artist of the Year award at the New Zealand Music Awards. In 2010 their 2nd album Alice by the Moon won Best Rock Album at the New Zealand Music Awards and they repeated the feat winning the same award in 2012 for their third album Deadly Summer Sway. They disbanded in 2012. Sven then went on to be part of Racing.

'Oasis first entered my orbit in the era of when New Zealand first got MTV and this was the peak of Oasis power so was continually on the telly. I even remember vaguely saying to my friend, if he got an electric guitar, he could play bass on it and we could start a band like Oasis. I watched the *MTV Unplugged* concert when Noel had to sing the whole thing while Liam was in the audience heckling him. Ed [Edward Knowles of The Checks] bought the 'D'You Know What I Mean?' CD single and I borrowed the *(What's the Story) Morning Glory?* CD from a friend of ours called Bill. That CD is in my car at this moment.

We were just out of school when The Checks got the call up to open for Oasis. I was washing dishes at a cafe in Mairangi Bay at this point in time. We'd opened for REM, but this was a different beast, a whole tour of Australia and Oasis have a different type of meganess. Our music got to Noel through the grapevine and he gave us the tick.

The first show in Brisbane we walked into the arena and Noel was sound checking by himself playing 'Strawberry Fields Forever'. It was an amazing sound to walk into and such a surreal moment to actually see him on the stage. Then the band slowly walked on the stage and they were playing 'Like a Rolling Stone' for ages, as we sat there in the empty arena and watched in awe. We sound-checked and Noel walked out and watched us for a bit, pretty out of it. Just Noel Gallagher watching us in an empty arena!

The first one we met was Liam who just waltzed into our dressing and went around shaking our hands and you could feel the megastar energy flying off him. We got comfier as the tour wore on. The guy that did our sound was called Nahuel who we hit it off with. He toured England with us a few years later and became one of our really good mates.

I don't know if I've ever seen such epic arena shows since, maybe only AC/DC. The way that people would sing and how the energy had lifted in these places was otherworldly. It was actually kind of religious, the hymn-like nature of those choruses. It was funny because even though these gigs were absolutely going off, they were getting panned in the papers because a previous time, Liam had punched someone, and with the patriotic Australia thing, the press had decided to go after Oasis. They would always open with 'Turn up the Sun', just a monstrous sound. Liam would cruise on the stage in this amazing white jacket and sunglasses and just fire start in 'I carry a madness....'

Over the years going to and from Australia lots of people that started bands were at these Oasis gigs and told us they saw us and started listening to us, such as the DMA's and others. The last night of the tour was in Melbourne so it was then we got into the drinking with them. It was such a great show and a great tour so we went to Cherry Bar on AC/DC Lane to celebrate. We were all drinking backstage and I remember chatting to Zak Starkey (Ringo's boy) about jazz and blues etc. and how it's like playing with Pete Townshend. It turned into a bit of a magic night, where we were smoking a spliff with Liam and then we went inside and Noel was singing the riff to 'Hunting Whales' off our debut album at us saying he liked that one.

I hit it off with Zak and he was like, 'You guys have to come to my studio in Brighton to jam.' So, we went to swap numbers and I was so drunk at the time I didn't notice but the next day when I looked at the number and I had written ##tomo#3sbv, something like this. Pre-social media. This drunken error gets bought up to this day. The son of a Beatle who also played in The Who.

We were 19, Karel [Chabera, bass guitarist for The Checks] was 17, when we played those gigs. So, they couldn't help but have been a big influence on us. The album that they were touring was called *Don't Believe the Truth* which was touted as the return to form record. Between that album and the touring, we got back into listening to Oasis.

The influence on us from Oasis pops up in many ways. The one that gets missed when people talk about Oasis' music is often the meganess of the slow grooves. There is also this spiritual stadium experience thing which if you get a glimpse of it in writing something, the Oasis thing to do is just really lean into it. Make it massive and magical which is not really a New Zealand ethos or an English one either. Also, the power of simplicity is always the goal, not unlike AC/DC. Surprising how few bands can actually light up a stadium, even apparently 'stadium' bands.

It was a cool full-circle moment when Racing got the call to open for Liam years later in 2019 in Auckland. He was great too.'

* * *

In later years Oasis would regularly tour Europe, Asia, and North and South America on the back of successful albums. The fanbase, especially in Europe and South America remained dedicated enough for them to sell out stadiums well into the 2000s. Their legacy in Australasia was very different. A loyal fan base remained, but only Australian fans were lucky enough to see them perform in the flesh again. Tours down under in 2002, 2005 and a Noel Gallagher acoustic tour in 2006 offered the band redemption following the now infamous 1998 tour. The 2005 tour was covered in the documentary *Lord Don't Slow Me Down*. In New Zealand, the band's four final studio albums would disappear off the chart in the blink of an eye with *Dig Out Your Soul* lasting only three weeks. Memories of the 1998 tour became the stuff of folklore. In 2015 *Stuff* named the Wellington show as the worst-ever concert in New Zealand history.[162] The recollections used to inform this analysis, however, inaccurately claimed that Noel sang most of the songs after Liam disappeared off stage. The details recorded in this book firmly call into question this version of events and the label of New Zealand's worst ever concert. But it wouldn't be Oasis without dividing opinions.

A backstage fight between Noel and Liam in Paris saw the eventual demise of the band in August 2009. The *Dig Out Your Soul* tour had two gigs left - one in Milan and one at a festival in Germany. Had they kept it together, another jaunt down under could have followed, this time including a trip to New Zealand. Talking to the fans who were there shows the band is firmly etched in their memory, even to this day. Oasis may be no more, but the tunes remain, their magic undiminished. Old and new generations of fans have been lucky enough to get a glimpse into what it might have been like to see Oasis live, thanks to Noel's and Liam's successful solo careers. Noel returned to New Zealand for the Big Day Out in 2012, and to support U2 in 2019. His planned 2016 solo show at the Aotea Centre in Auckland was cancelled as his equipment failed to turn up on time from South America due to stormy weather causing flight delays. Liam returned with his band Beady Eye for the Big Day Out in 2014, followed by solo gigs in 2019 and 2022 at the Spark Arena in Auckland.

Oasis has said very little publicly about their tour to New Zealand. In 2012 when interviewed by David Farrier on *3 News* ahead of his Big Day Out appearance, Noel said he was informed he'd had a sing-along with Joe Cocker at the hotel they were both staying at in Auckland but has no memory of it. In 2016 when interviewed by Sam Wicks of Radio New Zealand, Noel said he had no memory of the New Zealand tour. Liam Gallagher's *Rip It Up* interview in 2006 confirmed what had been thought by many - he was drunk, but still offering little insight into what actually went on behind the scenes.

The tour wasn't the all-conquering success you might expect from the biggest band in the world, but instead offered glimmers of brilliance marred by the constant and palpable tension of two brothers trying not to conk one another. In the end, this is what many remember from the tour.

Just two years after the 1998 New Zealand trip, Russell Baillie of *The New Zealand Herald* interviewed Noel and extracted insightful thoughts about the fateful tour. The final word on the tour, the opinion of Noel Gallagher:

'Oh it was horrible,' he admits. *'The singer was constantly drunk on stage. It had taken us six years to get there and I just think that we blew it when we got there and that was basically down to the singer.*

'It was horrible mate. It was worse than that. Don't make no bones about it man. We were a disgrace and that is all down to Liam and he knows that and the rest of the band know that and if we ever get out there again, it will be a damn sight better next time, but there you go. People wanted the Sex Pistols and we gave it to them.'

[Russell] So can we take that as an apology to those folks who bought tickets to the whole fiasco?

'Well I am apologising on behalf of the singer,' replies Noel, his tongue heading toward his cheek. *'I thought I was marvellous, personally.'*[163]

Appendix 1 – Oasis Discography & Chart Positions in New Zealand

Singles

Title	Entry	Peak	weeks
Supersonic	14/08/1994	28	10
Live Forever	13/11/1994	43	3
Roll with It	15/10/1995	17	6
Morning Glory	10/12/1995	29	6
Wonderwall	11/02/1996	1	12
Don't Look Back in Anger	14/04/1996	20	7
Champagne Supernova	30/06/1996	16	8
D'You Know What I Mean?	27/07/1997	4	9
Stand by Me	12/10/1997	31	3
All Around the World	08/02/1998	24	6
Go Let It Out	20/02/2000	31	4
The Hindu Times	19/05/2002	47	1
Little By Little	24/11/2002	46	1

Albums

Title	Entry	Peak	weeks
Definitely Maybe	16/10/1994	5	32
(What's The Story) Morning Glory?	29/10/1995	1	69
Be Here Now	07/09/1997	1	22
Standing On the Shoulder of Giants	12/03/2000	8	5
Heathen Chemistry	14/07/2002	16	5
Don't Believe the Truth	06/06/2005	12	6
Stop The Clocks	27/11/2006	18	4
Dig Out Your Soul	13/10/2008	6	3
Time Flies... 1994-2009	21/06/2010	13	4

Source: https://charts.nz/showinterpret.asp?interpret=Oasis – Published with permission from Recorded Music New Zealand

Endnotes

[1] Taite John, Issue 205, 1994, September, *Rip It Up,* Hark Entertainment, Auckland, p.20

[2] Bowes, Richard, 2020, *Some Might Say, The Definitive Story of Oasis,* This Day In Music Press, Huntingdon, p.29

[3] Bowes, *Some Might Say, The Definitive Story of Oasis,* p.78

[4] Haris, John, 2003, *The Last Party. Britpop, Blair and the Demise of English Rock,* Forth Estate, London, p.131

[5] Downie, S., 2001, May 18. 4 major firms heading west: [3 Third Edition]. *The Daily Telegraph,* Sydney, NSW, p.3

[6] Issue 6, 1994, June, *Swerve,* Source Magazines, Auckland

[7] McNickel, David, *Swerve,* p.26

[8] Kay, George, Issue 202, 1994, June, *Rip It Up,* p.39

[9] Taite John, Issue 205, 1994, September, *Rip It Up,* p.20

[10] Charts.org.nz – *Oasis - Supersonic -* https://charts.nz/showitem.asp?interpret=Oasis\&titel=Supersonic\&cat=s – Accessed August 4 2022

[11] Charts.org.nz – Oasis – Definitely Maybe - https://charts.nz/showitem.asp?interpret=Oasis\&titel=Definitely+Maybe\&cat=a – Accessed August 4 2022

[12] Laurie, Jock, Issue 8, 1994, December, *Pavement,* C & G Publishing, Hamilton (NZ) – p. 81

[13] Taite John, Issue 206, 1994, October, *Rip It Up,* p.26-7

[14] Designer, Paul, 1994, November, *Tearaway Magazine,* Tearaway Magazine, Wanganui, p.15

[15] Baillie, Russell, 1994, September 20, *The New Zealand Herald,* Horton and Wilson, Auckland, section 3, p.2

[16] Reid, Graham, 1994, October 21, *The New Zealand Herald,* section 2, p.1

[17] Kennedy, Paul, 2021, Airplay Lists from 1995-1998 [Email]

[18] West, Ken, 2022, *Happy 30th Birthday Big Day Out* [Online], p.37

[19] Billboard.com – Oasis – Chart History - https://www.billboard.com/artist/oasis/chart-history/mrt/ - Accessed August 5 2022

[20] Soap Studios, Big Day Out 1995 poster

[21] Reid, Graham, 1995, December 22, *New Zealand Herald*, Section 2 p.10

[22] Charts.org.nz – Oasis – (What's the Story) Morning Glory - https://charts.nz/showitem.asp?interpret=Oasis\&titel=\%28What\%27s+The+Story\%29+Morning+Glory\%3F\&cat=a – Accessed August 5 2022

[23] Wright, Geoff, Issue 14, 1995, December, *Pavement,* p.114

[24] Taite, John, Issue 219, 1995, November, *Rip It Up,* p.36

[25] Taimre, Ilmar, 1995, November, *Real Groove,* Real Groovy Records, Auckland, p.24

[26] 1995, November, Tearaway Magazine, p. 19

[27] Greenop, Matt, Issue 27, 1995, October, *The Strip,* Local Publications (Eastern) Ltd, Auckland, p.70

[28] Baille, Russell, 1995, October 20, *The New Zealand Herald*, Section 2 p.10

[29] Reid, Graham, 1995, December 22, The New Zealand Herald, Section 2 p.10

[30] Billboard.com – Oasis – Chart History - https://www.billboard.com/artist/oasis/chart-history/mrt/ - Accessed August 5 2022

[31] nzTop40.co.nz – End of Year Chart 1996 – Albums - https://nztop40.co.nz/chart/albums?chart=3885 – Accessed August 5 2022

[32] 1996, February 22, *Evening Post*, p.18

[33] Smith, Louise, 1996, March 3, *Sunday News*, Independent Newspapers, Auckland, p.54

[34] Berry, Ruth, 1996, March 31, Sunday Star-Times, Independent Newspapers, Auckland, F4

[35] Cotmore, Greg, 1996, July 4, *Evening Post*, Independent Newspapers, Wellington, p.16

[36] Issue 224, 1996, April, *Rip It Up*, p.12

[37] Reid, Graham, 1996, July 16, *The New Zealand Herald*, p. 3

[38] Issue 228, 1996, August, *Rip It Up,* p. 13

[39] Harris, *The Last Party. Britpop, Blair and the Demise of English Rock, p. 312*

[40] 1996, September 14, *The New Zealand Herald*, B13

[41] Phillips, Daniel – Copy of ticket from Phillips personal collection

[42] Issue 12 – 1996, January, *Rukkus, NZ's Hard Rock Magazine*, Rukkus Records, Auckland, p.6

[43] Issue 230, 1996, October, *Rip It Up*, p.7

[44] Matheson, John, Issue 1, 1996, October, *Music Press Magazine*, Box Office Magazines, Auckland, p.4

[45] Evans, Gareth, Issue 241, 1997, September, *Rip It Up*, p.20-21.

[46] Houlahan, Mike, 1997, July 2, *Evening Post*, p.2

[47] Herrick, Linda, 1997, July 6, *Sunday Star-Times*, F11

[48] 1997, September 13, *New Zealand Listener*, Bauer Media, Auckland, p.81

[49] Charts.org.nz – Oasis – D'You Know What I Mean? - https://charts.nz/showitem. asp?interpret=Oasis\&titel=D\%27You+Know+What+I+Mean\%3F\&cat=s – Accessed August 5 2022

[50] Issue 10, 1997, July, *Music Press Magazine*

[51] Issue 11, 1997, August, Music Press Magazine, p.12

[52] Issue 240, 1997, August, *Rip It Up*, p.23

[53] Issue 241, 1997, September, *Rip It Up*

[54] Evans, Gareth, Issue 241, 1997, September, *Rip It Up*, p.20-21.

[55] Adams, Cameron, Issue 25, 1997, October, *Pavement*, p.118-124

[56] Agnew, Margaret, 1997, August 27, *The Press*, Independent Newspapers, Christchurch, p.1

[57] 1997, August 26, *Waikato Times*, Independent Newspapers, Hamilton, p.1

[58] 1997, August 25, *Evening Post*, p.3

[59] Issue 19, 1997, September 1, *Nexus*, Nexus Publications, Hamilton, p.29

[60] Issue 21, 1997, September 16, *Nexus*, p.41

[61] Taite, John, Issue 241, 1997, September, *Rip It Up*, p.29

[62] Sampson, Desmond, Issue 25, 1997, October, *Pavement*, p.154

[63] Woods, Scott, 1997, October, *Real Groove*, p. 23

[64] 1997, November, *Tearaway Magazine*, p.41

65 Issue 20, 1997, September, *Canta*, Canterbury University Students Association, Christchurch, p.30

66 Issue 12, 1997, September, *Music Press Magazine*, p.26

67 Glasson, Gale, Issue 20, 1997, September 9, *Nexus*, p.27

68 Baillie, Russell, 1997, August 21*, The New Zealand Herald*, E1 and E5

69 Cleaver, Dylan, 1997, August 31, Sunday News, p.20

70 McCarthy, Bede, 1997, August 26, *Waikato Times*, Sounds exert

71 Houlahan, Mike, 1997, August 28, *Evening Post*, p.17

72 Armstrong, Alistair, 1997, August 29, The Press, p.26

73 Bollinger, Nick, 1997, September 20, *New Zealand Listener*, Bauer Media, Auckland, p.42

74 Harris, *The Last Party. Britpop, Blair and the Demise of English Rock*, p.347-8.

75 Bowes, *Some Might Say*, p.164

76 Dowling, Stephen, 1997, August 17, *Sunday Star-Times*, F2

77 1998, January 17, The New Zealand Herald, B5

78 1998, January 28, *North Shore News*, Wilson & Horton Newspapers Ltd, Auckland, p.5

79 Issue 17, 1998, February, Music Press Magazine, p.25

80 Houlahan, Mike & Simcox, Craig, 1998, January 21, *Evening Post*, p.1

81 1998, January 22, Dominion, p.8 – Photo by Dave Hansford

82 Queue for Oasis tickets. Photographer unidentified. January 21 1998. *Dominion Post* Collection]. Ref: Dom/1998/0121-01. Alexander Turnbull Library, Wellington, New Zealand

83 Queue for Oasis tickets.[Photographer unidentified.] January 21 1998. Dominion Post Collection. Ref: Dom/1998/0121-02. Alexander Turnbull Library, Wellington, New Zealand

84 Queue for Oasis tickets. [Photographer unidentified.] January 21 1998. Dominion Post Collection. Ref: Dom/1998/0121-03. Alexander Turnbull Library, Wellington, New Zealand

85 Charts.org.nz – Oasis – All Around the World - https: //charts.nz/showitem.asp?interpret=Oasis\&titel=All+Around+The+World\&cat=s – Accessed August 6 2022

[86] 1998, February 25, *Capital Times*, Unit Two Newspapers, Wellington, p.4

[87] Issue 247, 1998, March, Rip It Up, p.1, p.18-19

[88] Issue 247, 1998, March, Rip It Up, p.18-19

[89] Issue 18, 1998, March, *Music Press Magazine*

[90] Matheson, John, Issue 18, 1998, March, *Music Press Magazine*, p.6-9

[91] Oasisinet.com, 1998, February 23, Press Release – accessed via https://web.archive.org/web/19980613233531/http://www.oasisinet.com/prauck.htm - original formatting of press release retained

[92] Issue 2, 1998, February, Nexus, p.30

[93] Wilde, Flann, 1998, March 8, *Sunday News*, p.19

[94] Dowling, Stephen, 1998, March 8, *Sunday Star-Times*, Revue 1-2

[95] Bowes, *Some Might Say*, p. 169

[96] Flint, John, 1998, March 12, *South China Morning Post*, Hong Kong, p.3

[97] Kwan, C.F, 1998, March 12, *South China Morning Post*, Hong Kong, p.20

[98] Hewitt, Paolo, 1999, *Forever the People, Six Months on the Road with* Oasis, Boxtree, London, p.164-7.

[99] Coughlan, Annie, 1998, February 27, *Dominion,* p.1

[100] 1998, March 7, *Bay of Plenty Times*, NZME, Tauranga, p.7

[101] Shelton, Andree, 1998, March 6, *Rotorua Daily Post*, NZME, Rotorua, p.14

[102] 1998, March 8, *Sunday News, p.38*

[103] Logan Campbell Centre, Greenlane West, Auckland. Whites Aviation Ltd. May 2, 1988. Reference: WA-80307-F. Held by Alexander Turnbull Library, Wellington. Used under CC BY 4.0. Image has been cropped from original item. https://creativecommons.org/licenses/by/4.0/

[104] Taylor, Phil, 1998, March 9, *Manukau Daily News*, Horton Media Ltd, Auckland, p.3

[105] Liam and Noel Gallagher of 'Oasis' in Auckland, New Zealand, 1998 – Murray Job/ Shutterstock

[106] 1998, February, *Michael Coppel Presents Oasis. Australia & New Zealand 1998*

[107] Stace, F.N., 1990, *Engineering to 1990,* Engineering Publications Co Ltd, Wellington, p.8

[108] Stringleman, Hugh, 2010, *Agricultural Heritage, Auckland Agricultural and Pastoral*

Association Inc. 1843-2010, Oratia Media Ltd, Auckland, p.234

[109] Akl.showgrounds.q.co.nz – Auckland Showgrounds Schedule of Rentals – Accessed via https://web.archive.org/web/19980515133650/http://akl-showgrounds.q.co.nz/ - There is no indication that Oasis was charged this amount. These charges were what was published by the Auckland Showgrounds.

[110] New Zealand Exposition Centre, Greenlane, Auckland (1990) – *Archives New Zealand Te Rua Mahara o te Kawanatanga* – ABKB 8032 2293 R19846391 – New Zealand Tourism Board Photograph

[111] Johnston, Martin, 2018, April 16, *The New Zealand Herald* [Online] https://www.nzherald.co.nz/nz/a-crisis-recalled-the-power-cuts-that-plunged-the-auckland-cbd-in-darkness-for-five-weeks/IZBJMV3I4H4FOQIX3MIG5JBN3Y/?c_id=1\&objectid=12033654 – Accessed 31 July 2022

[112] 1998, March 7, *Evening Post*, p.1

[113] Leser, David, 1998, 18 April, *Sydney Morning Herald,* Sydney, N.S.W., p.16

[114] Jeffrey, Glenn, *New Zealand Herald Digital Photography*, 2004

[115] Russell, John, Issue 248, 1998, April, *Rip It Up*, p.12.

[116] Hogg, Nicola (Ministry of Business Innovation and Employment), 2022, 28 April -

[117] Snippet of Noel Gallagher on *Havoc* provided by Tony Rarere

[118] 1998, March 11, *The New Zealand Herald,* A24

[119] Perry, Keith, 1998, March 10, *The New Zealand Herald*, p.1

[120] Baillie, Russell, 1998, March 10, *The New Zealand Herald*, B5

[121] Welham, Keri, 1998, March 10, *Waikato Times*, p.1

[122] Taylor, Phil, 1998, March 11, *Manukau Daily News, p.11*

[123] Dinsdale, Mike, 1998, March 11, *The Northern Advocate*, NZME, Whangarei, p.14

[124] Issue 19, 1998, April, *Music Press Magazine*, p.3

[125] Taite, John, Issue 248, 1998, April, *Rip It Up*, p.32

[126] 1998, 22 January, Evening Post, p.14

[127] The Parkroyal Hotel, Wellington City, by Chris Coad (1989)– Archives New Zealand Te Rua Mahara o te Kawanatanga – ABKB 8032 2707 R19844251 – New Zealand Tourism Board Photograph

[128] 1998, March 2, Manukau Daily News, p.1

[129] Oasis at the Parkroyal]. [Photographer unidentified] 1998. Dominion Post Collection. Ref: EP/1998/881-885-01. Alexander Turnbull Library, Wellington, New Zealand

[130] [Liam Gallagher]. [Photographer unidentified]. Dominion Post Collection. Ref: EP/1998/881-885-02. Alexander Turnbull Library, Wellington, New Zealand

[131] 1998, March 10, Daily News Taranaki, Independent Newspapers, New Plymouth, p.3

[132] 1998, March 10, Dominion, p.1

[133] 1998, The New Zealand Business Directory 1997/1998, Universal Business Directories, NZ, p.S148

[134] 2005, April, Wellington Convention Centre, Wellington City Council, Wellington p.1

[135] 1998, March 20, The Western News, Capital Community Newspapers, Wellington, p.3

[136] Faulds, Matt, Queens Wharf, Wellington (2006) – Accessed via Flickr https://www.flickr.com/photos/mattandsarah/87281400/in/faves-194521711@N04/

[137] Hewitt, Paolo, Forever the People, Six Months on the Road with Oasis, p.173-176.

[138] Reid, Neil, 1998, March 11, Evening Post, p.1

[139] Shakermaker, Oasis - Live in Wellington (10th March 1998) - Speed Corrected, YouTube, 2022, April 8, 1:13.28 https://www.youtube.com/watch?v=hwG8H6SuuHQ

[140] Hewitt, Paolo, Forever the People, Six Months on the Road with Oasis, p.173-179

[141] Hunter, Martin, 1998, March 11, Dominion, p.1

[142] Fyfe, Anna, 1998, March 11, Dominion, p.16

[143] Houlahan, Mike, 1998, March 11, Evening Post, p.38.

[144] Sweetman, Simon, 1998, March 16, Salient, The Student Magazine of Victoria University of Wellington, Victoria University Students Association, Wellington, p.20

[145] Rock band Oasis perform at the Events Centre. [Photographer unidentified]. 3 October 1998. Dominion Post Collection]. Ref: Dom/1998/0310-08. Alexander Turnbull Library, Wellington, New Zealand

[146] Rock band Oasis perform at the Events Centre. [Photographer unidentified]. 3 October 1998. Dominion Post Collection]. Ref: Dom/1998/0310-03. Alexander Turnbull Library, Wellington, New Zealand

[147] Rock band Oasis perform at the Events Centre. [Photographer unidentified]. 3

October 1998. Dominion Post Collection]. Ref: Dom/1998/0310-04. Alexander Turnbull Library, Wellington, New Zealand

[148] Rock band Oasis perform at the Events Centre. [Photographer unidentified]. 3 October 1998. Dominion Post Collection]. Ref: Dom/1998/0310-02. Alexander Turnbull Library, Wellington, New Zealand

[149] Rock band Oasis perform at the Events Centre. [Photographer unidentified]. 3 October 1998. Dominion Post Collection]. Ref: Dom/1998/0310-05. Alexander Turnbull Library, Wellington, New Zealand

[150] Rock band Oasis perform at the Events Centre. [Photographer unidentified]. 3 October 1998. Dominion Post Collection]. Ref: Dom/1998/0310-06. Alexander Turnbull Library, Wellington, New Zealand

[151] Image of Lifestyle Sports, on Willis Street. Photographed by Wayne Shepherd ca. 1980s-1990s. Ref: PA12-6062. Alexander Turnbull Library, Wellington, New Zealand.

[152] Rock band Oasis perform at the Events Centre. [Photographer unidentified]. 3 October 1998. Dominion Post Collection]. Ref: Dom/1998/0310-01. Alexander Turnbull Library, Wellington, New Zealand

[153] 1998, March 11, *Evening Post*, p.3

[154] Vita, Simon, 1998, March 12, *City Voice,* Te Aro Publishing Cooperative Ltd, Wellington, p.15

[155] Fyfe, Anna, 1998, March 12, *Dominion*, p.1

[156] Gallagher leaves Parkroyal. [Photographer unidentified.] March 11 1998. Dominion Post Collection. Ref: Dom/1998/0311b-01. Alexander Turnbull Library, Wellington, New Zealand

[157] Gallagher leaves Parkroyal. [Photographer unidentified.] March 11 1998. Dominion Post Collection. Ref: Dom/1998/0311b-02. Alexander Turnbull Library, Wellington, New Zealand

[158] Gallagher leaves hotel in the back of a van. [Photographer unidentified.] March 11 1998. Dominion Post Collection. Ref: Dom/1998/0311a-01. Alexander Turnbull Library, Wellington, New Zealand

[159] Sampson, Des, Issue 314, 2006, December, *Rip It Up*, p.65

[160] 1998, February, *Michael Coppel Presents Oasis. Australia & New Zealand 1998*

[161] Official Charts Company –End of Year Artists Albums 1998 - https://www.officialcharts.com/charts/end-of-year-artist-albums-chart/19980104/37502/ [Online] – Accessed August 9 2022

[162] Hyslop Liam, 2015, February 20, *Stuff.co.nz,* [Online]

https://www.stuff.co.nz/entertainment/music/66436599/top-10-worst-new-zealand-concerts - Accessed July 31 2022

[163] Baillie, Russell, 2000, June 30, *The New Zealand Herald [Online]*, https://www.nzherald.co.nz/lifestyle/noel-gallagher-midlife-at-the-oasis/CJW6E6QDI43YQMNWV7B7WV4PDI/ - Accessed July 31 2022

About the Author

Karamdeep Sahota is an archivist based in Wellington, New Zealand. Originally from the Black Country in England, his interest in music spiked in the mid-1990s and his obsession with Oasis formed during the inescapable build up to the release of *Be Here Now*. This is his first book.

If anyone reading this book has a story to share with the author about the Oasis tour to New Zealand that isn't included, email balmansabooks@gmail.com

BS - #0014 - 301023 - C159 - 229/152/20 - PB - 9781738581702 - Matt Lamination